Eyewitness RAF

Eyewitness RAF

The Experience of War 1939–1945

James Goulty

Pen & Sword
AVIATION

First published in Great Britain in 2020 by
PEN & SWORD AVIATION
An imprint of
Pen & Sword Books Ltd
Yorkshire – Philadelphia

ISBN 978 1 5267 5237 6

Typeset in 10.5/13 Ehrhardt by Vman Infotech Pvt. Ltd.
Printed and bound in the UK by TJ Books Limited, Padstow, Cornwall.

Pen & Sword Books Ltd incorporates the imprints of Pen & Sword Archaeology,
Atlas, Aviation, Battleground, Discovery, Family History, History, Maritime,
Military, Naval, Politics, Social History, Transport, True Crime, Claymore Press,
Frontline Books, Praetorian Press, Seaforth Publishing and White Owl.

For a complete list of Pen & Sword titles please contact:

PEN & SWORD BOOKS LTD
47 Church Street, Barnsley, South Yorkshire, S70 2AS, England
E-mail: enquiries@pen-and-sword.co.uk
Website: www.pen-and-sword.co.uk

Or

PEN AND SWORD BOOKS
1950 Lawrence Rd, Havertown, PA 19083, USA
E-mail: Uspen-and-sword@casematepublishers.com
Website: www.penandswordbooks.com

Contents

Acknowledgements

I am deeply grateful to Pen and Sword Ltd. for agreeing to this project, and for their continued support. In this regard, Rupert Harding has been an excellent editor and I remain thankful for his sound council during the writing process. For her assistance as copy editor, Linne Matthews was invaluable.

The book employs various sources and readers will find full details in the accompanying chapter notes. I thank the National Archives at Kew for allowing me to consult Operations Record Books. The Department of Sound at the Imperial War Museum, London, graciously allowed me to quote from select recordings of oral history interviews with RAF veterans held in their collection. Anthony Richards of the IWM was especially helpful and offered advice on copyright issues. The Trustees of the Second World War Experience Centre, at Otley, West Yorkshire, kindly allowed me to quote from materials held in their archive. Anne Wickes and Amanda Herbert-Davies from the SWWEC provided assistance and made visiting the archive a pleasure.

Paul Carter kindly allowed me to quote from his late father's book: Alan Carter, *Survival of the Fittest: A Young Englishman's Struggle as a Prisoner of War in Java and Japan* (privately published, 2013). Wing Commander Harry Blee agreed to be interviewed for the book, which was a real highlight. Notably, we discussed his period as an RAF apprentice and later as a flight engineer, including experience of operational flying with 358 Squadron, based in Jessore, India. His son, Simon, kindly provided copies of wartime photographs relating to Harry's service in Britain and India. I am grateful to Helen, Simon and Harry Blee for their hospitality during my research trip. Thanks go to Charlie Wainwright, who let me use documents and photographs regarding the wartime RAF career of Reggie Wainwright (his late father). Reggie served as an NCO navigator with 38 and 24 Squadrons, and was later commissioned, before enjoying a career in civil aviation after the war. Alastair Fraser kindly loaned me several books on the RAF, and allowed me to employ photographs from the album of Major Maurice Alexander Fraser (his late father). Major Fraser joined the Territorial Army in 1928, and during the war served with a searchlight (SL) unit of the Royal Artillery. After the SL effort was scaled down, he became an air liaison officer (ALO) with 2 Group, a post he held from June/July 1944 until 1946. He experienced service during the campaign in North-West Europe, and pictures from that period provided much of the inspiration for his album. I also am extremely grateful to my brother, Robert Goulty, for the loan of books on the wartime RAF and photographs of Sunderland flying boat *C for Charlie* from his collection, two of which appear in this publication.

Last but not least, I remain immensely thankful for the love and support of my family, including Poppy the Boxer. On a personal note, my late grandparents served with the wartime RAF and WAAF, and I hope that they'd have appreciated this book. Like so many of their generation, they didn't talk too much about their war, but I know that they were proud to have served their country.

List of Illustrations

A group of RAF personnel eagerly inspect the remains of a Junkers Ju 88 shot down near St Osyth, Essex, in September 1940. (Author's collection)

Airmen from 38 Squadron in their full-length flying suits, flying boots, and parachute harnesses. NCO Navigator Reggie Wainwright stands at the back left wearing a field service cap. (Charlie Wainwright)

Reggie Wainwright (third from left) and his Wellington crew from 38 Squadron. They served in Europe before moving to the Middle East in November 1940. (Charlie Wainwright)

The WAAF made a major contribution towards the war effort. Maise Goulty was granted an emergency commission in April 1944, and promoted to section officer the following November. (Author's collection)

A WAAF band parades in Brussels shortly after the Allied liberation of Europe from Nazi occupation, 1945. (Alastair Fraser)

Sport was a major part of Service life, even in wartime. Here, the winning team from 2 Group, Brussels, 7-a-side tournament pose for the camera in May 1945. (Alastair Fraser)

Harry Blee on passing out as a flight engineer from RAF St Athan. After serving in the Far East, he was granted a permanent commission, and served until 1975. (Simon Blee)

Flight Lieutenant Anthony Goulty photographed at the end of the war, while serving with Number 7 IAU in the Far East, sporting the medal ribbon of the Burma Star. (Author's collection)

With 358 Squadron, Harry Blee (flight engineer, second from right) regularly flew Liberators with Chris Headley (skipper, far right), and Jack Tubb (navigator/side-gunner, third from right), India 1944. (Simon Blee)

Reggie Wainwright served as navigator aboard this Avro York, regularly used to ferry Earl Mountbatten (Supreme Commander South-East Asia, 1943–46), who has signed the photograph. (Charlie Wainwright)

The Mosquito, affectionately dubbed the 'Mossie', was one of the most successful and versatile of all the aircraft employed by the RAF during the war. (Author's collection)

A fine view of a Sunderland flying boat: 'C' for Charlie, registration SZ268, moored in a Norwegian fjord. The Sunderland proved especially useful in anti-submarine work. (Robert Goulty)

On 21 March 1945, Mosquitoes from RAF 2nd TAF, escorted by Mustangs, launched a daring low-level strike against the Gestapo archives in Shell House, Copenhagen – marked here by an 'X'. (Alastair Fraser)

The Short Sunderland flying boat was dubbed 'flying porcupine' by the Germans owing to its heavy armament. Landing and taking off from water could be tricky and required great skill. (Robert Goulty)

Air Sea Rescue operations helped recover trained aircrew so that they could continue the war effort. Here a Supermarine Walrus is greeted by an airman who's ended up 'in the drink'. (Author's collection)

An attack on German gun positions near Boulogne by RAF Bostons and Mitchells from 2 Group, 2 September 1944. (Alastair Fraser)

This photograph of the harbour at Kiel was taken on VE-Day by a Mitchell bomber from 139 Wing. (Alastair Fraser)

Cologne, as viewed from an RAF Mitchell on 8 May 1945 (VE-Day). The massive destruction caused by aerial bombardment is clearly evident. (Alastair Fraser)

This shot of Kiel was taken from a Mitchell bomber flown by Flight Lieutenant John Smith-Carrington (139 Wing). Note the effectiveness of the camouflage in breaking up the outline of the ship in the centre of the photograph. (Alastair Fraser)

Bomb damage at Kiel, May 1945. This provides a graphic illustration of the level of destruction caused by RAF Bomber Command's policy of area bombing against German cities. (Alastair Fraser)

Introduction

On 3 September 1939, Britain declared war on Germany for the second time in twenty-five years. In Hull, one RAF reserve unit listened sombrely to the wireless broadcast by Prime Minister Neville Chamberlain announcing the outbreak of hostilities. Afterwards, whether with 'bravado, embarrassment or uncertainty', someone exclaimed: '"Well, never mind, let's all meet up again here when it's over." And people said, "Oh yes, of course, what else?" About fifteen minutes later the air raid siren went and people didn't take a lot of notice.'[1] Regular RAF personnel were less sanguine. Wing Commander Guy Gibson, who was killed flying as Master Bomber in a Mosquito of the Pathfinder Force (PFF) during a raid in September 1944, noted how they 'became changed from peace-time Air Force play-boys to fellows faced with death many days in a year, every year, for four years'.[2] Even so, the 'Brylcreem Boys' of the RAF tended to be resented by the army and navy, owing to what one pilot described as the 'spurious glamour and adulation gained during the Battle of Britain … assisted by the biggest and best public relations department of all the services'.[3]

Before the war, RAF strength was 117,890, and on mobilisation in 1939 this was increased by 58,100 with the addition of reservists and auxiliaries, although a substantial number of these lacked training. From this relatively humble beginning, a large wartime force was fashioned that served around the globe. By 1944, when wartime recruiting was halted, around 1.2 million men and women were serving with the RAF, approximately 70 per cent of whom were employed in non-flying trades.[4] This demonstrates the immense effort that was required to support operational squadrons, and that trained aircrew held an elite status within the RAF, not least because only about 5 per cent of those who applied for aircrew training were successful. Recalling his flying training in 1940, bomber pilot Wing Commander Ken Rees rapidly discovered that aircrew had a 'special petrol allowance for leave' and 'special food rations, flying gear and medical care': 'There were changing rooms, dining rooms, briefing rooms, all with "Aircrew Only" on their doors.' In short, they were 'hot stuff'.[5]

Consequently, the experiences of aircrew loom large here, but hopefully the reader will come away with an appreciation that the wartime RAF was about more than flying. The emphasis of this book is on life at squadron level and below, based around the personal experiences of a variety of men and women. Chapter 1 focuses on recruitment and training, including what motivated individuals to enlist. Notably, it outlines the role of women serving with the Women's Auxiliary Air Force (WAAF), and the efforts of the flying training organisation, which is often overlooked. Chapter 2 discusses bombing operations, including examples from the campaigns in North Africa and Burma. However, although bombing was a feature of most theatres, central to this chapter are the experiences of personnel engaged in Bomber Command's prolonged offensive against Nazi Germany, and the increasing technological sophistication that this entailed as the war progressed.

Chapter 3 explores the operational experiences of fighter pilots, and illustrates the characteristics required by such individuals, plus the different roles performed by fighter aircraft. It highlights fighter tactics, and provides a flavour of the controversies that existed regarding the subject. Chapter 4 deals with operational flying, this time from the perspective of Coastal Command, whose efforts have tended to be overshadowed by those of the Fighter and Bomber Boys. Yet, among other activities, Coastal Command performed an important role in countering U-boats, which contributed towards winning the Battle of the Atlantic. Typically, Coastal Command aircrew encountered awkward conditions, were faced with lengthy, monotonous sorties, and frequently relied on ageing or obsolete aircraft.

Chapter 5 concerns flying, but from the viewpoint of ferry pilots, and personnel who served with Ferry (later Transport) Command. Bold plans were formulated to fly bombers manufactured in America across the Atlantic to Britain – no easy task in the 1940s, especially in winter. For those involved, the weather was a major issue, and as the chapter shows, the ferry organisation had also to return pilots to America so that they could continue their valuable work. Pilots and navigators were a mixture of civilian and military personnel, and this went some way towards forging the distinctive character of the ferry organisation. As the war progressed, other ferry routes were opened up, notably via the South Atlantic and West Africa, which proved invaluable in supporting the North African campaign. Another strand of the chapter discusses the experiences of aircrew that operated transport aircraft with Ferry/Transport Command. Many had already served one or more tours with Bomber Command. Although ferrying supplies might seem unglamorous, it was nonetheless an essential activity. Transport aircraft were also invaluable in supporting airborne operations, either by dropping paratroopers and supplies, or by towing glider-borne units into action.

Chapter 6 concentrates on the experience of ground crew. As indicated, 'flyers' simply couldn't have performed their duty were it not for the support of these dedicated individuals, who worked long hours to keep 'em flying. Accordingly, a close bond usually existed between ground crews, pilots and aircrew, and those maintaining aircraft were frequently only too well aware of the stresses and strains suffered by those actually flying on operations. Equally, the chapter highlights a host of other non-flying related activities performed by men and women in the wartime RAF. Sometimes, these were derided as chair polishing roles, but in their own way, all contributed towards the overall smooth running of the Service. Duties ranged from administration, such as in pay and accounts sections, to the risky, courageous and less well recognised work of bomb disposal squads.

For a fighter pilot or member of a bomber crew, one of the most frightening prospects was that of being shot down and trapped in a burning aircraft. Chapter 7 considers the experience of being shot down from the perspective of those who endured it, and survived. Many didn't. Similarly, when shot down, some airmen were successful in avoiding capture, and training in escape and evasion techniques improved during the war. Others endured a torrid time behind the wire in prisoner of war camps in Nazi-occupied Europe. Contrary to the popular image in films and novels, there was nothing glamourous about becoming a POW, although opportunities to intimidate guards or mount escapes helped boost morale. Conditions in the Far East, where the Japanese had no respect for the Geneva Convention, were equally as appalling, if not worse, for those captured there. Other themes of the chapter are crashes and accidents. Sadly, these were all too common features of wartime life that killed numerous personnel, frequently having a significant impact on those who witnessed them.

Chapter 8 illustrates the challenges facing the RAF during the immediate post-war period, when many regular personnel continued to serve, although they weren't necessarily involved with operational flying. The demobilisation process, including the liberation and repatriation of POWs, is outlined, plus consideration given to how individuals viewed their war service and what effects it had on them. Having survived the war, and done their bit, some personnel deeply resented being liable for further reserve service. Likewise, during 1946, a mutiny occurred in the Far East, largely because airmen were frustrated over apparent delays in their demobilisation.

This book is based on a variety of sources, from official documents to oral histories and memoirs. The accompanying chapter notes provide full references of material accessed. However, readers might also wish to consult the bibliography, which contains a further reading section for those interested in what is a vast subject. It is now seventy-five years since the end of the Second World War, and sadly, the numbers of surviving RAF veterans are rapidly dwindling. Consequently, it is important that we continue to respect their memory, and appreciate the sacrifices made by the wartime generation. Hopefully, this book will prove informative and enjoyable, plus act as a fitting tribute to the many ordinary men and women who served with the wartime RAF.

James H.R. Goulty
November 2020

Chapter 1

Recruitment and Training

When compared with the other Services, the Royal Air Force was widely perceived as 'hardly the sphere for a gentleman'.[1] Partly, such views were a reaction against the technological nature of the RAF. Nevertheless, as a youthful, modern-looking service, it proved popular with recruits from a wide variety of backgrounds. Not all were necessarily desperate to fly. For many who chose to enlist during the late 1930s and 1940s, the air force was imbued with a degree of romance, and being associated with aviation, even in a ground role, held tremendous appeal. Pip Beck, a former junior NCO in the WAAF, recounted how aircrew were 'admired and hero-worshipped'; on commencing service with Bomber Command, her 'heart beat a little faster and … imagination took wings' once she was surrounded by such individuals.[2]

In 1939, all training, air and ground, was overseen by a single command – Training Command, which had evolved from a pre-war reorganisation. To cope with wartime expansion, Training Command was disbanded in May 1940 and reorganised into two separate branches: flying, and non-flying activity. Technical Training Command dealt with schools covering everything from chaplaincy to bomb disposal, plus training on maintaining aircraft and their related equipment. In contrast, Flying Training Command controlled schools dealing with flying instruction for pilots and training members of other aircrew, such as observers/navigators.[3]

Motivations for enlistment

There were various different means of entering the RAF. In early 1939, Lawrence Wheatley was inspired by the sight of an RAF officer's uniform displayed in a London shop and applied for a regular short-service commission as a pilot. At Adastral House, on the corner of Kingsway and Aldwych, he was interviewed by a panel of RAF officers. He soon realised 'that my speech, inability to play rugby, and leaving school at fourteen doomed me from the start'. Although the selection panel approved of him attending evening classes, he wasn't granted a commission, and was instead 'offered training as an Air Observer with the rank of sergeant and 12s 6d per day on completing training'.[4] He eagerly accepted. Unfortunately, it was discovered that he suffered from airsickness and so was discharged, only to later remuster as an armourer for war service.

Lawrence Wheatley's experience demonstrated, albeit at a low level, how far in 1939 the regular air force was still bound by class and tradition. There was a widely held perception that the public school system provided the best material for pilots. This was because they seemed to produce young men who were fit, well motivated, keen on sports, and able to master the intellectual and physical challenges of learning to fly. This belief persisted during the war. Yet, although they had an important role to perform, once war was declared it wasn't practical to solely rely on public school entrants and pre-war professionals.

The Royal Air Force Volunteer Reserve (RAFVR) came to prominence in the late 1930s, and according to historian Patrick Bishop, was instrumental in transforming the RAF from a small elite, largely recruited from the financially privileged and privately educated, into an organisation that drew more widely from British society. Notably, the RAFVR sought to foster a meritocracy, as promotions were based on men's ability rather than their background. However, these factors were still deemed important, as education up to at least School Certificate level was usually preferred, given the technical nature of flying.

The RAFVR was less concerned with conventional military values or skills, such as strict discipline and drill. Instead, it appealed to young men by fostering their desire to learn to fly, building on their sense of patriotism, and maintained a significant social side. Much like the Territorial Army, training took place at weekends and evenings, with one full-time fortnight per year. Every pilot was given a maximum of twenty-five hours' flying per year in light aircraft. By the outbreak of war, about 5,000 young men had either undergone or were undergoing flying training with the RAFVR.[5] Initially, they held non-commissioned ranks such as sergeant pilots, although many later became officers. Additionally, reservist aircrew and personnel for medical, administrative and technical branches were recruited, 'to form an invaluable reservoir of trained manpower'.[6]

Despite this apparently being an asset, given the international situation by 1939, some hostility was demonstrated against reservists. This was partly because old sweats, who'd made it as NCOs after several years of service, resented these new boys entering the RAF with similar rank. Some regular officers considered that the existence of RAFVR officers on short-service or wartime commissions similarly threatened the exclusivity of their organisation. One fighter pilot who served during the Battle of Britain found 'a definite prejudice in the Air Force against Volunteer Reserve Officers'.[7]

In an effort to recruit suitable material for the RAFVR, newspaper advertisements appeared around the country. Another popular method was via air displays, which appealed to potential recruits for all types of trades, not just those who wanted to fly. As an 18-year-old in 1939, Eric Marsden:

attended an Empire Air Day air show at RAF Hucknall [near Nottingham] where the RAFVR had a recruiting table. So I got an application form and took it home. I was then employed as an apprentice fitter at Plowright, a colliery engineers in Chesterfield, filled in the paper work took it to work because like the Territorial Army the employers had to give approval as you were going to be asking for time off.[8]

In September 1939, he was posted to RAF Scampton, Lincolnshire, and assigned as a fitter/mechanic to 'A' Flight, No. 83 Squadron, which at that stage was operating Handley Page Hampden bombers.

Rupert Cooling moved to Hull in the mid-1930s, and was educated at Hymers College before becoming an apprentice pharmacist. With war looking likely, he enlisted in the RAFVR, under somewhat fortuitous circumstances:

I joined the RAF because the chain came off my bicycle. My father had been in the Honourable Artillery Company and was called up at the beginning of the First World War. And I said oh I was going to join the Territorials. That was the gung-ho business where every lad in his early teens was talking about joining some military formation. And there was an artillery unit in Hull.

One February I was coming back from work in the evening, and there was a howling easterly wind with heavy showers and I had a bicycle which I didn't look after that well and every so often when you put too much weight on the pedals the chain came off and that's precisely what happened when I came to the corner of the Beverley Road and Cottingham Road, the chain came off and as I put it on again there was a ghastly shower, it really was vicious and I looked up above, just above my head there was a board that said: 'No. 8 Reserve Centre RAFVR'. So I darted up the path, opened the front door and a chapel mate I knew as Corporal Lance seized me with open arms and said: 'Ah just the sort of young man we are looking for!'

So I said: 'please tell me more?' At that time I was an apprentice pharmacist and was being paid Ten Shillings or twelve and six per week. And he said right what you do is sign here and we'll teach you to fly. For one day only you'll be an Aircraftsman Second Class on Two Shillings per day the next day you'll be a Sergeant Pilot U/T [Under Training] on ten and six a day, and when you've got your Wings it goes up to twelve and six a day. ...

So I took the papers home and went through them and my father and mother were saying 'yes, yes', but my mother was not that enthusiastic at the idea of her sole fledgling flinging himself into the air. This was at a

time when newspapers made great play of aircraft plunging out of the sky
and bursting into flames.[9]

Despite his mother's reservations, he commenced his pilot training in March
1938, going solo after thirteen hours on the Miles Magister, the first monoplane
training aircraft to be employed by the RAF. Subsequently, he piloted Wellington
bombers on active service during the war.

Additionally, front-line units were supported by amateur fliers of the University Air Squadrons and Auxiliary Air Force (AAF). The AAF was a corps d'elite,
comprised of socially exclusive units, such as 601 (County of London) Squadron.
Founded by Lord Grosvenor in the late 1920s, it initially solely recruited its
members from Whites club bar. As Patrick Bishop highlighted, theoretically, the
AAF could have formed the basis for establishing the RAFVR, but it resisted
attempts to do so over fears that it would lose its exclusive character. Under
wartime conditions, such an outlook proved unsustainable, and AAF squadrons
had to absorb whoever was posted to them as replacements, which watered down
much of their pre-war character.

Elements of the pre-war ethos were strongly maintained by the entire wartime
RAF, particularly in terms of the character of the organisation. Most airmen,
regardless of rank or background, tended to dislike 'show-offs and insouciance
and understatement were the form'. Whether they were pre-war professionals,
reservists, auxiliaries or conscripts, all 'were united in all-but-unquestioned
willingness to face any odds and accept any risk'.[10] An airman from the Polish Air
Force who fled to Britain in 1940 and joined the RAF was surprised by the 'easy-
going' nature of the airmen he encountered. Whereas most Poles were motivated
by revenge against the Germans, 'old fashioned RAF flyer types' seemed to view
flying an aeroplane 'like a sport'.[11]

Conscription provided another source of manpower. On the first day of war,
the National Service (Armed Services) Act came into effect. Under it, all males
aged 18 to 41 were liable for call-up, although there were significant exemptions.
Later, the upper age limit was extended to 51. Initially, men had to register, and
most did so at their local Labour Exchange, where they were asked which branch
of the armed services they wished to join. The RAF proved universally popular,
but only a relatively select few had the necessary qualities to be trained as aircrew.

Rather than wait for their call-up, many chose to volunteer. At the outbreak
of war, Morton Charlton from Hexham, Northumberland, was too young for
military service. However, 'anxious to become involved in some worthwhile
cause', he joined the men's detachment of his local British Red Cross branch.
In March 1941, this enabled him to enlist in the medical branch of the RAF.[12]
In 1939, Wing Commander Artie Ashworth, a New Zealander, explained that like
many of his contemporaries, he didn't want to wait to be conscripted, especially as

war appeared imminent. He longed for adventure, had a 'desire to learn to fly' and was deeply envious of those who'd already successfully joined the RAF.[13]

It is difficult not to overemphasise the popularity and impact that flying had on the generation who grew up between the wars. Despite the economic climate, many were eager for news about the various speed records being set in the air. Aeroplanes, when flying was still in its comparative infancy, held an enormous fascination. Fiction – notably the *Biggles* books by former RAF pilot W.E. Johns – instilled in a host of youngsters, especially boys, a romantic fascination of flying. Fifteen were published between 1932 and May 1938, and many who read them served as young adults with the wartime RAF. Similarly, magazines covering flying were popular, and the subject regularly appeared in the press. Battle of Britain ace Bob Doe confessed that he kept a scrapbook of cuttings on aircraft and flying related matters, right up until he actually learned to fly with the RAF.[14]

During the 1930s, flying was portrayed in an exciting manner at air displays. Squadron Leader Jack Currie recounted that ever since the Hendon Air Display of 1937, he'd been wedded to the idea of flying a bomber. At that event, Vickers Wellesleys and Armstrong Whitworth Whitleys from Blueland made a 'steady, menacing approach, through puffs of ack-ack and swarms of Hawker Demons' as they plunged 'into the heart of Redland, and into mine'.[15] In this case, a force of friendly bombers from 'Blueland' sought to attack enemy territory, or 'Redland', while enemy fighters and anti-aircraft gunners attempted to intercept them. Others were drawn to the exciting prospect of flying fighter aircraft in combat, with the apparent onus on individual skill. As Richard Hillary believed, the fighter offered a way 'to return to war as it ought to be, war which is individual combat between two people, in which one either kills or is killed'.[16] Alternatively, some recruits were motivated by a desire for revenge against the Germans. Ivor Broom, a future air marshal, volunteered on 11 May 1940, having witnessed the German onslaught against the West and had 'become familiar with the sight and sound of Blenheims and other RAF aircraft flying low overhead' on operations against the enemy.[17]

However, the shadow of the First World War, and particularly the experience of trench warfare, still haunted the interwar generation. Many had fathers or other relatives who'd fought in it, and suffered. The 'Phoney War' of 1939–40 initially appeared to offer a repeat of First World War conditions, with the British Expeditionary Force (BEF) holding static positions on the Continent. Eighteen-year-old William Goodman volunteered for aircrew duties and recalled there was 'no way I was going to fight on the ground if I could help it', and thought that, compared with soldiering, 'the war in the air might result in a cleaner death'.[18]

By comparison, the RAF uniform may have seemed a trivial reason for enlisting. Yet, Albert Smith, who became a navigator, recorded that there was a lad in his street in Salford who'd joined the RAF and 'looked good in his blue uniform …

all the girls fancied him'.[19] The RAF appeared an especially attractive prospect for ex-grammar school boys, as most roles required a reasonable standard of education and the Service was concerned with a form of warfare based around cutting-edge technology, seemingly more suitable to 'the intelligent'. A common perception existed, perhaps falsely, that the RAF attracted a better standard of recruit, and that on joining up, the individual was liable to be in better company, particularly when compared with the army.

Most recruits underwent some form of selection process, even if it was simply a short interview on enlistment. Often this took an individual's previous experience into account. Shortly before the war, Mike Henry aspired to become a flight mechanic but lacked the necessary mechanical/engineering experience. Instead, he was persuaded by the NCO interviewing him to become a wireless operator, especially as he had been serving with the Royal Corps of Signals (TA).

Notably, potential officers came in for a particular grilling by Air Ministry Selection Boards, comprised of senior officers, who could ask surprising questions. Wing Commander Ken Rees was confronted by the president of his selection board, an elderly squadron leader and First World War veteran, who enquired: 'Can you ride?'[20] Although taken aback, he replied positively, having grown up with horses on a Welsh farm. Having applied for a commission as a Meteorology Officer (RAFVR) in 1941, F.R. Chappell discovered that his selection board considered 'that a Cambridge degree in Geography, London Diploma of Education and experience as a school master (thirty-two years of age) with interests in physical education and games were not sufficiently scientific background for Meteorology'.[21]

Instead, he was recommended for training as a bomber intelligence officer, a role he came to find extremely rewarding.

Another strand of selection was that recruits received a medical. This could be daunting. One Lincolnshire farmer's son found that:

> The MO made me strip to the waist and gave me a thorough examination—heart, lungs, eyes, ears throat and limbs. Then he ordered 'Drop your trousers…And your underpants.' Timidly I did as ordered. The officer then conducted the most intimate inspection of my private parts, finally taking a firm grasp he ordered 'Now cough.'[22]

Others recalled that they were inoculated against various awful sounding diseases, although to some, it appeared as if standards had relaxed in wartime. In 1940, Ivor Broom 'had a swollen TB gland in his neck' but after treatment was passed 'fit for pilot training', without having to undergo any further testing.[23] Similarly, Morton Charlton attended a medical in Newcastle in March 1941, and was informed that he was 'a little underweight' but that 'service life would soon put that right'.[24]

Induction into the RAF

Recruits were first posted to a reception centre, such as RAF Cardington, Bedfordshire. For Albert Smith, this was nerve-wracking. He'd only previously left Salford to watch Manchester United play Port Vale in a cup tie, and once been to a school camp in Wales. He underwent various tests to determine his suitability as aircrew, including the mercury test, where recruits had to blow mercury up a glass tube and keep it level for at least sixty seconds. On volunteering, Ronald Pate was extremely surprised to be directed to London Zoo, near his home. Conveniently, an Aircrew Reception Centre had been established there, which was all about 'getting involved with the air force'.[25] This entailed introducing personnel to military discipline via drill, so recruits became accustomed to efficiently obeying orders without questioning them and fostering the necessary corporate identity.

At a Receiving Wing at Babbacombe, a holiday resort adjoining Torquay, aircrew recruits worked a twelve-hour day starting at six o'clock in the morning, although there were breaks between instruction/training when they could enjoy cafes along the sea front. Much time was spent on keeping their kit in perfect order to try to satisfy their NCO instructors, and getting in shape via route marches, PT sessions, and plenty of squad drill. The NCOs deliberately generated an intimidating atmosphere, even picking on specific individuals. Consequently, men soon learnt to appreciate that as a recruit, or 'sprog', they were effectively 'the lowest form of Service life', even though technically they were designated 'UT/P or Pilots Under Training', and could expect to be addressed by officers as cadets.[26]

Another form of instruction entailed lectures, some of which were more stimulating than others. Subjects included mathematics, the elementary theory of flight, hygiene, gas warfare and RAF organisation. However, a curious policy existed in that personnel who failed flying training were posted back to Receiving Wings, as seniors to recruits who were in the system. This hindered morale. As one former trainee explained, these individuals highlighted 'the difficulties and dangers of flying, leaving us with the impression that those who escaped death would almost certainly meet disaster in failing the course'.[27]

Conditions could also be tough for tradesmen under basic training. Albert Bennett became an instrument repairer, or 'basher'. At RAF Cardington, he was issued kit before being hurriedly sent to Great Yarmouth for a few weeks' 'square bashing', a situation he found strange because frequent air raids would curtail their training and they seemed to spend all their time sheltering from bombs.[28] Although Ron Smith wanted to be an air gunner, in June 1940 he was told by a recruiting officer to enlist as a ground gunner. Soon afterwards, he commenced basic training in Blackpool and was 'marched – it seemed incessantly – up and down the sunlit promenade' and fired an obligatory five rounds on the range with 'a vintage rifle'.[29]

Cyril Clifford ended up posted to No. 1 RAF Depot, Uxbridge, to train for the Service Police. Here, senior NCOs regularly appeared ready to castigate anyone for what seemed relatively minor infringements, such as stepping off a path or having a button undone. Such individuals usually found themselves on fatigues in the cookhouse, scrubbing out baking tins for lengthy periods after a full day's training. The Station Warrant Officer (SWO) was usually the most feared NCO. As Cyril Clifford recalled, their SWO would conduct inspections and run his finger along the top of a door, where, upon finding a few specks of dust, he'd shout: 'This place is not fit for pigs to live in!'[30] Yet, as Eric Marsden discovered on becoming a fitter at RAF Scampton, SWOs didn't always come across as fearsome characters, and many were specially selected owing to their fatherly qualities.

Neither was air force discipline always as strict as might be supposed, even for an Aircraftman Second Class (AC2) such as C.A. Faulks, who found he was effectively the 'lowest form of animal life'. Nicknamed 'Guy' for obvious reasons, he underwent training as a wireless operator in Blackpool during 1940, and recalled that they learnt:

> Morse code but also attended lectures on various subjects of Air Force life, and learned how to drill. Learning the Morse code came fairly easily to me – it was in a way similar to figures in that one had to translate hieroglyphics or sounds into figures and words, but at speed. The corporal in charge of our squad couldn't have been more than 5' 6" and had very little idea of discipline. There were about 30 in our squad, the marching formation being the usual 'tallest in the front and rear, shortest in the middle'. Being one of the tallest, I was in the front row. He gradually instilled into us some semblance of order, and usually on the command: 'ATTENTION' there was a ragged sound of stamping boots. Our drills were always spoilt by someone turning the wrong way, or missing the command, or of course being out of step. We hadn't joined up to be soldiers.[31]

During basic training, individual identities were subsumed under name, rank and number. David Mattingley, an Australian, transferred to the RAF. On enlisting in the Royal Australian Air Force, he was known simply as: 'Mattingley, C.D. Aircraftman Class 2, 408458'.[32] A short haircut was important in helping men assume a military identity. One airman described how they 'had the quickest haircut of our lives', when a civilian barber was brought onto their station and faced with a large queue, hastily set about them with his electric shears.[33] The issuing of uniform was also significant in helping to generate a feeling of esprit de corps, when recruits first donned distinctive RAF blue. Males were initially issued with two sets of No. 1 Dress uniforms, one of which was kept especially for parades. As the war progressed, a No. 2 uniform was introduced that closely resembled the 'battledress' issued to the army, albeit in blue. This could be used for everyday duties and training. Trainee aircrew were expected to always wear their uniform, even on leave, and sported a distinctive white flash in their forage caps to denote they were aircrew cadets.

With its attendant medical inspections, kit issue and atmosphere of discipline, one trainee pilot described induction into the RAF as 'a levelling experience'.[34] What was apparent to many recruits was they were joining a new world, complete with its own language and customs. Most quickly became familiar with the RAF slang that permeated all aspects of life. Rumours were significant in wartime, and information was termed 'gen' by airmen, short for 'intelligence'. Hence, 'ace' or 'pukka' gen was information that bore relation to the truth, whereas, 'duff gen' was always false, often failing to bear any relation to the truth. Somewhere between the two lay 'ordinary gen'. Enemy aircraft were 'bandits', and 'kite' was a generic term for any aircraft. 'Gremlins', as made famous by former wartime RAF pilot Roald Dahl, were imaginary, mischievous sprites blamed for failures with aircraft or equipment. Cakes or buns were universally termed 'wad'. The warrant officers' badges of rank were 'Tate & Lyle', as they resembled the trademark employed by that well-known manufacturer of golden syrup.[35] Another feature of RAF slang was that it provided a ready supply of euphemisms covering less pleasant aspects of wartime, such as 'Gone for a Burton', signifying a pilot had been killed. Some, including Pip Beck, felt RAF slang was 'silly', but soon adjusted 'to speaking the "language" fluently'.[36]

On joining the RAF, recruits rapidly became acquainted with Service cuisine. At one Receiving Wing, this included 'squares of a vivid yellow block cake' that appeared to contain 'a high percentage of sawdust'. This was the famous 'NAAFI wad', and to accompany it were 'heavy cups of newspaper-flavoured grey tea'. If they were lucky, given rationing, recruits might additionally be offered tarts of 'a grey cloying pastry' filled with a sickly sweet, brightly coloured and 'tasteless jam'.[37]

Coping with relatively primitive accommodation and living communally were further issues that had to be faced. Hotels and boarding houses were frequently requisitioned for Initial Training Wings (ITW), usually kitted out with Service-issue furniture. Some were comparatively pleasant, whereas others were drab and unwelcoming. One Spitfire pilot recalled that at his ITW in the West Country, they lived in 'crummy old hotels and boarding houses', and the food was simply 'ghastly!'[38]

For many men and women, joining up meant leaving the security of home and their regular employment and taking a leap into the unknown. This was more of a culture shock for some than for others, especially when faced with brutish NCO instructors and a disciplined atmosphere. Recalling his wartime service, Squadron Leader Denis Peto-Shepherd reckoned that recruits with a public school background tended to cope far better with the conditions than those without such experience. He was surprised at how difficult some without such backgrounds found physical training. Largely, he considered this was because the public schools of the period provided pupils with comparatively harsh conditions and plenty of opportunities for sport, plus they ran Officer Training Corps (OTC), geared specifically towards preparing young men for the military. Those with prior experience of serving with the LDV (Home Guard) found that this often helped them cope with the discipline, drill and general conditions on joining the RAF.

The Women's Auxiliary Air Force

At the outbreak of war, women could opt to serve either with the Women's Royal Naval Service (WRNS), Auxiliary Territorial Service (ATS) or the Women's Auxiliary Air Force (WAAF). The Army's ATS included companies specifically designated to co-operate with the RAF, and in June 1939, these were given a separate identity as the WAAF, which on the eve of war comprised about 8,000 officers and airwomen.[39]

The primary object of the WAAF was to release men for combatant roles, and recruits were accepted between the ages of 17½, and 44. Described as 'extremely nice girls' by one male RAF officer, early recruits were volunteers and signed up for the duration of hostilities.[40] In contrast, under the National Service (Armed Services) Act, from December 1941, single women and childless widows aged 20 to 30 were expected to make themselves available for war service. Faced with conscription, many chose the WAAF in preference to the other women's services. In July 1943, the Service reached its peak numerical strength of 181,835 airwomen of all ranks.[41]

There were numerous reasons why women chose to join the WAAF. Muriel Pushman confessed that 'as a blue-eyed blonde, I had always been besotted with blue', and this was almost reason enough to choose the air force.[42] Others, including Joan Rice, were motivated by a sense of 'doing one's bit', although the prospect of adventure, opportunity to lead an independent life, and 'swank around in a uniform' all influenced her decision.[43] For Laura McGeown, guilt at leading a comfortable civilian life, replete with domestic help, spurred her to enlist. Moreover, she'd attended a co-educational school and was 'distressed by the number of my class mates killed in the war', so 'joining the WAAF was revenge in a small way, for their deaths'.[44]

Initially, the Service simply wasn't prepared for an influx of volunteers, and demand for uniforms outstripped supply. Gwendoline Saunders became an NCO and trained as a teleprinter operator. Having enlisted in 1939, she was posted to RAF Old Sarum, Wiltshire.

I don't think we even had our 'hussif' ['housewife' – armed forces-issued sewing kit]. I don't think we had anything. ... I took up my little sewing box and materials from home. I had a nice suit, it was grey, and much to mother's disgust I had it dyed so it would be of navy blue. I bought some very nice brogues with crepe soles and I had those dyed. The first uniform we had were air force mackintoshes and a navy blue beret with air force badge. The 'macks' had what was called a teddy bear lining, most welcome on the edge of Salisbury Plain, but underneath we wore our own clothes, shoes and stockings.[45]

However, by 1940–41, the situation improved. Irene Storer recounted being issued with an impressive array of uniform items, including: four shirts with several matching collars; one black tie; two blue serge skirts and jackets; two caps; one cap badge; two pairs of black lace-up shoes and a pair of plimsolls; plus vests, bras and several items of undergarment. The latter were a mixed blessing, especially Service-issue knickers, which were regarded disparagingly and dubbed 'passion killers' or 'blackouts' in the case of the winter-issued ones, after their colour.[45]

There was also the food to contend with. After route marches, Mable Payne discovered that she was so hungry that she even developed a liking for liver and onions, a dish she'd hated before joining up. Equally, on entering the cookhouse armed with their irons (knife, fork and spoon), WAAFs often faced having to eat their entire meal from the same plate. Under these conditions, women soon learnt to eat quickly. As Irene Park recalled, hopefully servings didn't meet in the middle, 'jam from one side, and kidneys perhaps floating across from the other side'.[47] At RAF Old Sarum, Gwendoline Saunders found the 'food quite good', despite the 'girls having to concoct meals in a First World War era cookhouse'.[48] Alternatively, some women found they were able to scrounge foodstuffs from generous locals or rely on comrades for assistance. Pip Beck spent some of her service at an RAF station at Barford, Oxfordshire, where she gathered quantities of blackberries and elderberries from the surrounding countryside when off duty, and was allowed to pick as many apples and plums as she wished from an old man's orchard. She fondly remembered that sometimes coming off duty at midnight, the duty signaller would give her his fried egg to go with her cold meat and chips.

On enlisting in the WAAF, like their male counterparts, women were routinely faced with relatively spartan accommodation. Shortly after arriving at RAF Old Sarum, Gwendoline Saunders encountered:

these rather decrepit billets, because walking up from the Guard Room I could see some rather nice little brick buildings, that were obviously married quarters and the Headquarters were brick. Obviously they'd been built in the early 1930s but we were directed onto these sub-standard or contract sort of built places that are being condemned now. These were First World War ones because this station was a First World War one. Anyway I was directed to this huge quarter, obviously meant for a big family, and given a brass bed with a mattress and so on. And then I was escorted back to another ancient building that was the canteen and cookhouse for the WAAF.[49]

Her mattress turned out to be sodden wet, but she was later able to scrounge a replacement, and with help from a couple of other WAAFs who'd been Girl Guides, light a fire and make their quarters as comfortable as possible.

Owing to the technicalities of a legal ruling, during 1939–41, WAAF personnel weren't treated equally in disciplinary matters compared with their male counterparts. This included serious offences, such as desertion and going AWOL. Whereas an airman might be court-martialled, WAAFs had to agree to a suitable punishment, and if they declined, could leave the Service without charges being brought against them. The situation was resolved by the implementation of the Defence (Women's Forces) Regulations in late April 1941, which ensured WAAFs were considered members of the Armed Forces of the Crown and subject to the Air Force Act, although provision was made 'for specifically feminine items of routine Service life'.[50]

Like men enlisting in the RAF, most women underwent basic training, with an emphasis on drill. In mid-October 1939, Joan Rice recorded how 'I shall be tough what with marching, early rises and hard beds'.[51] There were lectures on topics designed to hold women in good stead once they were posted to an RAF station. These included hygiene, the history and organisation of the RAF and WAAF, and instruction on military courtesy, such as who to salute and why.

A degree of social integration was another feature of WAAF life, especially after conscription was introduced, when women from differing backgrounds could find themselves thrown together. One WAAF recruit was surprised to discover herself sharing a hut with two prostitutes from Liverpool Docks; they had lice, but proved very engaging characters and 'broadened my horizons a lot'.[52] Another commented that, particularly with relation to boyfriends in the RAF, 'in wartime the pace of life was speeded up so tremendously … it might take months or even years in peacetime to get to know someone really well – yet in wartime it often took only days or weeks.'[53]

Women weren't permitted to fly operationally, although throughout the war, some accepted offers to accompany male colleagues on flights. However, women proved they could perform admirably as pilots with the Air Transport Auxiliary (ATA), a separate organisation tasked with delivering a wide variety of aircraft to where they were needed – a role not always granted the recognition it deserves.[54]

Initially, women were employed in administrative or domestic roles, such as clerks, cooks or drivers. Some became balloon fabric workers, which entailed repairing large, unwieldy barrage balloons, and could be dangerous owing to the harmful effects of the dope varnish used to coat the fabric. Women were entitled to a free glass of milk from the NAAFI, in the belief that this counteracted the ill effects of the dope. As the war progressed, a host of other trades were opened up to women, and they became involved in most aspects of RAF activity, apart from actually flying. This included intelligence work, serving as plotters in operations rooms, helping run radar sites, and even working as flight mechanics.

Wherever possible, 'substitution' would occur, i.e. replacing male personnel with female. By late 1945, women had been successfully 'substituted' in fifteen officer-related roles and fifty-nine airmen trades, in addition to those trades specifically created for the WAAF. Typically, recruits were assessed by a trade test board at training depots, and once their basic training was completed, women embarked on their trade training. One highly important role was that of WAAF watchkeepers, who were an integral part of the operations room at many RAF stations. Usually trained as sergeant telephonists, these women had to receive operational messages from Command, break these into their constituent parts and ensure that each piece of information reached its proper destination. Messages to pilots, the armoury and cookhouse all had to pass through the watchkeeper.

Signals relied heavily on the WAAF. Aileen Morris was the daughter of a civil servant and was a fluent German speaker, having spent time in Germany before the war. After enlisting, she was eventually posted to the 'Y' Service, which intercepted German radio communications. These were painstakingly logged and sent via the Air Ministry to Station 'X', the codebreaking centre at Bletchley Park, Buckinghamshire.[55] At Leighton Buzzard, over 1,000 WAAFs spent their war in close proximity to 'the clatter of the tele-printer rooms' in what was 'the central signals station and exchange for all landline communications of the RAF, and the main inter-command W/T receiving station'.[56]

Pip Beck was posted to Bomber Command and served at RAF Waddington, Lincolnshire, as an R/T (Radio Telephony) operator. There were normally five operators, and they'd each work 'a shift system consisting of a four-hour watch and an eight-hour watch', covering a twenty-four hour period. She rapidly had to learn the correct procedure or 'set replies and instructions to use in any contingency by both air and ground operators', plus how to log all communications correctly, employ the phonetic alphabet, and signal in Morse code with an Aldis lamp. 'It all sounded rather formidable, but I was certain I'd be able to cope with it – given time.'[57]

While the majority of WAAF personnel served in Britain, some volunteered for overseas service. By 1944, as part of 45 Group, about seventy code and cypher officers were serving in Canada. Another organisation that famously employed WAAF as agents overseas was the Special Operations Executive (SOE), the secret service established to aid the resistance movement. Numerous other WAAF personnel performed diligently and bravely, often under dangerous conditions. At RAF Biggin Hill during the Battle of Britain, 'two telephone operators, Sergeant Helen Turner and Corporal Elspeth Henderson, continued to maintain communications even after the operations block in which they were working received a direct hit.' Their behaviour was deemed not only inspirational to airwomen on other stations, but also to their male comrades.[58] Corporal Daphne Pearson received the Empire Gallantry Medal (later George Cross) for her action after witnessing a crash. She rushed to the burning aircraft and rescued the injured pilot, then shielded his body with her own as the bombs it was carrying started to explode.[59]

Initial Training Wings

Initial Training Wings (ITWs) were established in several towns as well as at some Oxbridge colleges. The latter were highly sought-after. Sam Pritchard was posted to No. 2 ITW in Cambridge University, and revelled in the experience of mixing not just with grammar school boys like himself, but with those from public schools, even university, plus Commonwealth personnel.[60] Another aircrew cadet remained puzzled and frustrated: 'How was I going to learn to fly in the middle of Cambridge?' Yet, as he rapidly discovered, the RAF expected him to undergo a swift regime of discipline and instruction before he could commence flying training as a pilot or observer/navigator.[61] According to Air Commodore Cyril Brown, who'd joined the RAFVR as a sergeant pilot before the outbreak of war, the ITWs:

> served two purposes really, to knock some discipline into us and really to keep us occupied until the flying training schools could accept the increasing intakes of people that had been called up. People's stay there varied from two or three weeks [usually more like six to eight], and some unfortunate ones two or three months until they could be absorbed into the Service flying training organisation.[62]

The fact that many trainees came from public schools and were destined to become officers was deeply resented by some instructors, owing to the social divide between those with such backgrounds and the average NCO instructor. At No. 7 ITW at Newquay, Cornwall, NCO instructors 'within their limited sphere ... instituted, with relish, a regime of absolute hell'. Uniforms and equipment had always to be kept up to a high standard, but this seldom satisfied the instructors. Consequently, cleaning buttons and polishing boots occupied much time, and this had to be fitted in around aircrew cadets' studies and other training.[63]

Along with the discipline, drill and inspections, there was an accent on promoting physical fitness. Leslie Biddlecombe, who became a pilot, found that he 'revelled' in the physical demands of his course, 'and enjoyed a fitness he had never known before'.[64] Physical training was similarly important in building up anyone who'd remained undernourished after growing up during the Great Depression.

An idea of the intensity of the courses can be gauged by the experience of an aircrew cadet at No. 9 ITW, Stratford-upon-Avon. He described how his first day started at 6.15 am with a parade before breakfast and a mile march there and back to his quarters. This was followed by another parade at 8.00 am, before they were marched to a requisitioned school 'for 2 hrs of maths, all back as fast as possible, then to the Memorial Theatre for an address by the CO', followed by instruction on aircraft recognition, lunch, another parade, a lecture by the MO, and 'parade after parade until 6'. This was followed by an evening meal and a period of private study before going 'for a swim in the river, and then polish buttons and boots and shave for the morning'.[65]

As courses progressed, against a constant background of discipline, aircrew cadets studied subjects such as mathematics, aerial navigation, meteorology, signalling, armaments, aircraft recognition, and seemingly 'funny ones like Air Force Law, hygiene and gas thrown in for good measure'.[66] Clearly, many topics had relevance to aspiring aircrew. It was essential in combat, for example, to be able to differentiate between friendly and hostile aircraft. Even so, some aircrew cadets, including Richard Hough, remained perplexed at some of their lectures and instruction. How was Morse by Aldis lamp supposed to work when flying an aircraft? 'Did one stand up in the cockpit at night, coming in to land, and flash permission – Shot through ... like a colander – must pancake?' Stripping down and reassembling machine guns while blindfolded fostered images in his mind of unrealistically repairing guns 'in the heat of combat', while under enemy fire.[67]

Despite the conditions, and their comparative lowly status, many aircrew cadets appear to have valued their ITW experience. Although not all would agree, the food and accommodation in commandeered boarding houses and hotels was reasonable, by wartime standards. Locations such as Cambridge or Newquay were generally pleasant, especially when compared with towns and cities that experienced the brunt of German bombing. There was a strong feeling of comradeship among intakes from various backgrounds who shared the common desire of wanting to fly. Years later, Squadron Leader Jack Currie reflected that it was the 'intercourse with the hearts and minds of others that was the best part, for me, of the ITW experience'.[68] Others developed a respect for their instructors, particularly those who were First World War veterans. Group Captain W.G.G. Duncan Smith fondly remembered that at his ITW they 'came both to fear and love' Warrant Officer 'Timber' Woods, a former RSM of the Grenadier Guards, and 'stickler for discipline' who regularly stressed its importance in all forms as 'a prerequisite in enabling one to beat the enemy'.[69]

Flying training

If they passed their ITW, aircrew cadets would learn to fly, either as pilots or navigators. Typically, successful personnel were posted to an Elementary Flying Training School (EFTS) for ten weeks of basic flying instruction and ground-based lessons. This was followed by sixteen weeks at a Service Flying Training School (SFTS), where they would undertake advanced flying training before being posted to an Operational Training Unit (OTU), where they received four to six weeks' experience on the type of aircraft they'd be flying operationally. As aviation historian Chaz Bowyer stated, this ensured that on average, wartime pilots logged around 200 flying hours before embarking on operations.[70]

As the war progressed and heavy bombers were introduced, training for their crews was extended to incorporate a period at a Heavy Conversion Unit (HCU), intended to adapt them to such aircraft. Crews of Lancasters even underwent training at a Lancaster Finishing School (LFS), designed to deal with the demands of operating that specific aircraft. Consequently, many pilots, especially in Bomber Command, eventually logged well over 300 hours' flying before they embarked on operations.

Given the demands placed on the wartime RAF and its rapid expansion after 1939, many aircrew completed their flying training overseas, often as part of the Empire Air Training Scheme in Canada and Rhodesia (Zimbabwe). In America, the Arnold Scheme, with the help of the US Army Air Corps, produced nearly 4,500 RAF pilots between June 1941 and February 1943, while British Flying Training Schools (BFTS) established across America may have trained as many as 7,000 pilots by August 1945. Over 1,000 RAF navigators were similarly trained by the Pan-American Airways Observers' School during 1941–42, and under the Towers Scheme, the RAF trained crews for flying boats, although many of these were diverted to Bomber Command.[71]

In mid-1941, Tony Tooth was relieved to be posted to No. 1 BFTS in Texas, after having been held for a lengthy, frustrating period at his ITW in the West Country because poor weather ensured flying schools in Britain were behind schedule. Having endured an arduous voyage to North America, he eventually found that the training set-up was strange.

> All the facilities were supplied by the Dallas School of Aviation based at Love Field, including all instructors ground and flying, whilst aircraft were on loan from the US Army Air Corps. The only RAF personnel were the CO, a Squadron Leader, the Adjutant, a Flight Lieutenant, and a Sergeant Armament instructor.[72]

Initially, he learnt to fly the Boeing-Stearman PT-18, a two-seat biplane trainer of interwar vintage.

A really lovely little biplane, a real classic and still sixty years later a great favourite, were hangered at Love Field but the flying was mostly done from an auxiliary landing field about twenty miles away. Half the courses would fly in the morning while the other half had lectures in the ground school, changing over at lunch time. Lectures could be bit of a mixed blessing by mid-summer because it was so hot we couldn't stay awake, in fact the only way to keep us awake was to turn on a very powerful fan, the only problem being it was so noisy we couldn't hear the lecturer!

This part of the course called Primary was to consist of seventy hours' flying and last ten weeks. The flying proved very enjoyable and at times was very exciting, apart from learning how to get the aeroplane off the ground, and down again, there were important things like navigation, formation flying and aerobatics that are vital for a military pilot to master. The reason for this is that a military pilot has to be able to make an aircraft do anything that it is physically capable of. This is known as flying to the limits. I do not mean to imply that this was expected of us at this stage but it was to prepare us for what was to come later.[73]

In Britain and Commonwealth countries, the de Havilland DH 82 Tiger Moth, equivalent to the Stearman PT-18, was widely employed as a two-seat elementary trainer, with the two cockpits connected by a rubber mouthpiece to allow for in-flight communication between an instructor and his pupil. A robust biplane, it had a maximum range of about 300 miles and top speed of 109 mph, and was ideally suited to its training role.[74] According to one former RAF pilot who encountered the Tiger Moth in Kenya, it 'suffered innumerable heavy landings from incompetent beginners without turning a hair'.[75]

Ivor Broom and countless other trainees soon discovered that prior to take-off in a Tiger Moth, you had to learn how to swing the propeller correctly to start the engine. As there was no self-starter or brakes, 'if the propeller was incorrectly handled', the engine would start too soon, and risked slicing 'off a hand, or even the head, of its prop swinger!'[76] Most trainees received an 'Air Familiarisation' detail, a short flight during which their instructor endeavoured to acclimatise them to the feeling of flying, part of their job being as early as possible to weed out anyone suffering from air sickness or any other defect that could only be detected once airborne.

At an EFTS, trainees were expected to rapidly progress by learning how to taxi, take off into the wind, climb, fly straight and level, recover from stalls, turn to the left and right, and make a glide approach and safe landing. Usually this was done via a series of progressive exercises, with pupil copying instructor. These followed a pattern such as: Exercise One: Air Experience or Acclimatisation; Exercise Two: Taxiing and Handling the Engine; Exercise Three: Effects of the Controls; and

Exercise Four: Straight and Level Flight.[77] Skills were then practised repeatedly until they had been mastered satisfactorily. The ultimate aim was for all trainees to fly solo, something most did after about seven to ten hours' instruction.

Even so, many found flying difficult, and holding the control column too tightly was a common fault. Yet another awkward area was landing, something most trainee pilots took time to master. Squadron Leader Jack Currie found that trying to operate the pedals and the stick, and associate their movements with those of the aeroplane, 'was like putting your hands on a pianola's keyboard and pretending you were playing'.[78] A former fighter pilot recounted how at first he found the art of taking off especially difficult: 'I am just totally unable to control the swing and I career all over the airfield in ever-increasing ugly great swerves. No matter how hard I try I just cannot keep the beastly aeroplane straight.' Overall, he considered that learning to fly was 'an intriguing business'.[79]

The Miles Magister, or 'Maggie', was another two–seat elementary trainer in which the pupil sat in a separate cockpit behind the instructor. It was produced from 1937–41, and despite initial teething problems, proved an excellent aircraft. Unlike the Tiger Moth, it was a low-winged monoplane, something that made it especially valuable in training fighter pilots. Constructed of wood with a plywood covering, the Maggie was powered by a single 130 h.p. de Havilland Gipsy Major I inline piston engine, giving it a top speed of 132 mph.[80] One trainee pilot discovered that the Maggie was comparatively easy to operate, including when conducting a turn, something he started to learn on his second day at an EFTS. 'To come out of a turn, opposite aileron and when straight, rudder. After a time you do both together. As for straight flying, that comes automatically, much the same as you joggle the wheel of a car.'[81]

Some trainee pilots, including Wing Commander Ken Rees, discovered that after flying, they experienced an exhilarating emotional and physical release, and this reoccurred on completion of later operational sorties. Contrastingly, others were struck by the demands of flying training, including Leslie Biddlecombe, who was overwhelmed by 'a deep, all-pervading weariness', the like of which he'd never experienced before.[82]

All trainee pilots needed to find their instructors compatible. Many instructors in Britain were pilots who'd exhausted themselves on operations or felt they could best serve the war effort by training others. Inevitably, there were sometimes personality clashes or cases where the chemistry between pupil and instructor simply wasn't right. Often this could be rectified by a change of instructor. Group Captain Duncan Smith trained in Britain and found that he had a cautious flying instructor who offered little encouragement, even when he felt ready to fly solo. Luckily for him, the chief flying instructor (CFI) was aware of the situation and paired him with another, after which he 'never looked back'.[83] Spitfire pilot Tony Tooth found that staff in Flying Training Command were generally 'unwelcoming and unfriendly', in stark 'contrast to the attitude of operational outfits'.[84] Richard Hough, who was taught to fly in America, reckoned flying instruction was 'not a profession celebrated for gentleness, good manners and patience', and that he was far from being the only pupil 'half paralysed with fear of these scarred, cursing American instructors', many of whom were former crop-duster or stunt pilots used to frighteningly low-level flying.[85]

According to Squadron Leader Jack Currie, good flying instructors taught their pupils to do what they found difficult, and to do these things well, often via relentless practice. This included performing awkward manoeuvres such as putting an aircraft into a spin and recovering from it, or flying solely by instruments. This approach sought to prepare pilots so that the appropriate actions for any situation became second nature. If a trainee pilot 'could make a lovely steady barrel roll' but his snap rolls were never as good, the instructor would insist these were practised until of a comparable standard.[86] After flying operationally, Tony Tooth qualified as a flying instructor training RAF personnel in Rhodesia (Zimbabwe), where he had:

> to be able to demonstrate any manoeuvre impeccably to a student, without any risk of it going wrong, whilst at the same time explaining it clearly and accurately. Not the easiest of things to do. Maintaining the Patter, as the talk was called, through any exercise that was not going according to plan could be a real challenge, calling for ingenuity and a bit of cheek.[87]

Instruction was also provided on the ground-based Link Trainer, a static machine shaped like a miniature aeroplane, employed for simulated instrument flying. One trainee pilot found that these were highly beneficial 'in sharpening accuracy with the instruments and procedural knowledge'.[88]

However, trainees' experiences differed according to where they learned to fly. In particular, weather was a major factor, as was the constant potential for accidents. Having gone solo successfully in a Tiger Moth at an ITS in Nairobi, Roald Dahl was given the freedom to fly around in clear blue Kenyan skies. While doing so he observed a host of game, including 'huge herds of buffalo and wildebeest which would stampede in all directions as I whizzed over' at heights of 60 to 70 feet.[89] In California, Richard Hough found that he was similarly blessed with perfect flying conditions for much of his training. This contrasted sharply with the cloudy, damp conditions many personnel encountered during flying training in Britain, mainly in the west so as to avoid the attentions of the Luftwaffe. At No. 16 EFTS, RAF Burnaston, near the Pennines, pilots undergoing training routinely had to fly between rain showers. Dealing with clouds could be tricky. For Richard Hillary, diving into a cloud formation over Scotland was 'intoxicating', but the resultant poor visibility meant he had to rely on his instruments. Having performed a 'strictly forbidden' slow roll, he nearly went into a spin, dramatically losing height. Fortunately, he regained control, and exited the cloud formation at sufficient height to make it home safely, 'another lesson learned'.[90]

Having completed a course at an Elementary Flying Training School, trainee pilots were usually posted on to a Service Flying Training School, or the equivalent, where they honed their skills with plenty of time in the air, either with an instructor or flying solo. This provided a chance to practise advanced formation, aerobatic and instrument flying. Often they encountered more advanced training aircraft. Having mastered the Stearman in America, and done a forty-hour basic flying course on the Vultee BT-13A, Tony Tooth was introduced to the North American AT-6A Texan, known as the Harvard by the RAF. Initially, it 'looked huge and menacing and was quite a bit more complicated' than the other aircraft types he'd experienced.[91] It was a modern-looking, low-wing monoplane with a retractable undercarriage, flaps and constant-speed airscrew. Geoffrey Wellum remembered being cautioned by his instructor at RAF Little Rissington, Gloucestershire, to treat the Harvard 'with respect and you will find it a very pleasant and safe aircraft to fly' but if you 'pull it about' the sky like a Tiger Moth, especially at lower speeds, 'it will turn round and bite you'.[92]

Ronald Pate also learned to fly in America, under the highly disciplined conditions of the US Army Air Corps. Eventually, he completed around sixty hours on the Harvard, flying from Maxwell Field, Alabama. There were 'no radios. Everything was done by signs. One of the big things in the American air force was formation flying, because it was what was needed by bombers especially B-17s in defensive formations.' He vividly remembered one exercise late on in his training. The instructor said:

> Now in this exercise I want you to follow me very closely and do exactly as I signal. To read his hand signals we had to be in close formation. And up we went stooging around the clouds, and in and out and so forth, very tight formation all the time. Then he gave his first signals reduce speed, put down your undercarriage, some flaps and so forth. It's difficult to believe but I can promise you it's so, that so concentrated in exactly what you are supposed to do and you are really tight in like this. All of a sudden I felt a bump and we had landed and I hadn't even seen the ground. It was an incredible experience. Now of course when the CO found out what happened he really tore this fellow [the instructor] off, but he'd proved his point i.e. if you do exactly what I say you'll be alright.[93]

Trainee pilots selected for bombers underwent advanced training on twin-engine aeroplanes, including the Airspeed Oxford. This was a two-seat general purpose trainer, usually crewed by three men at any time, which not only leant itself to training pilots, but could be configured to train air gunners, bomb aimers, camera operators, navigators and radio/wireless operators. Power plants varied according to mark, but one of Ivor Broom's abiding memories was of having to climb onto the ice-laden wings and hand-crank the Oxford's two Cheetah X engines during the bitterly cold winter of 1940/41. 'That really scared me. I was terrified of slipping off into the whirling propellers as the engines fired up.'[94]

Rupert Cooling had mixed feelings about the Oxford, a type he first encountered as a 19-year-old sergeant pilot U/T at RAF Lossiemouth in early 1940, having qualified as a pilot with the RAFVR.

> I did one circuit with an instructor where he showed me the way around. We did another couple of circuits, landed and taxied in. Then he said: 'Right off you go.' And I said: 'What, by myself?' He replied: 'Yes' 'But this is the first time I've flown an Oxford.' He said: 'So what, you've got those wings on, go and fly it!' It was an excellent training aeroplane but it was a cow of an aeroplane because they expected you to three-point them and the Oxford didn't like three-pointing. It was the old nose wheel, main undercarriage, tail wheel sort of thing, a porpoise.[95]

Like in the American air force, formation flying was deemed important in the RAF. Initially, it was considered that bombers armed with a rear gunner and machine-gun turrets could protect themselves against attack by enemy fighters when flying this way. Learning formation flying was part of the fighter pilot's remit. After completing his flying training in America, Richard Hough was posted to RAF Watton, near Norwich, where during 1942 he got to grips with the Miles Master Mk II as part of an Advanced Flying course. This aircraft was intended to replicate the performance of existing fighters, and proved 'unfriendly and ferocious'. Training was rarely cancelled owing to poor weather, which could be hair-raising and required intense concentration. Unlike in America, Hough found that he was constantly enveloped in cloud, and there were far fewer recognisable landmarks when compared with the Antelope Valley, California, with its towns, mountains and straight roads and railway tracks. Typically, his course entailed formation flying, learning aerobatic manoeuvres, flying at low level 'to get under enemy radar', as well as mock dogfights, using cine cameras rather than guns.[96]

As Wing Commander Ken Rees recorded, a fighter pilot was akin to a boxer, heavily reliant on rapid, instant reactions, and as a military pilot had to be able to fly an aircraft to its limits and shoot with the right deflection to hit an enemy aircraft flying at an angle across him, i.e. 'judge the distance and speed to shoot ahead, anticipating the time it takes for the bullets to get to the target, not unlike shooting a pheasant'. However, bomber pilots, or skippers, had responsibility for their crew as well as for themselves, and needed to understand their roles. Often they had to show the same level of determination and courage as fighter pilots, but over much longer periods, if they were to successfully hit a target and make it back home.[97]

Another skill all pilots picked up as their training advanced was the art of night flying. In America, this was relatively straightforward because, with no blackout, navigation and visibility were not especially problematic. Contrastingly, in Britain, conditions were more challenging owing to having to fly in total or near-total darkness. Rupert Cooling experienced his first night flight while stationed at RAF Lossiemouth, something he never forgot.

> it was magical. I remember taking off there to the north, and there was the Murray Firth there and there was very thin moonlight, and it was just the light playing on there, and you swung round and you could see the flare path behind you, and it was a crystal clear night, and you just seemed to be hanging there looking at the lights sliding by. And then came and lined up and you got the green [light] and thought this is it. And you watched out and were sort of feeling for the ground, and all of a sudden I felt this rumbling and knew I was down.[98]

On completion of SFTS training, pilots usually reported to an Operational Training Unit, where they gained experience on the type of aircraft they'd fly operationally. Prior to the war, such experience would have been gained with front-line squadrons, but losses sustained during the French campaign in 1940 ensured that this was often impractical. Consequently, Spitfire pilots, for example, could be posted to either No. 5 OTU at Aston Down in Gloucestershire or No. 7 OTU at Hawarden, near Chester.

Group Captain Duncan Smith spent eleven days at No. 7 OTU in 1940, during which he converted to the Spitfire Mk I, first sitting in the cockpit and learning what all the instruments did, until he could master it with his eyes shut. Subsequently, via dogfighting practice in the air, he 'came to explore every part of her handling characteristics, till eventually flying her was second nature'. Ground-based training included men pedalling around the parade ground on tricycles armed with compasses and battery-powered radio sets, while controllers vectored them onto an enemy tricycle, which must have been a hoot to watch, especially as it 'usually finished with a free-for-all with the enemy being rammed from all angles'. Instructors were operationally experienced pilots who were being rested, and although they'd pass on valuable experience, they weren't necessarily well-motivated for this role. Training was dominated 'by a feeling of here today, gone tomorrow' and trainees realised that ultimately, 'personal ability' and 'guts' might count for much and ensure they became successful fighter pilots.[99]

As a sergeant pilot in May 1941, Ivor Broom was posted to No. 13 OTU at Bicester, where he converted onto the Bristol Blenheim, a twin-engine high performance light/medium bomber with a top speed of 266 mph. These aircraft suffered shocking losses, often deployed on low-level bombing sorties, and it was reckoned crews stood only a 25 per cent probability of surviving their first operational tour. However, trainees tended to discount the likelihood that they might actually become casualties. Pilots also found that it could take time to acclimatise to the new aircraft they encountered at OTUs. One who eventually flew a Wellington bomber trained for this during 1942 at No. 24 OTU on the obsolete Armstrong Whitworth Whitley, also a twin-engine medium bomber. These proved 'immensely stable', yet simultaneously they were 'clumsy cows. If a wing drops ten degrees, you need full aileron to pull it up.'[100] This was a marked change from the Oxford he'd been used to flying earlier on, and the Whitley tended to prove more physically draining to fly, especially when trying to keep the nose down when landing.

Another experience of OTUs for bomber pilots was that this was where they'd 'crew-up' with those they were to fly with on operations. To fly the Blenheim, Ivor Broom teamed up with Sergeant Bill North, navigator, and Sergeant Les Harrison, wireless operator/air gunner (WOP/AG).[101] Typically, crewing-up was an informal, even slightly chaotic process, with seventy or more men milling about a hanger. Former navigator Albert Smith recalled that at his OTU, 'there was no system and we just mingled around nervously', most of them being sergeants with a smattering of 'sprog Pilot Officers' who'd been commissioned at the end of their flying training.[102] For Bill Goodman, an air gunner, the process seemed a little more structured. At No. 20 OTU, RAF Lossiemouth, he trained on Wellington bombers, the backbone of Bomber Command early in the war. During this time, personnel flew with a 'mixture of different members of the different categories and got to know them in their flying duties', and also saw them in the mess or local pubs. Consequently, when the order came to 'crew-up', Goodman and the five others needed for a Wellington crew rapidly coalesced, having already possessed 'a fair idea of the strengths and weaknesses of each other'.[103]

Usually at an OTU, bomber crews were engaged on intensive cross-country exercises that provided plenty of further flying experience for pilots, practised navigators and radio operators in realistic conditions. Likewise, there was bombing practice over designated ranges to hone bomb aimers' skills, and usually scope for air gunners to practise against towed targets or to fire into the air. Fighter affiliation, particularly for medium and heavy bombers, was important as well, when crews practised their defensive skills against mock attacks by fighter aircraft.

Whether as a fighter pilot or member of a bomber crew, by the end of training at an OTU, personnel were deemed ready for operations. As an Australian navigator with Bomber Command stated, it was as if the RAF had said: 'We are teaching you no more. Armed with your present knowledge, you are to navigate a plane to Germany. If your knowledge is inadequate, the fault is your own. And this was just. The training had been full and fair.'[104]

Chapter 2

The Experience of Bombing Operations

The bombing of Guernica in April 1937 by the German Condor Legion on behalf of the Nationalists during the Spanish Civil War, and the devastating raid by the Luftwaffe against Rotterdam on 15 May 1940, appeared to support contemporary thinking on the deployment of air power. Squadron Leader Denis Peto-Shepherd volunteered for the RAF in July 1940 and recalled that Italian General Giulio Douhet seemed to suggest that bombing would 'destroy cities in rapid hammer blows, causing the collapse of the social structure and disintegration of a nation', and that war would become 'a slogging match between rival bomber forces'.[1] British policy between the wars stressed that indiscriminate bombing, aimed at achieving a 'knock-out-blow', would be central to the next major war. To counter it, Britain required its own bomber force as a deterrent.[2]

Historian John Terraine observed that an 'attack on morale', whatever phrases might be employed to describe it, 'really means only one thing: putting the fear of death into individuals'. Senior RAF commanders were well aware of this, and in undermining morale, bombing simultaneously offered a means of dislocating German industry and oil production.[3] Although Britain had invested in bombers during the late 1930s, all that was feasible, once war started, was for RAF Bomber Command to commence limited raids on German urban areas in an attempt to weaken the morale of the enemy's civilian population. This was justified by the Air Staff, who 'presented industrial workers as a factor of production which had to be rendered ineffective like transport or fuel. Thus the attack on morale merged into an attack on the economy.' Moreover, the British viewed morale as a viable target, 'without whose reduction' the Allied plan to eventually invade Continental Europe simply wouldn't have been possible.[4]

From the relatively humble efforts of 1939–41 emerged a concerted policy of 'area bombing' that would characterise the RAF contribution to the Combined Bomber Offensive of 1943–45. This effectively entailed 'the unloading of high explosives and incendiaries directly over German city centres' in the hope that some of this tonnage of bombs would hit industrial targets, while the rest flattened housing and amenities, weakening the resolve of workers to continue the war effort.[5] Most of this bombing by the RAF was done by night as daylight bombing had proved too costly. Air Marshal Arthur Harris, who took over Bomber Command in February 1942, has forever been linked to 'area bombing'. Yet it is important to appreciate that he didn't instigate the policy, but ran with it after it had been established. Known as 'Butcher' or 'Butch' Harris by aircrew, because of their high casualty rate, he was typically a remote figure. Nonetheless, 'he possessed a single-mindedness or, alternatively, a myopic strategic vision, which made the conduct of the British offensive' different from that of the Americans, with their emphasis on daylight precision bombing against industrial targets, theoretically minimising collateral damage.[6]

Early bombing efforts suffered from the vagaries of the weather and relatively primitive methods of navigation. The decision to bomb by night offered protection to crews, but without moonlight, it was extremely difficult to locate targets. A report by the British civil servant D.M. Butt, compiled for Lord Cherwell (Churchill's scientific adviser) during the summer of 1941, questioned the accuracy of Bomber Command operations. After examining photographs taken during raids on Germany, and looking at statistics for each operation, Butt reckoned 'that only one aircraft in three got within five miles of its target area', and that the figure was 'a mere one in ten' against industries in the Ruhr. On 'hazy nights', or when there was less moonlight, this 'fell to one in fifteen'. On average, the overall 'proportion of aircraft that managed to make an attack within the 75 square miles surrounding a target was a mere 20 per cent'.[7]

During the war, there were significant improvements that raised Bomber Command's efficiency, including the introduction of better aircraft and navigational aids, and the establishment of the dedicated Pathfinder Force, tasked with accurately locating and marking targets. As well as the strategic bombing offensive, the RAF mounted several precision bombing raids, notably those operations by the elite 617 Squadron of 'dam-busting' fame that have rightly received much attention.[8] Yet, there were others, including the daylight raid against the Gestapo Headquarters in Oslo, mounted in late 1944 by Mosquitoes from 627 Squadron.

In Europe, bombers were employed on other tasks, including anti-shipping strikes, minelaying (gardening) and tactical support of ground troops. Bombing was a significant feature in other theatres, including the Mediterranean and Burma. On 13 January 1945, Liberators from 358 Squadron conducted a successful operation against Mandalay.

> The bomb run was at 12 o'clock. The basic issue was the Japanese in Mandalay, which is on fairly high ground and the British were sadly down at the bottom of the hill and the Japanese were parked in trenches half-way up, easy shooting down-hill. So the arrangement was the British would all pull back some considerable distance, and we were given a bomb line [line based on geographical features in front of friendly troops, beyond which it was safe to bomb] to follow with map references. … That would get the Japanese out of town and the British would run up the hill.

It worked, we ended up taking Mandalay back, but without us intervening it would have been a very expensive exercise. ... We knew where the bomb line was and made sure we got over it.[9]

In North Africa, crews from 205 Group Desert Air Force flew Wellington bombers on night sorties against enemy units, transports, supply routes, airfields and ports, and later supported the Allied invasion of Italy. F.R. Chappell, a wartime RAF intelligence officer with 104 Squadron, 205 Group, noted: 'there are definite signs of tiredness among the crews and who can wonder after their terrific efforts?'[10] Losses were as much a feature of their war as they were for units bombing Nazi-occupied Europe. By August 1943, his wing had 'lost fourteen Wellingtons since 1 July, eight from 104 Squadron and six from 40 Squadron'.[11] Each had a crew of five, so this equated to the loss of at least seventy airmen, including forty from Chappell's squadron.

Impressions of their aircraft

Most aircrew, as Wing Commander Ken Rees discovered, tended to 'develop a certain fondness' for the specific aircraft they flew, because for long hours it was their 'place of work' and 'home'.[12] Sometimes, championing aircraft types was borne out of genuine affection and admiration for their capabilities. One Australian pilot, after his first flight in a Lancaster, commented that it was 'a really beautiful kite, by far the best I have flown. She is remarkably manoeuvrable for her size and is light on the controls.'[13] Contrastingly, the Lockheed Vega Ventura, which for a period served with 2 Group, was christened 'pig' by crews owing to its ungainly appearance. It suffered heavy casualties in daylight missions over North-West Europe because it was slow and inadequately armed. Yet even if aircraft exhibited disappointing characteristics – and several did – there was still a tendency on the part of crews to outwardly view them favourably, not least because drawing attention to faults was bad for morale.

During the war, the RAF operated a number of different types of bomber manufactured according to British designs, as well as some American types.[14] Each had its own distinctive characteristics, but for aircrew, most were cramped and cold, and lacked adequate armament, as .303 machine guns proved of limited defensive use. Typically, Luftwaffe fighter pilots learnt that machine guns were ineffective beyond ranges of about 400 yards and remained out of range, from where they could easily outgun British bombers with their cannons.[15]

The Fairey Battle was a low-winged monoplane that earned an unenviable reputation. Designed during the mid-1930s, it had been revolutionary owing to its light alloy-stressed skin construction, making it surprisingly robust. It had a three-man crew, top speed of 257 mph, and could carry a maximum 1,000lb bomb load.[16] Mike Henry, an air gunner, encountered it during his training, and recalled that by 1940, it was 'becoming obsolescent because of its smallish bomb load and single in-line, liquid cooled engine ... which made it vulnerable to flak and fighters alike'.[17] When Battles went into action with the Advanced Air Striking Force (AASF) during the French campaign, they typically suffered grievous losses. On 10 May 1940, a German column advancing through Luxembourg was spotted, and the pilots had 'to make a very low approach to the target, and to attack at 250 feet, using bombs fused for eleven seconds' delay'. In total, thirty-two Battles mounted the attack, thirteen of which were lost and all others receiving damage without severely hindering the enemy's advance.[18]

The Bristol Blenheim, various marks of which served with the RAF during the early part of the war, was a three-seat light bomber, heralded as one of the fastest aircraft around in the late 1930s. The Mk IV had a maximum speed of 266 mph at 11,000 feet, and could carry a bomb load of 1,000lb in its bomb bay, together with up to 350lb of light bombs carried externally. This wasn't particularly impressive, and neither was the Blenheim well armed. It was used widely on low-level daylight bombing raids, and similarly suffered heavy losses. Aircrew tended to demonstrate a healthy respect for the Blenheim, as it had a high accident rate and was relatively frail. 'Banking before adequate airspeed had been obtained on take-off killed scores of novices.'[19]

As a young pilot in 1941, Air Marshal Sir Ivor Broom was posted to 114 Squadron with 2 Group, which was equipped with the Blenheim. Despite its weaknesses, if he'd been given the choice he would have always opted for a Blenheim squadron because he'd trained to fly twin-engine aircraft, and owing to its speed regarded it 'as a more exciting prospect' than Wellington, Hampden or Whitley bombers. By comparison, these appeared 'lumbering giants which operated at night and night flying was something that, throughout his training, had been regarded as dangerous and ... to be avoided'.[20]

One air gunner discovered that, as with most contemporary aircraft, crew comfort was at a premium in the Blenheim. The 'biting cold slipstream fairly whipped into his turret', where there was 'a large aperture' to enable the guns to move vertically and traverse horizontally. Goggles were ineffective as they easily misted up and froze, and 'condensation from one's oxygen/microphone mask dripped and froze into a beard of icicles'. Dealing with bodily functions was a further challenge. Taking along an old empty glass bottle was usually advisable, although some aircraft had toilet facilities. Alternatively, as with the Blenheim, crew could try 'aiming through the camera hatch', a hole, 1 foot in diameter, with a Perspex cover that was removable. This could be tricky. Mike Henry attempted it, and recalled, 'I got the whole lot back in my face!'[21]

One of the most successful and versatile aircraft of the war was the de Havilland Mosquito, or 'Mossie'. Again, it was a twin-engine design, but constructed almost all from a mix of ply and balsa wood, giving it a high power to weight ratio. It had a crew of two (pilot and navigator), a maximum speed of over 360 mph, and long range. Despite its small size, it could carry a 4,000lb 'blockbuster' bomb, ensuring that Mosquitoes could inflict much damage on cities, including Berlin, leading it to be dubbed 'the greatest little aircraft ever built'.[22] One pilot reckoned it looked good, 'as though it ought to fly well with two, great, sharply-pointed engines slung below the tapered wings; the typically towering tail that said de Havillands had made it; and the narrow fuselage'.[23]

Navigator Albert Smith had flown Wellingtons before transferring to Mosquitoes, and found 'the cockpit was very cramped – there was no movement that did not mean brushing against something'. Yet flying a Mossie was to experience 'sheer joy'.[24] Another boon was that it had a cockpit heater, meaning crews didn't have to wear cumbersome flying kit, and the cockpit was pressurised on several models, so crews didn't have to wear oxygen masks. Even so, many did, 'rather than risk an explosive decompression which would follow after a rupture of the pressurised shell'.[25]

In July 1944, Ronald Pate was posted as a pilot to 627 Squadron, an elite Pathfinder unit equipped with Mossies, having already amassed over 1,000 flying hours. He remembered the type fondly.

> It was a fantastic aeroplane. On the other hand I always think about her as a female. They are very loyal and so on, but if you mishandle them they can kick you in the butt. You have to treat them softly because they can react but they can take an amazing amount of punishment too and of course it was the fastest aircraft.
>
> You entered it through a trap door in the floor and a little metal ladder that collapsed and fell back into the unit. There wasn't a great deal of room, just enough to sit a pilot and a navigator. ... And there was a space where the entrance/exit was and a space where you could get up into the nose although we never did. So it was very cramped from that point of view and you couldn't move. The longest trip I did was 5 hours 40 minutes and I was quite knackered at the end of that because you've got nowhere to exercise and you've got to concentrate, concentrate all the time.
>
> Even though it was made of wood, it had incredible strength ... and you could fly quite easily on one engine and not mean you were doomed. Beautiful to fly ... no problem at all.[26]

The Handley Page Hampden was extremely cramped, leading to it being dubbed 'the flying suitcase'. It had a strange-looking narrow fuselage with a sort of podlike compartment for the pilot and crew. One historian described it as a 'grotesque-looking flying glasshouse'.[27] It had a comparatively slow cruising speed,

The Experience of Bombing Operations   33

but by contemporary standards it possessed reasonable range, and could carry up to 4,000lb of bombs. Classed as a twin-engine medium bomber and conceived to operate by daylight, early experience demonstrated that daylight operations were too costly. As Wing Command Guy Gibson, who flew Hampdens with 83 Squadron discovered, it was 'to be used for night raiding only'.[28] Other drawbacks included a lack of power-operated turrets, and an inability to absorb much punishment.

Another bomber that formed the backbone of Bomber Command early on was the Armstrong Whitworth Whitley, resembling 'a rather pedantic middle-aged pipe-smoker, with its jutting chin mounting a single Vickers K gun' and distinctive high-tailed flight.[29] Classed as a five-man long range night bomber, it could carry a 7,000lb bomb load. When posted to command 77 Squadron, Air Vice-Marshal Donald Bennett was 'disappointed to find it equipped with twin-engine Whitleys, aircraft which I had thought were completely obsolete many years before', but he soon 'learned to respect this very good work-horse, which did a job quite as well as the more famous Wellington'.[30] For another distinguished pilot, it was 'homely and simple' to operate.[31]

Compared to the Whitley, a pilot from 12 Squadron considered the Vickers Armstrong Wellington, or 'Wimpey', was 'all cockeyed, the throttle, the pitch control etc. being on the left-hand side. Like trying to write left-handed.'[32] It was a twin-engine, mid-wing monoplane medium bomber, with a five-man crew, and became one of the outstanding aircraft of the war, not least because it could absorb much punishment owing to its geodetic construction, specially designed by Doctor Barnes Wallis. Eventually, over 11,400 were produced. Many served as night bombers with Bomber Command, after suffering catastrophic losses as day bombers, and the type served extensively overseas. On 1 April 1941, a Wellington from 149 Squadron dropped the first 4,000lb 'blockbuster' bomb during a raid on Emden, and during Operation Millennium, the so-called '1,000 bomber raid' against Cologne on 30 May 1942, nearly 600 of the aircraft that took part were Wellingtons.

During 1940–43, bomber pilot Rupert Cooling completed two operational tours, one with 9 Squadron based in Britain, and another with 142 Squadron in North Africa.

> I flew the Wellington Mark I, Ia, Ic, III and X, and each was better than its predecessor. The Mark X was a joy to fly because you had the Hercules engines that would hum like Singer Sewing machines. I flew the Mark X in North Africa where the climatic conditions were a bit more arduous. You had to watch cylinder head temperature and so on. I remember taking a load of 6,500lb with an outside temperature of 28 degrees, so by the time I got up to about 10,000 feet the cylinder heads, the collector ring on the front of the engines, was glowing a bright pink, cherry red. It

really was a bit off-putting. Even then we went out over the coast to get altitude. That was a bit difficult so I shed one of the 500 pounders so I could get a bit higher. Apart from that, the Hercules engine was a delight. Once the bombs were gone you'd fly home and bring RPM down to 1,600. All you had to do was keep it above 1,500 to keep the generator going for electrical power. She just scythed through the air.

The Wellington was a perfect partner. If you treated her with the respect of a very gracious, willing lady, if you like, she would do whatever you wanted. I wouldn't care to take liberties with her but provided you realised there were certain things you shouldn't do you were alright.

She wasn't easy to fly on one engine, so you didn't try that too much. You had things like flaps there were so many odd things about the 'Wimpey'. When you were on the ground and looked out you saw the engine nacelles next to you and that was fine. When you were airborne you saw the engine nacelles and the wing tip and as you flew along you saw this sort of 'sea-gull action', the wings flapping. But it was a thoroughly good aeroplane that was relatively easy to fly. It was heavy, slow in response ... but robust.[33]

The Short Stirling was the first of the four-engine monoplane heavy bombers to enter RAF service. Bill Goodman, a rear gunner with 7 Squadron, had previously been used to the Wellington and found it 'massive' by comparison, at over 22 feet tall and 87 feet 3 inches long.[34] The Stirling completed over 18,000 sorties, dropping in excess of 27,000 tons of bombs, plus 20,000 mines. Crews found it a surprisingly manoeuvrable aircraft, but it was slow, had short range, and suffered from poor performance at high altitude. Consequently, as the war progressed, it was relegated to less demanding roles, such as a transport aircraft or glider tug.

In contrast, the Avro Manchester, a seven-seat medium bomber that entered service during 1940–41, was beset by technical problems. There were a number of flaws with the airframe, and the Vulture engines proved chronically underpowered and unreliable. In March 1942, 106 Squadron was busy replacing its Hampdens with Manchesters when Wing Commander Guy Gibson assumed command. He was told: 'These Manchesters. They're awful. The actual kite's all right, but it's the engine. They're fine when they keep turning but they don't often do so. We've had an awful lot of prangs. ... If you are hit in one engine you've had it.'[35]

The Avro Lancaster was altogether different, despite the prototype being based on a converted Manchester airframe. Like the Spitfire, the Lancaster became an iconic aircraft of the Second World War, and was one of the best heavy bombers produced by either side. At least fifty-nine RAF Bomber Command squadrons operated the type, and these flew over 156,000 sorties, dropping 608,612 tons of high explosive bombs, plus in excess of 51 million incendiary bombs. For

Don Charlwood, an Australian navigator with 103 Squadron, the Lancaster was 'clean-lined and lady-like, a contrast with the more robust, masculine lines of the Halifax' he'd previously flown.[36] Squadron Leader Jack Currie gained an equally favourable impression of the 'Lanc'. It 'looked good from every angle, strongly shaped and well proportioned. In flight she appeared both powerful and balanced.' Some aeroplanes appear awkward in flight, but 'the Lancaster rode the air easily and steadily'. Moreover, the 'cockpit smelled good, and the pilot's seat was comfortable, with a good view from port quarter to starboard beam'. His crew were happy with their positions, particularly the bomb aimer, 'who had a panoramic view through his Perspex blister in the nose'.[37]

Compared with the Lancaster, the Handley Page Halifax, another seven-seat heavy bomber, 'was all solid bulk' without any of the 'arcs and curves'. Neither was it necessarily as easy or as comfortable to fly. One pilot recalled how the controls for the flaps and undercarriage were so close together that 'fumbling for them in the dark, down beside your right thigh, you could be forgiven for mistaking one for the other, and that might make an overshoot more exciting than it need be'. Whereas, the Lancaster always seemed 'eager to be airborne and never keen to land', the Halifax was 'a mite reluctant to take off and fly' and felt as if it were 'waiting for the moment when you set it on the ground again'.[38]

Initially, the Halifax suffered from a fatal flaw. As Don Charlwood remembered, 'the story' circulated that 'the Halifax Mark I had a viscous rudder stall that few of those who experienced it came out alive'.[39] Once this was rectified, it proved robust, and was fondly referred to by crews as the 'Halibag'. One flight engineer recounted: 'She could take a lot of damage. We had no starboard elevator, half a rudder, and half the port elevator was gone, but we managed to get it down, to crash-land.'[40] Another useful feature was the large escape hatch that many crews valued when shot down.

Bomber crews

Aircrews in Bomber Command were volunteers, and typically well-motivated, although it was characteristic of the wartime generation to downplay the skill, courage and devotion to duty required on operations. Many had been at school or university when hostilities commenced, while others were pre-war regulars who'd continued to serve. Walter Thompson joined the Royal Canadian Air Force (RCAF) in 1941, and flew Lancasters with 106 Squadron RAF before joining the elite Pathfinder Force. He highlighted that Bomber Command tended to adhere to an 'unofficial motto' of 'Press on Regardless'. This was alright:

> if one's chief concern is a Kipling-like keeping of a stiff upper lip,
> while all about one are being shot to pieces ... but if one wishes to

fight intelligently and to create an atmosphere in which air supremacy and victory can be achieved then one doesn't press on regardless – one arms oneself and gets assistance from professional gunfighters and then presses on.[41]

He considered many other aircrews agreed with his views, but didn't voice them for fear that they be regarded as afraid.

Equally, Leslie Mann, a rear gunner with 51 Squadron, equipped with Whitleys, who was shot down and captured in 1941, reckoned some personnel weren't motivated so much by patriotism as by a willingness 'to risk dying for the sake of their pride and their conscience', effectively to show that they'd done their bit.[42] However, as one pilot explained:

> If you're on a bombing raid it's a job to be done. You cannot allow other things to implode on your concentration because to do so would probably mean something happening which shouldn't happen and would cause more problems. The training is to concentrate absolutely on what you're doing.[43]

Another distinctive feature of Bomber Command was the cosmopolitan nature of its aircrews, as personnel came not just from Britain, but from all over the British Empire. For example, by January 1945, about half of its pilots came from Canada, Australia and New Zealand. Numerous personnel also came from countries occupied by Nazi Germany. While serving with the WAAF at RAF Waddington, Pip Beck was especially taken with the airmen from 44 (Rhodesian) Squadron. They 'were so unmistakably not English', with their more relaxed appearance, 'air of tough independence, skins bronzed by warmer suns than ours, and eyes used to wider distances', plus their 'disregard for the finer points of discipline was a by-word on the camp'. Their 'accent was clipped and unfamiliar' and speech 'littered with romantic sounding phrases in Afrikaans'.[44] Contrastingly, 76 Squadron, based in North Yorkshire during 1943, had a dedicated contingent of Norwegian airmen, who 'flew with Norwegian flags pinned in the cockpits'. Drawn from escapees from occupied Norway, they were single-minded in their determination to fight Nazism, always wanting to know 'how many Germans per acre' were at a target, rather than details on its economic significance. Serious minded, less interested in the antics of the mess, 'on evasion exercises on the moors, they were always back first'.[45]

Squadron Leader R.C. Rivaz, an experienced tail gunner with 102 Squadron, encapsulated the dynamic between the individual members of a bomber crew. All had to work together in achieving the same purpose, i.e. reaching the target, 'identify and bomb our target – doing as much damage as possible – and reach home safely. Our lives depended on each other, and each one of us was indispensable.' The pilot's job was to fly the plane to the target and back, 'and make a safe landing, avoiding flak and searchlights as best he could'. Navigators had to tell their pilots what course to fly, 'and to do this ... calculate and check', and especially 'know the exact strength of the wind at whatever direction' they were flying. The wireless operator had to constantly 'keep a listening watch at his set', and be prepared to send messages and assist the navigator by obtaining 'loop bearings or fixes', something that was awkward, especially for novices. Early on, a second pilot, or second 'dickey', was often employed. Usually, he was inexperienced, and might map-read or fly part of the way. However, primarily he was there 'to learn, and will be watching and noting all that goes on'. Air gunners had 'to keep a continual look-out for enemy fighters; to report on the movements of searchlights and positions of flak bursts'; effectively acting as 'a driving mirror for the pilot'.[46]

Despite the bond between the different members of a bomber's crew, experienced Wellington pilot Rupert Cooling highlighted that in larger aircraft, they tended to fight a separate war from each other.

> Each individual in the crew experienced his own particular war because we were all in various compartments ... the rear gunner was 70 feet away down the backend in a cubicle and all he was, was a disembodied voice over the intercom. The wireless operator had his head phones on and a mass of dials – couldn't see a damned thing. The navigator was in his compartment. The bomb aimer was the only chap I remember and I would be flying the aircraft and Bill would be standing next to me looking out the window. Then when you came up to the target I could see what was going around up there. Bill was looking straight down into it, and could see what was going to come up. The others couldn't see anything except the rear gunner and he saw it when we were on our way out.[47]

A sense of the camaraderie that existed can be gained by the experience of Squadron Leader Denis Peto-Shepherd, who completed an operational tour as a pilot on Lancasters with 90 Squadron based at RAF Tuddenham, Suffolk, in 1944. This entailed not only partaking in the strategic bombing offensive against Germany, but in a variety of other sorties, including bombing transportation targets, supporting ground forces in Normandy, hitting 'V' weapons sites in France, and dropping dummy paratroopers during the Battle of Arnhem.[48] His crew included Ron Hitchcock as bomb aimer, 'a charming and egocentrically inclined individual who took himself and his deep interests in the arts most seriously'. Len Stretton, an Australian, was the wireless operator, and 'turned out to be a tough but kind, thoughtful and gentle personality' blessed with 'a calm competence' and 'easy-going self-confidence'. The navigator was Alec Mitchell, who was 'studious and reliable' with 'the semi-aloof attitude of the intellectual' who didn't 'approve of the crew's somewhat rumbustious goings on'. Gunners consisted of Ormerod Suddall, or 'Sue', a tough lad from Preston, who'd been a butcher's assistant 'and knew how to look after himself', and Samuel, or 'Sammy', a school-leaver from South Wales. They all had to be moulded into an effective fighting team.[49]

On heavy bombers there was also a flight engineer instead of a second pilot. As Bill Goodman explained, on the Stirling they were responsible for dealing with any faults that developed while they were airborne, and if possible, repairing damage resulting from enemy action. Flight engineers would 'look after the engines and controls in use – the hydraulic systems and electrical circuitry and oxygen supplies for the crew'. They'd monitor fuel consumption and 'get the best possible economy or increased power during combat, thus ensuring a sufficiency of fuel to get us home again'. Consequently, flight engineers had to be prepared to 'move fuel from a damaged tank to an undamaged one', there being eight tanks in each wing, which were all under his control. Another job assigned to the flight engineer entailed dropping the photoflash from the rear of the aircraft 'to coincide with the dropping of the bombs to illuminate the target at the times the bombs detonated'.[50]

The crew dynamic differed in smaller bombers, such as the Mosquito or Blenheim, where two or three men operated in close proximity without the compartmentalisation associated with larger aircraft. Yet there was still an intense sense that personnel were working together as a team. As Ronald Pate found in 627 Squadron, 'most of the aircrew were officers and the camaraderie was wonderful. We relied on each other and respected one another.' The Squadron 'was small, approximately 42 flyers, and there was a good relationship with ground crew'.[51]

It was accepted in the RAF that the pilot was always the captain or skipper of an aircraft, regardless of his rank. As Squadron Leader Rivaz observed, because there were a number of NCO pilots in most squadrons, it followed that some aircraft were flown by NCOs with officers in their crews. 'Rank in the air, in a sense does not count'; rather, what was important was the competence of the pilot and the faith the rest of the crew put in him, and gunners were often particularly attached to their pilots. In larger bombers, tail gunners sat with their back to the direction of travel, and communication with the pilot was vital. If the tail gunner saw something on his left-hand side, he always referred to it as starboard to avoid confusion, and let the pilot know what he'd seen was on the right-hand/starboard side of the aircraft, not the gunner's right-hand side.[52]

Another important factor for air gunners to appreciate was how to fire a deflection shot. Bill Goodman remembered the only time that it was possible to aim successfully was when 'you and the target were flying in line'. Otherwise, a deflection shot was required, and 'according to the angle between the courses of the aircraft, the gunner had to calculate the differential and use the gunsight to fire at the other aircraft'. Maximum deflection entailed the gunner aiming 'some distance ahead of the target', as both aircraft were on the same course and speed. With practice, such skills became second nature.[53]

One of the most stressful and difficult jobs was that of navigator, given that he had to make complex calculations in the midst of aerial combat, and if the aircraft was flying at speed, this complicated his task. Often there was a reliance on dead reckoning, whereby the navigator drew a compass course and attempted to direct the pilot to follow it, with corrections from deviation and variation, flying over known places termed 'check points'. Initially, there was an absence of direction-finding aids. One navigator likened the situation to 'sitting in a freezing cold stair cupboard with the door shut and the Hoover running and trying to do calculus'.[54] Rupert Cooling recorded how navigation was conducted with 9 Squadron in 1940:

> You didn't identify a target by careful map reading and so on, but saw where all the muck and filth was and thought that must be it. Navigation was not a fine art in 1940. It was by guess and by God, dead reckoning and astronavigation if you were lucky. None of us were good at that, we were grotesquely undertrained. We could fly the aeroplanes but where we flew them and what we did when we got there was in the lap of the gods. ...
>
> Go find an oil refinery at Gelsenkirchen, which was a favourite target ... was about the size of the car park in Henley in a mass of smog and fog in a built-up area and being shot at all over the place. ... You just believed what the navigator said: 'I think that's it,' right bombs gone thank God, let's get home.[55]

As the war progressed, a number of navigational aids were introduced that radically improved the situation. Flying Officer James Hudson completed two operational tours as a navigator, one flying Blenheims with 101 Squadron, and another over two years later on Lancasters with 100 Squadron. By 1944, he'd witnessed the introduction of 'Oboe', an electronic navigational aid 'dependent on ground signals' for transmissions. Although it wasn't successfully jammed by the enemy, 'its range was governed by the earth's curvature, restricting its use for targets beyond the Ruhr'. The pilot was guided to the target by dots or dashes so that bombs could be released accurately on receipt of a radar signal. Gee radio navigation was another useful innovation, although it could be jammed once an aircraft was over hostile territory. Typically, the navigator could 'fix position by consulting the Gee Box after reading the pulse signals on the radar screen received from three ground stations', which were interpreted with the aid of a 'latticed Gee chart'. This information was then transferred 'to the Mercator's projection chart on which the navigator plotted all courses to and from the target'.

Another system, H2S, was independent of ground control, had great range and couldn't be jammed – although it could be homed in on by the enemy – as a means of directing his defences against an oncoming bomber stream. The device beneath the aircraft transmitted radar signals, and these were displayed on a cathode ray tube in the navigator's position. Effectively, 'a map of radar images' could be constructed on the screen by a diligent navigator, with the aircraft at the centre, and 'to plot position, readings by distance and bearing could be taken of the images'. Equipment dubbed 'Fishpond' was operated by the wireless operator, akin to 'a radar scanner looking backwards'. It monitored other bombers, which showed as steady blips, and indicated hostile aircraft, normally appearing as rapidly moving blips. However, as many crews discovered, the signal from 'Fishpond' could be picked up by radar in enemy night fighters. Another navigational aid was the Distance Reading Gyro-Magnetic compass, or 'DR' compass. It was accurate 'as the instruments combined the properties of a gyro and compass and were not affected by sudden aircraft changes in direction, or accelerations'.[56]

Components of a sortie

The period prior to an operation was characterised by tension and uncertainty, as aircrew didn't know whether they'd successfully make it back to their base or not. Bruce Lewis trained as a wireless operator/air gunner with Bomber Command and completed thirty-six operations. According to him, for any given 100 aircrew, from September 1939 to May 1945, the following casualties occurred: 'Killed on operations 51; killed in crashes in the UK 9; seriously injured 3; prisoners of war 12; evaded capture 1; and survived unharmed 24.'[57] Men's reactions varied depending on the sortie they were tasked with conducting. During the spring and summer of 1941, Blenheim crews from 2 Group were repeatedly involved in low-level anti-shipping strikes in the English Channel and North Sea. 'On average, a unit lasted a fortnight before being withdrawn, decimated.'[58] Likewise, 'trips' to industrial targets in the Ruhr, dubbed 'Happy Valley' by Bomber Command aircrew, or Berlin, 'the Big City', tended to be greeted with fear and trepidation. Dick Starkey, a pilot with 106 Squadron, completed nine trips to Berlin during 1944–45, and reckoned that beforehand, aircrews 'were like men going to the gallows'.[59]

An officer with 90 Squadron recorded that, by 1944:

> The build-up to an operational sortie was long, complicated, and left more than enough time for contemplation of what lay ahead. It began with the Battle Order which for a night operation would normally be published before lunch. This order named the crews for that night's squadron effort, detailed with any temporary changes and the number of aircraft the crew was to fly. Lunch was likely to be a cheerless meal with the desultory

conversation of those pre-occupied with their thoughts – the paramount thought being what was the target? On this mainly depended the crews' chances of survival and, despite much conjecture and supposedly inside information, the target would not be known until briefing began. After lunch, wisdom dictated a brief rest before briefing and I for one used to lie on my bed at first in a contemplative wakefulness, but later [in his tour] was so exhausted as to be able to sleep at once in this brief period.[60]

Briefings early in the war could be relatively relaxed, and not necessarily that informative. A member of 83 Squadron recounted how before a raid against Hamburg docks, they were told their bomb load and fuel supply, and were permitted to 'attack at any height from which the target is visible', bearing in mind that 'the moon is in the south-west, so the best direction for attack would be to come in from the north-east side'. And, 'on no account are you to bomb towns or villages indiscriminately'. This was the only target to be attacked, so if aircraft couldn't find it, they had to bring their bombs home. Aircrew were free to navigate their way to the target by what route they saw fit, and that concluded their briefing.[61]

Such informality 'when a cluster of pilots and navigators assembled around the central table in the Ops Room' disappeared with the introduction of the heavy bombers, when briefings became serious and lengthy affairs.[62] In North Africa, intelligence officers prepared displays of the target and its defences, compiled route maps for navigators and bomb aimers, and gave briefings to bomber crews on particular targets while 'emphasising the value of our bombing attack as a contribution to the war effort'. Former schoolmaster and wartime intelligence officer F.R. Chappell was 'conscious of my own ignorance and deficiencies, and became tense and worried by the strain of briefing ... these groups of young men not much older than sixth-form boys but now involved in the deadly business of war'.[63]

Invariably, from 1942 onwards at British airfields, each specialist member of a crew was briefed independently. Entire crews also received briefings with the aid of a large wall map and were told by a senior officer, 'Gentlemen, your target for tonight is...' Bomber Command veteran Squadron Leader Peto-Shepherd outlined the atmosphere and conditions at briefings late in the war.

The difficulties and dangers of the attack depended mainly on the depth and penetration into occupied France and Germany, with the defences to be breached. This could be assessed at a glance, for the particularly hazardous targets and areas such as the Ruhr were well known. Attacks on such targets were usually greeted with an uncanny silence. The Squadron Commander would give a brief introduction to the target and then hand over to a succession of specialists, the Intelligence Officer, the Meteorological Officer followed by the Navigation, Bombing, Signals Engineer and Gunnery Leaders. Each one of these would give information and instructions for the attack, which concerned his particular subject or aircrew category. Overall it was a lengthy dissemination of information which had to be memorised, or noted in a form unrecognisable to the enemy. A final summary would be made by the Squadron Commander, or frequently the Station Commander. The crews then left to empty their pockets into little numbered canvas bags [so that nothing of intelligence value might fall into enemy hands if they were shot down], to don flying kit, and draw parachutes, escape-kits, foreign currency and flying rations.[64]

Crews would then be driven by WAAF personnel to dispersal bays where their aircraft waited, and pilots commenced pre-flight checks. There was always a chance that an operation might be scrubbed at the last minute, which heightened the anxiety felt by aircrews. Alternatively, a general recall signal might be received owing to some change or an individual aircraft have to abort owing to mechanical failure. One Australian pilot found it best to 'engender a sense of confidence' in his crew by 'suppressing my own feelings, and this certainly eased the tension in the air'.[65] Last-minute chats with the station padre, or receiving good luck pep talks from senior officers, could allay the apprehension before take-off.

When the time for take-off arrived, invariably groups of WAAFs and other airman might congregate to wave at lines of taxiing bombers. Pilots hoped to be given a green Aldis lamp signal from the runway control caravan, denoting that they were 'clear for take-off', then carefully manoeuvre onto the runway and slowly open the throttles before releasing the brakes and move forwards, gradually building up each engine to full power. Ron Smith served as a rear gunner with 626 Squadron, based at RAF Wickenby, Lincolnshire, and from his position at the back of a Lancaster, it felt like being catapulted backwards. He'd watch 'the tarmac fast slipping away, raising my hand in salute, as I always did, in the superstitious belief that, if I forgot the gesture, we should not return'. Then there was a 'sinking feeling' as the wheels left the runway, and the lumbering bomber hesitated slightly before gaining speed, followed by a 'dull thud' as the undercarriage retracted, and the skipper ordered 'flaps up'. The aircraft then gained height, and there was a palpable sense among its crew that they were on their way, so 'the tension eased and I was more relaxed than I had been since briefing earlier in the day'.[66]

Assuming a bomber embarked successfully on a sortie, and survived contact with the enemy's anti-aircraft defences, it would eventually navigate its way to its designated target. The pilot then had to hold the aircraft as steady as possible while the bombs were released. Initially, this was done by the navigator, but with the arrival of the heavy bombers, the job fell to a specialist bomb aimer, who'd direct the pilot onto the aiming point and deal with any related problems, such as if a bomb hung up in the bomb bay. On 10/11 May 1940, Rupert Cooling flew his first operational sortie with 9 Squadron from RAF Honington, Suffolk, acting as second 'dickey', tasked with hindering the German Blitzkrieg. His was one of thirty-six Wellingtons ordered to bomb Waalhaven airfield, while nine Whitleys bombed bridges across the Rhine, as well as enemy columns near Goch and Geldern. No losses were reported.[67] Even so, it wasn't straightforward, and coming under fire for the first time proved especially traumatic.

> We took off about five in the evening. It was still daylight and we got over Holland, Waalhaven, the airfield for Rotterdam was the target because the Germans had seized it and landed gliders and God knows what, and the Dutch were supposed to go in and retake the airfield, and we were to act like the artillery bombardment. And I remember Dougie [the pilot] saying: 'right, you go back in the astrodome and keep a look-out for fighters or anything and I'll fly it.' And I went back in the astrodome, looked around and my heart stopped as I saw another aircraft and recognised it as another Wellington. Then straight ahead of us, you know those bead curtains you see on beach huts in the summer, well there was a coloured one of these hanging across the sky, and it was light flak. And we just went straight for it. I remember sitting there like a petrified rabbit watching these coloured lights going left and right. As we got to them they appeared to separate and there was a thwack and a hole came up in a piece of fabric in the starboard wing. And I remember saying to Dougie: 'We've been hit!' 'Right, where?' And I said: 'Starboard wing.' 'Anything?' 'No it's just torn fabric.' And we pushed off through, out to the coast and came out to the North Sea again and Dougie said: 'Right you fly. I'll go back and take a look.'
>
> And Dougie stood beside me and we crossed the British coast and saw the beacon. Dougie took over and we came in and landed. We were very unpopular as we were one of the first to land and the light flak had punctured the starboard tyre, so we touched down and then came to a stop 90 degrees across the flare path. And they got us out and you could smell the sweet smell of petrol and we went out and there was a sort of gunge like a pustule or carbuncle on the side of the wing where the self-sealing had been pushed through and petrol was dripping from it. You could hear the engines ticking and once you moved away you could smell the burnt exhaust disappearing and God the grass felt lovely under your feet.
>
> Anyhow, that was it. They pumped us into a wagon and drove us for a debriefing and down to the mess. We were probably half-way through our first beer by the time the next man landed.[68]

By 1944, the situation was infinitely more complex. Not only had technological developments aided navigation and bombing, but a series of ground and air-based radio countermeasures (RCM) had been introduced against German radar.[69] One of the most widely used was 'Window', a relatively simple device that achieved impressive results. As one Canadian pilot noted, it became routine for bomb aimers to drop Window: 'strips of silver paper ... which rendered the Wurzburg radar sets virtually useless', although not the Freya radar sets that had longer range.[70] To jam these early warning radar sets, a device known as Mandrel was employed, including against Kiel on 23/24 July 1944, when Bomber Command resumed its attacks on German cities after the Battle of Normandy. Aircraft equipped with Mandrel formed a screen off the Danish coast, and coupled with Window, this ensured the bomber stream reached Kiel virtually unmolested. Out of 629 aircraft that took part, only four were lost, the German defences having been totally disorientated by these countermeasures.[71]

Aircrew learnt that 'the invisible bomber stream' that surrounded them afforded protection from enemy fighters, if they kept up with it. To stray out of it usually meant that a crew were 'easy meat for marauding fighters, vectored onto [their aircraft] by the enemy controllers in their sections that ringed the coast of Europe'. As one rear gunner recalled, there was much sense in the posters at their base, which proclaimed: 'Don't be proud – stay with the crowd.'[72] Knowing the vulnerability of isolated bombers, some aircrews chose to fly just above the main bomber stream with the aid of 'Fishpond', operated by the wireless operator and bomb aimer.

An idea of the threat German night fighters posed can be gauged by Warren Thompson's recollections as a Lancaster pilot with 106 Squadron, and later, Pathfinder. As soon as the H2S sets were switched on at dispersals, invariably the German monitoring service noted this, and had advanced warning of a raid. 'Wild Boars' single-engine fighters and/or 'Tame Boar' twin-engine machines equipped with radar were then despatched to protect likely targets. By late 1944, a 'shadower' aircraft in conjunction with a ground controller was employed to home in on the H2S transmissions of Pathfinders spearheading an attack. The assembled fighters would then 'follow the shadower's radio beacon until they too found themselves in the bomber stream', where they could do immense damage. Although different methods of attack were evolved by the Germans, one of the most common was the '*von unten hinten*, i.e. from-under-and-behind'. This involved a long approach on radar, then a visual sighting, at which point the fighter 'approached from a little below and astern in a slightly nose-up attitude, aiming and firing its fixed forward guns at the bomber's fuselage and bomb bays'. This caused a massive explosion, especially if a bomber carried a thin-skinned 4,000lb bomb, or 'cookie'.[73]

On 18/19 August 1944, Bremen was targeted by 288 aircraft from Bomber Command. The raid was conducted with good visibility over the target and perfect marking by Pathfinders. Over 1,100 tons of bombs were dropped. Worst hit was the port area, north-western parts of Bremen and city centre, and over 8,600 houses were recorded by the Germans as burnt out.[74] One of the Lancasters that flew on this raid was piloted by Squadron Leader Peto-Shepherd from 90 Squadron. During it he resorted to desperate measures, when 'conned' by German searchlights, and was angered to witness several bombers jettisoning bombs early – something he suggests was widespread, and hardly in keeping with the 'heroic image' of Bomber Command.

Our attack on Bremen at twelve minutes past midnight on the night of August 18/19 was inescapably another fire-raising raid as we were carrying one 4,000lb bomb and twelve 30lb incendiaries. We crossed the English coast – out at a height of between 4 and 6,000 feet above the Diver Belt [the zone protecting southern England from Hitler's V-1 flying bombs]. I no longer wondered at the heavy flashes in the North Sea on our course out ... I had previously imagined to be a major naval engagement. ... These flashes were the explosions of 4,000lb bombs jettisoned in the North Sea by our own aircraft. Or possibly the photo-flash which Bomber Command, suspecting this dumping had wired to fire automatically on release of the 4,000lb bomb ... but it was possible to avoid ... incriminating evidence by immobilising the camera. The 4,000lb had a very thin skin, the case being constructed from one-quarter-inch mild steel plate, and could be detonated by shell splinters. It was therefore unpopular to the extent that many crews disposed of it (hopefully unobserved) at the earliest. Such disposal had the added advantage of increasing the aircraft's maximum height and speed.

We climbed to some 15,000 feet over the North Sea before crossing the Dutch coastline. The bomber stream was shrouded in Window, continually discharged from a point out in the North Sea until well into the North Sea again on our return. Our climb continued to run in onto the target at a height of 18,000 feet, in the clear, from which we bombed. When running up onto such a target, the scene of awful violence was daunting. In the darkness below was what might have been a great cauldron of boiling metal, seething under a rugged crust of darkening dirt and flotsam, through which bubbled and burst countless splashes and pinpricks of brilliant molten light, some living on and some dying as others sprung up and multiplied beside them. From a distance this glowing, pulsating mass seemed to be throwing high into the sky above it, a huge canopy of twinkling sparks and colours. It was tempting to dismiss it all as some gigantic, light-hearted and inconsequential firework display, and to evade the reality that it was a stricken city blazing amidst clouds of bursting shells, falling target markers and hundreds of tons of bombs shrieking into the billowing smoke of dreadful destruction.[75]

For Peto-Shepherd's crew, all went well, with Window having proved effective, and they made a successful bombing run. On leaving the target:

> we were suddenly held in the icy blue brilliance of a master searchlight beam, and were faced with the certainty of having been singled out for the kill. This beam was directed by a Wurzburg radar tracking station below, which 'locked' onto us, and the chance of escaping such radar tracking was remote. ...
>
> We had been singled out either for the attentions of predicted AA [anti-aircraft] fire, or fighters, or more likely both. My plan in these circumstances had always been to attempt to corkscrew out of the concentration of beams hoping, by the rapid changes of course and height in this comparatively violent manoeuvre, to evade the predicted AA fire and confuse radar tracking. I threw the aircraft into a diving corkscrew – it was desperately heavy work and as I laboured on neither the thudding and thumping of bursting shells around us, nor the intensity of the lights seemed in anyway diminished. It was impossible to keep this up for long, and as the cone of light built up with perhaps 40 or more searchlight beams directed onto us in the master beam, came the sickening realisation we were well and truly trapped. ... One chance remained – speed and I decided on a desperate expedient of a maximum-speed dive on changing courses. ... To put the aircraft into a fast dive was one thing, but to keep the speed below maximum safe diving speed in a fast turn, would be another. I was flying purely on instruments and the two master instruments would topple or spin if ... I exceeded their limits. ... The maximum safe diving speed for a Lancaster was 360 mph, but in no time in a steep banking dive we were well above this speed. ...
>
> As we roared twisting earthwards we were still in the grip of the lights and seemed doomed, until I noticed that both the intensity of the AA and lights seemed to be decreasing. Within seconds some of the lights appeared to be wavering. I could no longer delay, and in the hope that we had them beat, began the long slow struggle with the controls to bring the aircraft very gingerly out of dive without overstressing it.[76]

Via a combination of skill and luck, they survived their ordeal. Many other aircrews didn't. Although anti-aircraft fire was unnerving, as Reg Fayers of 76 Squadron discovered, it could appear 'worse than it was as you were seeing bursts over a large area'.[77] Contrastingly, many aircrews were more fearful of night fighters and searchlights, given the damage they could do. Men died in horrible ways, such as a result of mid-air collisions, being hit by bombs from another aircraft, in crashes, or when they failed to survive parachuting from a stricken aircraft. A second 'dickey' in a Halifax bled to death when a piece of German shrapnel from heavy flak, 'no more than a couple of inches across, that had shot up through the bottom of the aircraft capriciously to sever' the main artery in his thigh.[78]

The return leg to base was one of the most awkward parts of any sortie. Even if they experienced relief on reaching the halfway home point, aircrews still often faced challenges such as 'running the gauntlet of enemy fighter intruders awaiting the return of the bomber stream; of difficult weather conditions; of landing a damaged aircraft, or landing on a runway obstructed by damaged aircraft'.[79]

An important development in assisting with bad weather conditions was FIDO (Fog Investigation and Dispersal Operation), consisting of large petrol burners installed along either side of runways, the heat from which lifted fog, allowing aircraft to operate safely.[80]

After landing, concentration was still needed for taxiing to a dispersal point, usually in the dark, and embarking on the process of running down the engines and related systems correctly before it was safe to leave the aircraft. On returning to base, Ron Smith found the 'mental relaxation' encountered after hours of tension brought 'euphoria that brings me near to tears with the knowledge that I have survived again'.[81]

Typically, crews were relieved of their parachutes and Mae Wests (life jackets) while WAAFs handed them welcoming mugs of coffee laced with rum. As one veteran recorded, 'both the WAAF and the coffee were wonderfully comforting and as reassuring as the firm ground under our feet after those long hours in the air.'[82] The process of debriefing would then commence. In North Africa, intelligence officers found they 'could depend more upon' the opinions of experienced crews regarding 'the success and failure of attacks'.[83] Presumably, their counterparts with Bomber Command had particularly high regard for the opinions of veteran crews who'd learnt the hard art of survival. A first operational tour with Bomber Command became set at thirty sorties. When pilot Jack Currie joined his squadron, the odds against 'finishing the tour were about seven to one', but once he'd reached the halfway mark, the odds 'shortened to better than four to one'.[84]

Pathfinders

Bomber Command's war involved a highly technological struggle against the enemy. While the RAF introduced systems such as Gee, Oboe and H2S, as well as better aircraft with greater bomb loads, simultaneously the enemy sought to improve his defences along the Kammhuber Line, and institute ever more deadly night-fighter tactics. The Kammhuber Line, as the RAF called it, was the enemy's air defence network intended to protect the Third Reich's air space, and incorporated thousands of anti-aircraft guns, searchlights and Würzburg radar sets. It was arranged in a series of belts or zones, stretching from the Belgian-Dutch coast into Germany, and named after Generalmajor Josef Kammhuber, who in 1940 was tasked by Hitler with organising and implementing the night defence of Germany.[85]

One of the most significant developments for Bomber Command was the instigation of a dedicated Pathfinder Force in late 1942 under the command of a tough, highly experienced pilot and navigator, the Australian AVM Don Bennett. The PFF led major attacks on Germany by helping to direct the main force of bombers onto their targets. Initially, Wellingtons were employed by the PFF, but in some squadrons, Mosquitoes proved better for the role. While they had no armament, Bennett considered they were 'very fast little craft', and 'had a bomb bay big enough to take four of our five hundred pound Target Indicators, and it seemed to me if they could achieve the ceiling we required they would be perfectly suitable'.[86] They could also carry sophisticated electronic equipment, notably Oboe, to act as a navigational and bombing aid.

PFF crews were all volunteers, and were required to complete tours of at least forty-five operations, the rationale being that the force needed to be based on the skill, dedication and experience of longer-serving crews. All would eventually qualify to proudly 'wear the PFF emblem – small, gilded metal wings, worn below the Air Crew brevet'.[87]

Typical tasks included acting as 'Finders', where aircraft dropped flares at crucial points to aid the navigation of the main bomber stream. In poor conditions this could be done 'blind', relying on H2S. 'Illuminators' would simultaneously fly in front of the main force and drop Target Indicators (TIs) on the designated aiming point, and this was done using H2S if conditions were poor or by Mosquitoes using Oboe. The TIs were designed to burn with different colours, and were given names such as 'Pink Pansies' or 'Smoke Puffs', making it much more difficult for the Germans to employ decoys. 'Markers' subsequently dropped further markers onto the TIs to assist the main force of bombers. 'Visual centres' estimated 'the mean point of impact of all the primary markers', and dropped TIs on that point, usually of a different colour, and ensured 'the target was illuminated at all times'. Master bombers were introduced, normally a senior PFF officer who would 'continuously circle the target broadcasting radio instructions to both Pathfinders and main force aircraft, correcting aiming points and generally co-ordinating the attack'. He was ably supported by a 'deputy master bomber' who took over if necessary. Both ran a high risk of being hit by falling bombs from above or flak from below, as they circled targets at low altitude directing operations.[88]

As Wing Commander Artie Ashworth explained, there were three main techniques by which PFF identified targets. In a 'Parramatta', TIs were dropped by aircraft employing H2S or Oboe to identify a specific location. The target would then be continuously marked by a follow-up marking force, and this worked well with large targets. Secondly, a 'Newhaven' was when an aircraft dropped flares over a target to illuminate it. Once the aiming point had been visually identified by other aircraft, these would employ TIs using the Mk XIV bomb sight, a stabilised vector sight widely employed by the RAF that performed well in active service conditions, and could even be used when an aircraft made a banking turn or went into a glide. Finally, a 'Wanganui' was used when a target was obscured by either clouds or a smokescreen. The Pathfinders identified the target via H2S or Oboe, then released TI flares suspended below parachutes, which provided the main force with aerial aiming points.[89]

Ronald Pate vividly recounted his experience as a young Pathfinder officer piloting a Mosquito on raids from his base at Woodhall Spa, Lincolnshire.

> The 'Mossie' pilots would go out on co-ords from Britain and where they crossed them was the target. And the pilots had to listen out for this and when the sound changed [presumably, he's referring to using Oboe] they had to release the TIs which was a pyrotechnic which was shaped like a bomb but when it left the aircraft it would explode after two or three seconds and there would be a huge pyrotechnic red, green or yellow. But marking targets was done in red TIs and these pyrotechnics would drift to earth and mark the target for the bombers that were coming subsequently. So you had several Mosquitoes all doing the same job at the same time, so there was a huge expanse of red fireworks on the ground which the bombers were told that was the target. But wind would drift TIs when we dropped them from 20,000 feet.
>
> H Hour was the time the first bombs were going to be dropped. There was a Master Bomber controlling the operation. H-13 the Lancasters put green TIs down. At H-11 the first flare went down, followed by another flare. Mossies down around 600 feet and first pilot to identify the target would shout 'Tally Ho' go in and drop TIs. There was nine minutes to identify the target, mark it and get out. You couldn't hold the heavy bombers back under anti-aircraft fire etc.[90]

Coping mechanisms

Early bombing operations were characterised by 'dogged amateurishness'.[91] Yet for the individuals concerned, sorties proved equally as intense as those experienced by bomber crews later on. From September 1940 to June 1941,

Reggie Wainwright undertook over thirty operational sorties as an NCO navigator with 38 Squadron, flying Wellingtons in Europe and North Africa, receiving a Mention in Despatches (MID) in the process. His service included 'trips' to targets as daunting as Cologne and Berlin, and over North Africa his aircraft was attacked by a fighter, and hit by flak.[92]

Wellington pilot Rupert Cooling completed tours in Europe and North Africa. He put his 'survivability' down to 'the learning curve' on operations, which included an appreciation of suitable tactics. This included avoiding 'the herd instinct by flying in at a different height and so not giving anti-aircraft gunners a chance to recalibrate'. Luck and faith, or a belief in God, played a role too. 'People say do you believe in God? I say I was a pilot in Bomber Command. That doesn't mean I believe in religion.' Most important was the development of a mindset that helped him to cope with the stress of active service, and in this he was far from alone. 'You might talk about your next leave but never next month. It was almost a tacit acceptance that was never manifested more than you never looked forward, because you didn't know if there was anything to look forward to.'[93]

Typically, aircrews experienced a surreal existence when compared with other combatants. One day they could be enjoying the comforts of an airfield with its mess and accommodation, the next they'd be facing the prospect of death or mutilation in the skies. Bomber Command suffered over 50,000 fatalities during the war: 47,000 died on operations, and about 8,000 were killed as a result of non-operational or training accidents.[94]

An Australia airman described life on a bomber squadron as being a 'strange mixture of comradeship, heroism and fear', and most seemed to accept this.[95] Having completed two tours during 1943–44, a Canadian Lancaster pilot and former Pathfinder outlined the mental coping strategy he developed. After experiencing a few sorties, aircrew:

> had to develop a philosophy with which to deal with the casualty figures and probability of one's death. ... One had to learn to accept death and become used to the idea of it. One had to consider oneself already dead. In that way one could live in honour, without fear of cowardice or death.[96]

Even so, many airmen lived in fear, even if they kept their feelings private. It wasn't just a fear of dying; some worried about receiving a serious wound. As one Lancaster pilot explained, after seeing 'the wicked orange flashes of shell bursts' on operations, 'of all the possibilities, I felt to be feared most was the loss of vision. Who would then see for me all my heart saw in life?'[97] Others wondered whether they'd withstand the repeated strain of operations. Rupert Cooling recounted how 'the time that your name went up on the board to the time that you became airborne was always the most anxious', but once flying on an operation, 'you were less worried'.[98]

Aerial combat brought its own pressures. Rear gunner Ron Smith recalled feeling 'bruised and battered and not a little queasy, after the almost continual evasive action' after his bomber was persistently attacked by a German night fighter. Afterwards, the determined nature of it left him shaken and made his 'imagination run riot'.[99]

Ultimately, the entire experience of operations was extremely draining, particularly in Europe. Navigator Albert Smith was involved in a raid on Essen in early March 1943, involving over 440 bombers. He found it was 'impossible to comprehend how all of us [he means the seven aircraft from his squadron] had come unscathed through' the 'frenzy'. Later he was mightily relieved to learn he wasn't the only airman who was 'Shit scared' on flying to 'Happy Valley' and back.[100] Squadron Leader Jack Currie observed that one of the greatest fears youthful airmen faced was 'of showing cowardice'.[101]

For many, the 'stiff upper lip', in keeping with their upbringing and schooling in Britain and the Commonwealth, was one way of handling fear. Despite suffering from severe airsickness and nasal bleeding, Harold Chadwick, an eager volunteer, became an accomplished bomb aimer.

> he would be plagued with the stench of his own vomit, while his oxygen mask would be slimy with blood. Yet lying in the dark isolation of the Lancaster's front compartment he was able to conceal his suffering from the rest of the crew.[102]

Squadron Leader Peto-Shepherd became aware that 'crushing exhaustion and depression', plus relief on completing an operation, forced some men to cry.

> My upbringing had led me to believe that it was unmanly to cry, or to whine in adversity, as the first of these was weakness and the second cowardly. On account of these widely held beliefs such weeping is rarely admitted and never referred to amongst men, making it impossible to know how widely it may have been experienced.[103]

Yet there were cases where an airman's courage ran out. When this happened, he ran the risk of being branded 'LMF – Lack of Moral Fibre – with its dreadful stigma'.[104] A member of 103 Squadron remembered hearing of a man 'over the target [who] … had screamed. He was ashamed and apologetic, but they had taken him off ops immediately.'[105] Another NCO pilot, when his squadron was tasked with flying several sorties to Berlin, returned early to RAF Wickenby, complaining he was feeling ill, not once but at least twice. Squadron Leader Jack Currie observed his plight. His crew 'may have thought that some of us would vilify him, but no one except officialdom did that. We knew what was wrong: the so-called lack of moral fibre and most of us had felt that at times.'[106]

Most LMF cases were treated harshly, in keeping with the RAF's mentality, with its strong emphasis on 'gentleman fliers' making the best aircrew. Faced with wartime conditions, the authorities were unable to countenance that men might, for psychiatric or other reasons, refuse to fly, particularly as masses of resources had been put into training them. Additionally, the RAF was desperate that individuals displaying signs of LMF should be removed quickly, less they contaminated others. As Bill Goodman noted, an airman suffering from LMF 'would be stripped of his rank and posted away to some menial duty. It was looked on as cowardice, but to go LMF required more guts than was appreciated by officialdom.'[107]

An idea of the scope of the challenge LMF presented can be gauged by one study of Bomber Command, which postulated that about one man in ten was lost owing to medical or morale reasons, between the Operational Training Unit stage and the completion of an operational tour.[108] Alternatively, men might be regarded as 'waverers', which was deemed less serious than LMF, but still of concern. It meant that although they'd continued to serve, despite signs of stress, they had lost the confidence of commanders. Many 'waverers' were posted to an Aircrew Refresher Centre to rehabilitate them for flying duties or to be remustered for ground duties.[109] These centres 'were no rest cure', plus personnel had 'to explain to the folks back home why you ain't flying no more, and how you came to lose your stripes and brevet'.[110]

At the other extreme were personnel who were considered 'flak happy'. Often, these were experienced veterans who'd already demonstrated their courage, and exhibited a devil-may-care attitude. Don Charlwood encountered one such airman on an operational tour with 103 Squadron. He was a flight lieutenant, a trained pilot and navigator, and holder of the Distinguished Flying Cross with Bar, who 'seldom wore pilot's wings in case he was made a flying instructor'. He'd completed 134 operations, 'was a maniac', and after being taken off flying duties, his 'one ambition ... was to get back on ops'. Later he managed to become a fighter pilot and was never heard of again.[111]

Benzedrine tablets were issued to bomber crews to stave off fatigue on operations and keep men sharp. These tasted bitter, and according to one rear gunner, 'would keep your eyes firmly open when your body was exhausted, mind ever alert, but sometimes distant, unbelieving'.[112] For many aircrew, alcohol was a major source of relief, although that didn't mean all drank to excess off duty. Several towns and cities across Yorkshire, Lincolnshire and East Anglia, where many bomber airfields were located, were accessible to RAF personnel. In Scunthorpe, personnel from RAF Elsham Wolds 'could get drunk at the "Crosby", or see a floor show and get drunk at the "Oswald", or dance and get drunk at the "Berkley"'.[113] Related to this was the singing that was a part of many nights out, and escapades such as 'borrowing' any available transport home when the last bus had long since departed.

The antics of the mess offered similar relief from the prolonged stress of operational flying, and for what might be termed 'male bonding'. Vigorous games included 'Flarepath', where men had to dive 'across the floor between two lines of human beacons clutching flaming newspapers'.[114] Alternatively, 'Are you there Moriarty?' involved two players laying face-down on the floor, blindfold and clasping a rolled-up newspaper in their free hand. Each 'took his turn to speak the [above] formula; thereupon, the other might take a swinging swipe with a rolled-up newspaper at the point where he judged the speaker's head to be.'[115]

The 'charisma of squadron life', and the comradeship that this entailed, tended to hold a special place in the hearts of airmen, leading many, including Ron Smith, to opt for further tours rather than be posted away as instructors.[116] Life was often enhanced by the prevalence of particular characters, even if such individuals didn't survive long. The war hero Leonard Cheshire explained how, as a young pilot flying Whitleys, his squadron had a 'tall, blond, mad Irishman who crowded more laughter and more action into five weeks than anyone would have thought possible'. Eventually, he was shot down, and died after spending days adrift at sea in a dingy.[117]

Ultimately, bomber crews were a tight-knit group, who depended on each other for their survival, and routinely faced the prospect of a violent death. One pilot noted:

> While my own experience would not allow me to say that there was no such thing as chance, or good fortune; in operational flying the survival of a crew was chiefly dependent upon unity of purpose, discipline, professional competence, close co-operation, concern and interest for each other and sustained determination to destroy the enemy. These breed confidence, the success of which should never be confused with luck.[118]

Yet many crews or individuals did believe in luck, and this helped them cope. Bill Goodman recalled a fellow air gunner who'd man the mid-upper turret on his Stirling, replete with his rabbit foot talisman, and one crew in 103 Squadron believed in the superstition that they all had to pat their 'cookie' prior to a sortie. Some of them kept 'a grimy toy rabbit' christened 'Nunc Nunc' that 'swung like a pendulum' over the instrument panel, and when an operation was completed it was kissed on the rear, before being safely stowed away until the next flight.[119]

Pre-operation routines were important to many, virtually to the point of being ritualistic. Although he didn't personally believe in attaching much significance to luck, Squadron Leader Peto-Shepherd noted that for many, such behaviour as always leaving your bicycle in the same place before a briefing 'became a process vested in an unfathomable, mystic importance, as if it was the repetition of previous actions in continuing normality that resulted in safe return'.[120]

Since 1945, debate has raged about the conduct and effectiveness of the strategic bombing offensive against Germany. However, it forced the Germans to divert valuable resources from other fronts, especially in Russia, to defend the Reich, including manpower and artillery. The Luftwaffe was degraded, and German aircraft production became unbalanced in favour of fighters as a result of attempting to counter the bombing. Although Nazi Germany's war-making capacity wasn't halted, its economy was severely dislocated, plus several factories had to produce material for air defence rather than other items. Crucially, bombers also helped in other areas. In support of D-Day, several transportation and communications targets were hit, hindering the Germans' ability to react, with decisive results for the overall campaign in Normandy.[121]

Even so, aircrews' attitudes towards bombing varied and certainly not all shared the enthusiasm of Arthur Harris, their commander-in-chief for area bombing, with all that implied. Ahead of a raid on Brunswick in 1944, one officer was disturbed to learn at a briefing that the emphasis wasn't on military targets but:

> on the destruction of the workers' dwellings in which the aiming point was centred and which, we were informed, 'should burn well'. I was profoundly shaken as I did not know that Bomber Command had since mid-1943 begun methodically to bomb German cities and suburbs, often taking the city centre as its aiming point.[122]

After the war, Rupert Cooling professed:

> I volunteered for a second tour overseas because I did not like the idea of area bombing, slash and burn or whatever you like to call it. That didn't appeal to me at all. I thought there are some ethics surely and the fact that some people have none doesn't mean to say I shouldn't either.[123]

In contrast, Ronald Pate reflected:

> I think the general bombing strategy was OK. I know that since the war you get criticism, and the Dresden raid is the most obvious one. [He is referring to the 'infamous' raid on 13/14 February 1945 – Operation Thunderclap, designed to target the already hard-pressed German war

machine and civil administration, in which thousands were killed.] But then what people don't appreciate is that there were armament factories in Dresden. It also was a main train traffic area. And it went into areas towards Russia. ... And it was strategically in a very important place. ...

Although I know it's caused a lot of conflict in people's attitudes, we didn't start the war and it had to be completed. Don't forget the reverse was true during the Blitz in London.

There was always a target which we had to attack. It was not a case of we are going to attack civilians. There was never any suggestion that we were just going to attack a town, albeit civilians might get killed in the process.[124]

Chapter 3

Flying with Fighter Squadrons

Fighter Command will forever be associated with the Battle of Britain (July–October 1940), when Hitler's planned invasion Operation Sea Lion was thwarted owing to a combination of the skill of RAF pilots, the ability of the British to replace aircraft losses, and the unsuitability of the Luftwaffe's training and preparations for the strategic task thrust upon it. Yet as an American pilot who flew with the RAF commented, 'I'm not sure that we knew there had been a Battle of Britain. I never heard the term used until it was all over.'[1]

Air Vice-Marshal 'Johnnie' Johnson noted, on the eve of the Battle of Britain, the RAF's fighter tactics generally lagged 'a long way behind those of the Luftwaffe'.[2] With recent combat experience from the Spanish Civil War, German pilots had developed more flexible formations, notably 'widely spaced units of four called a Schwarm'. Each of these consisted of two Rotten, or pairs, which formed the standard combat unit. Within each pair, the leader, or Rottenführer, was tasked with making kills, while his wingman, or Rottenflieger, protected his leader's tail, especially when he was making a kill.[3] The advantages of the system were that two pilots operating in this manner were invariably more effective and much less vulnerable than a single fighter, even one flown by a skilled pilot.

Modern aircraft, such as the Hawker Hurricane and Supermarine Spitfire, also called for a rethink on fighter tactics. The greater speeds of these aircraft initially led many experienced pilots to question whether dogfights were feasible, 'due to the excessive forces involved in turns at speeds in the 400 mph range', although both aircraft could perform well at slower speeds, and owing 'to the very low wing loading of these aeroplanes they could turn in very tight circles' at about 140 mph 'and continue to do so indefinitely'.[4] Issues also arose regarding gunnery. A wartime fighter pilot who saw action during the Battle for France in 1940 explained that the official line considered, 'at 400 yards range bullet velocity was still high enough to prevent tumble, maintain accuracy and penetrate armour (which seemed unlikely), the spread produced by aiming, shooting and random errors combined would be more than enough to drop lethal density below the minimum required for a kill', particularly against a small target such as an enemy fighter. Consequently, his Hurricane squadron 'secretly harmonized all ... guns on a spot at 250 yards' range' before operations in France, where 'we shot down every enemy aircraft we'd attacked'.[5]

As the Luftwaffe turned from daylight operations against Britain to bombing targets by night during what became termed the Blitz, the emphasis for the RAF switched from daytime aerial battles to night fighting, a function for which it was initially ill-equipped. Another major role performed by fighters was launching sweeps across the Continent, primarily intended to tie down the Luftwaffe in the west. During Operation Jubilee, the Allied raid against Dieppe on 19 August 1942, there was another significant air effort, as the RAF was tasked with providing an air umbrella to protect the invasion forces. Although the operation as a whole was a costly failure, several lessons were learnt. Notably, the RAF's role was deemed significant and effective because it kept the Germans at bay while the landings occurred. Fighter Command alone contributed approximately 60 per cent of the 2,955 individual sorties flown by the RAF on that day.[6]

Fighter Command steadily increased in size during the war, and by spring 1941, it comprised eighty-one squadrons, sixteen of which were designated as specialist night-fighter units. Daylight tip and run raids by fighter-bombers that whizzed in for low-level attacks before attempting to rapidly fly away were another strand of the Luftwaffe threat, and proved awkward to counter. By 1943, better aircraft types became available, and the Allies were gearing up for the opening of the Second Front. This prompted a reorganisation, including the formation of Second Tactical Air Force (2nd TAF), which absorbed numerous fighter squadrons from Fighter Command. Protecting Britain then fell to Air Defence of Great Britain (ADGB), which comprised twenty-one squadrons, eleven of which were night-fighter squadrons. The ADGB was also tasked with providing protection for the invasion forces being built up in Britain ahead of D-Day.

Major concerns of 2nd TAF were the provision of reconnaissance and close air support, or hitting tanks, troop concentrations and other targets at the behest of ground commanders. Often this entailed using a cab rank system of waiting fighter-bombers, armed with powerful cannons and bombs, or even rockets. These loitered close to the battlefront, and were brought into action via a forward air controller based on the ground. Effective methods of close air support/ground attack were forged in North Africa, and proved equally as important in Normandy, North-West Europe, and South East Asia.

The RAF also had to counter Axis air power in the Far East and Middle East, where it had long-standing and geographically widespread responsibilities. Typically, in these theatres units relied on ageing or obsolescent aircraft, until improved types became available. Another challenge during the latter stages of the war was how to counter the V-1s, or doodlebugs – flying bombs that the Germans launched at southern England from across the Channel. By 1945, the RAF had also entered the jet age, with the introduction of the Gloster Meteor, a first-generation jet fighter, which was a stark contrast to the Gloster Gladiator biplane that still equipped some units on the outbreak of war.

Fighter pilots and their aircraft

Like Bomber Command, Fighter Command was a highly cosmopolitan organisation. Not only were there pilots from Britain, but personnel came from around the globe. American James Goodson proved himself an adept Spitfire pilot with the RAF during the Battle of Britain. Later he was posted to 133 (Eagle) Squadron, comprised of American nationals, before transferring to Fourth Fighter Group, United States Army Air Force (USAAF), and became a leading ace.[7] When Air Commodore Cyril Brown joined 253 Squadron at RAF Kenley in November 1940, at the end of the Battle of Britain, he discovered:

> it was made up of a hotchpotch of people. In order to provide reinforce-
> ments at a critical stage people were being transferred from all sorts of
> other roles. ... one of the flight commanders had been an ex-Fleet Air
> Arm pilot and I think he'd been flying Walrus seaplanes. The other flight
> commander was a very colourful chap who'd been a very successful night
> fighter pilot on Blenheims ... but got himself transferred to Hurricanes.[8]

Additionally, there were escapees from Nazi-occupied Europe.

> In 253 Squadron we had two Czechs, a Pole and two Free Frenchmen,
> only recently arrived from Europe. Some of them didn't speak English
> at all but they picked up the standard R/T [radio telephony] phrases,
> but sometimes when they were in the air and got excited they'd talk in
> their own language which was chaotic. So it really was very interesting
> and there was a mixed bunch of people all wearing their own uniforms in
> those days.[9]

According to the station commander at RAF Warmwell, Dorset, in October 1940, the Poles were 'keen and enthusiastic about flying for its own sake, and would rather fly and fight than do anything else'. Whereas he considered Czech pilots 'as hardworking and conscientious as the Polish personnel but not usually so good from the flying point of view and the pilots I have met seem to be less enthusiastic than most fighter pilots'.[10] Even so, another officer thought that when his squadron received Poles and Czechs, it was akin to 'manna in the wilderness' and 'what they lacked in English, they more than made up in with experience and spirit', not least because 'most of them were regulars in their own services and more experienced than our own crowd'.[11]

   Boleslaw Henryk Drobinski escaped to Britain via Rumania and France, was later promoted to squadron leader, and received the Polish equivalent of the Victoria Cross. Posted to commence operational flying with 65 Squadron, equipped with

Spitfires, he was, according to ace Gordon Olive, who served alongside him, a 'youngster, with blond, curly hair and a pinched look due to enduring fantastic hardships in escaping overland from Poland. ... He had the appearance of a prematurely old man who had suffered greatly. We called him Gandhi-ski, but he was a most intrepid boy.'[12]

Having flown the Tiger Moth and Hawker Hector biplanes, Drobinski completed 'three take-off and landings on the Fairey Battle' at an OTU at Hawarden, then spent eighteen hours on the Hurricane. Consequently, his posting to a Spitfire squadron during the Battle of Britain was a shock.

> We hadn't even seen a Spitfire, so we went to the mess and saw a senior officer in charge of training and told him we hadn't seen a Spitfire. So he says OK and took us in a car down the side of the airfield where the Spitfire training took place to show us what's what etc. And we each did three take-offs and three landings.[13]

At the political level, the various governments in exile were typically keen for their countries' air forces to remain independent, but with a degree of reluctance, the Air Ministry considered it would rather the RAF absorbed these foreign flyers. Yet the pilots concerned were just as keen as their British counterparts to do their bit in confronting Nazi Germany. Many served in separate squadrons, organised along national lines, which remained part of the RAF. Polish airman Kazimierz Budzik recorded the daunting moment in 1941 when as a rookie fighter pilot he joined the famous 303 (Polish) Squadron.

> I was only little and had nothing to say because these chaps had been at the Battle of Britain and were all experienced, so you couldn't open your mouth. All you had to do was listen to what they say and do exactly what they say. They told you stories about the Battle of Britain when they were quite a successful squadron.[14]

Sometimes the change to independent squadrons was resented. When 133 (Eagle) Squadron was established from American flyers who'd been serving with the RAF, many, including James Goodson, who'd been serving with 416 (Canadian) Squadron, were unhappy at leaving their old units. He commented:

> the thought of flying with pilots we didn't know, and the depressing facilities at Great Stamford, and the fact that we were stuck off there, while the other two Eagle Squadrons relaxed in the luxury of the main station at Debden, all combined to create an atmosphere of depression and cynicism.[15]

In contrast, 331 and 332 Squadrons, both Norwegian fighter squadrons, were notable because their morale and esprit de corps was invariably classed as 'excellent' or 'exceedingly high'.[16]

Like their British counterparts, many foreign airmen resorted to humour to help them cope with the conditions they faced. Jokes were typically directed at political figures or even the British for their supposed stuffiness. One popular anecdote, said to have originated from a Dutch squadron, played on the language barrier. It concerned an Allied pilot being disciplined for 'cowardice in the face of the enemy'. The senior British officer present stated: "'You were told there were bandits at three o'clock, and yet you immediately flew back to the station. Why?" Came back the nonchalant reply: "Because it was only half past one."'[17]

Fighter pilots were renowned for their off-duty antics; again, these acted as a coping mechanism, given the pressures they faced. Most were aware that peacetime flying was dangerous, but operational conditions could be worse. Consequently, they resented 'idleness because it means waste of time from which pleasure might be wrung. ... The gaiety of pilots has always been that of men who were prepared to die at any moment, in return for the privilege of enjoying beauty and danger in flight.'[18] Yet matters could get out of hand. In October 1942, Peter Hearne was stationed near Edinburgh with 65 Squadron. He recounted the celebrations marking the arrival of a new flight commander with the Distinguished Flying Medal (DFM) – a sign he was an experienced pilot.

> one chap took off his shoes and socks, placed his feet in the dead embers in the fireplace and, by using tables and chairs, was able to leave the imprint of his soles on the very high ceiling of the mess. He then autographed his masterpiece. Others followed suit. ... The only culprit identified received an immediate posting.[19]

The intelligence officer with 43 Squadron observed that fighter pilots and their ground crews tended to 'speak, laugh and think in their own secret tongue' and 'are satisfied with this secrecy and are shy and even suspicious of any attempt to intrude upon it'. This added to a squadron's character, and 'isolates a Service mess from civilian life'.[20] Developing a distinctive style of dress was another means of cultivating a visual identity symbolic of the fighter pilot's profession. Accordingly, many pilots adopted 'the squashed hat, sweater protruding below tunic, silk scarf and – of course – battledress jacket top button undone'. The silk scarf 'became a trophy of some distinction sought by more adventurous young women', but served an important purpose as it prevented pilots from suffering a chaffed neck when wearing their flying kit.[21]

During the early 1930s, the RAF lived up to its unofficial tag as the best flying club in the world. '[There] were few tactical lectures, a serious approach had not been made to instrument flying, and squadron training seemed based on pretty aerobatics and tight formations rather than on the lessons of air fighting.'[22] The Gloster Gladiator, a hangover from this period, was the last of the great British biplane designs employed by the RAF. Entering service in 1937, it introduced modern features, such as an enclosed cockpit. Two squadrons of Gladiators were posted to France in 1939 as part of the Advanced Air Striking Force, and it was flown by 263 Squadron during the Norwegian campaign. A handful famously assisted in the defence of Malta, April–June 1940, plus it saw active service in the Middle East.[23]

As a recently qualified pilot in North Africa with 80 Squadron, Roald Dahl first experienced the Gladiator. He marvelled at 'how two machine guns firing thousands of bullets a minute could be synchronised to fire their bullets through a propeller revolving at thousands of revs a minute without hitting the propeller blades'.[24] Australian Squadron Leader Gordon Olive 'loved the old Gladiator' and volunteered for operations in Norway, although reflected he was relieved not to have been posted there because of the heavy casualties.[25] He found the Gladiator a joy to fly, and once it had been withdrawn from front-line service, appreciated using one for meteorological reconnaissance flights at RAF Northolt. Regularly he'd climb:

> to thirty thousand feet, taking wet and dry bulb thermometer readings at intervals of a thousand feet and calling these figures on the transmitter at two-minute intervals. In this way the operations room was able to work out wind velocities at the various altitudes … It was, however, very exacting flying as the conditions were frequently almost impossible, with a cloud base below five hundred feet and visibility below half a mile.[26]

The Hurricane was the backbone of Fighter Command during the Battle of Britain, and inflicted severe losses on the Luftwaffe. During the war, various marks of the Hurricane were produced. As well as a day fighter, it was deployed as a night fighter, performed ably as a fighter-bomber (Hurribomber) against shipping and other targets, and when fitted with underwing 40mm cannons, acted as a tankbuster, notably in North Africa and the Far East. A Battle of Britain pilot recounted how 'we learned to love the rugged, solid old "Hurry"', although it struggled to cope with 'high-level reconnaissance planes, and sneak raiders' because 'our Hurricanes couldn't reach the altitudes of most of the recco planes; and the intruders used bad weather and cloud cover so effectively, that, even with radar, which in any case was only really effective over the sea, they were seldom caught'.[27]

Reflecting on his posting to 253 Squadron at RAF Kenley in November 1940, Air Commodore Brown considered the Hurricane:

was a nice aeroplane, easy and straightforward to fly. Hardly any vices and so for a new boy it was really quite an easy and pleasant aircraft to fly. Of course as always with most pilots they tend to think that their aircraft in their squadron was the best aircraft ever made.[28]

A pilot who started his combat career with 151 Squadron in 1940 held an equally favourable opinion.

It was a stable aeroplane. Quite easy to land once you got the sort of feel for it. You had to land in your semi-stall position otherwise you would start bouncing, but once you'd leaned all that, it was a delightful aeroplane to fly, stable, and you could pull a very tight turn, and we were taught all that, and we were told that we could out-turn a Messerschmitt 109, as long as you saw him coming. The good thing about the Hurricane, it had a big mirror above the cockpit, so if you were looking around you would, with luck, not get somebody on your tail.[29]

Not all pilots agreed. Tony Tooth was briefly posted to 175 Squadron at RAF Warmwell to convert to Hurricanes, having previously flown Spitfires. The squadron wasn't being employed in its normal fighter-bomber role on anti-shipping strikes, so he faced relatively peaceful conditions. Still, he found it 'big, seeming much bigger than the Spit, and altogether clumsy feeling, being much slower and having much slower reactions. I felt that I would not like to go to combat in it.'[30]

In the summer of 1938, the Spitfire Mk I entered service with 19 Squadron at RAF Duxford, Cambridgeshire, and by the outbreak of hostilities, nine Spitfire squadrons were operational. In August 1940, as the Battle of Britain raged, there were nineteen such squadrons, and by December, the Spitfire Mk II became available. Some saw action on Rhubarbs – fighter sweeps across occupied Europe. These were later joined by the Mk V, which became the workhorse of Fighter Command during the middle of the war. Later models followed, including the Mk XIV Spitfire, which was recorded as being the first Allied fighter to successfully shoot down a Messerschmitt 262 jet. Spitfires served in all major theatres as both an interceptor and fighter-bomber, and with their graceful lines became one of the most iconic aircraft of the Second World War. One pilot commented: 'in a Spitfire we're back to war as it ought to be ... to individual combat, to self-reliance, total responsibility for one's own fate.'[31]

Squadron Leader Drobinski considered it:

a marvellous plane. I think it was the apex of fighter planes. Slight movement and it follows the right way. The Spitfire had a smaller cabin

[cockpit] than the Hurricane and when you're belted in you feel like one
and it's like a race horse … the aristocrat of fighter planes.[32]

A pilot with 92 (East India) Squadron found he experienced 'a sensation of being
part and parcel of the aircraft, as one'.[33] The commanding officer of 64 Squadron
impressed upon his pilots that 'you buckled on the Spitfire', rather akin to putting
on armour in 'days of old'.[34]

For Kazimierz Budzik, his first flight in a Spitfire during 1941:

> was exciting … the biggest worry you've got to come back and land the
> plane. So what we used to do was to find your stalling speed, climb over a
> Cumulous or something and you find it … but it didn't take long, it was
> such a lovely plane to fly and more powerful than anything I'd flown …
> it was really something and you felt that you'd got something here. It was
> fantastic. You could see lovely … climbing and turning was superb.[35]

Group Captain Duncan Smith flew Spitfires over Britain, France, Malta, Sicily,
and Italy, and remembered how before going into action for the first time he'd
come to know his aircraft via continuous practice of dogfighting. 'With full power
in a steep turn and at slow speeds she would judder and shake, rocking to and fro,
but so long as she was handled correctly she would not let go and spin – surely
a unique feature for a high performance aeroplane.' Owing to 'her clean lines
with minimum drag', the Spitfire had a tendency to 'float', but 'with a powered
approach, nose well up controlling engine power and forward speed with positive
use of the throttle', she could be landed safely in a short space.[36]

Polish flyer Antoni Murkowski found the Spitfire 'manoeuvrable and enjoyable
to fly'. His favourite model was the clipped wing version of the Mk V, as 'it didn't
have the tendency to fly one wing down like those with the original wing design
at low altitudes'. In contrast, the Spitfire Mk II 'could be a bit tricky', not least
because 'the undercarriage had to be pumped up by hand and it was awkward
because the selector was on the right-hand side of the cockpit and the hand
pump lever on the left. To work this you had to change hands after take-off; it
was awkward.' The Spitfire Mk IX, by comparison, was more powerful and 'a
very good kite at high altitude', although initially plagued by engine trouble as the
supercharger, which was supposed to work automatically at 18,000 feet, would fail,
sending the aircraft nose-down into a spin.[37]

Although the Spitfire performed well at high altitudes, pilots still faced
numerous challenges, especially when in 'an unheated and unpressurised cockpit',
which 'froze hands and feet in minutes'. By approximately 30,000 feet, 'the Perspex
and windscreen frosted up badly due to the condensation of the water vapour in
the breath and it was only possible to see at all by continuously scraping off frost

as it formed.' Pilots' discomfort was further hindered by crudely designed oxygen masks that were 'far from efficient'. At high altitudes, aircraft also risked forming distinctive vapour trails that easily gave away their position to enemy fighters.[38] Likewise, flying at night could be challenging in a Spitfire because 'the engine produced spectacular amounts of flame exactly in the direction the pilot would be looking when landing'.[39]

Mud was a further problem, especially on grass air strips in Britain or on primitive airfields, such as those employed during the campaign in North Africa during 1942–43. In Tunisia, Tony Tooth flew the tropicalised version of the Spitfire Mk VB with 152 (Hyderabad) Squadron.

> The Spitfire hates mud, mainly because of the very heavy engine sticking out so far in front that it is liable to tip over on its nose, breaking the propeller, also the propeller whips up mud and plasters it into the radiator, blocking it and causing the engine to overheat. This meant that all the squadrons at Souk-el-Arba were virtually grounded for some days.[40]

Initially, the cannons on the Mk VB, which was armed with four .303 Browning machine guns and two 20mm cannons, were problematic. Stoppages made it extremely difficult for pilots to engage targets successfully. One pilot recorded that if one cannon stopped, aircraft would be twisted sideways by the recoil of the other, which had kept firing. 'We had to put up with this sort of snag during the early days with the Hispano 20mm cannons till we sorted out the stoppage problems. It was very annoying when a stoppage threw one off-balance because of the sudden change in trim.'[41]

A less well-known aircraft type was the Boulton Paul Defiant. First deployed operationally in May 1940, it achieved total surprise, accounting for about sixty-five enemy aircraft that month. It was a low-wing cantilever monoplane of all-metal construction, with a crew of two: pilot and gunner, who sat behind him in a hydraulically operated turret equipped with four .303 calibre machine guns. Its success as a day fighter was short-lived as Luftwaffe pilots swiftly learned to attack the Defiant head-on or from below, from which angles it was a sitting duck. Consequently, by late 1940, it was relegated to night defence, and proved rather successful. As one pilot recounted:

> for that purpose it was very good. I think it should have been used initially for night fighting. We had to get a method of actually detecting the German. And if searchlights did that, the Defiant was the ideal aircraft to shoot him down. Instead it was used as a day-fighter which was ridiculous and they got shot down left, right and centre.[42]

Another aircraft that achieved a good reputation as a night fighter was the Bristol Beaufighter. Conceived as a night-fighter/long-range escort/anti-shipping strike fighter, it was a large twin-engine monoplane with a maximum speed of over 300 mph. There was room for radar equipment, and with four forward-firing 20mm cannons, plus six forward-firing .303 calibre machine guns, it packed a fearsome punch. As Squadron Leader Tony Spooner explained, 'when a Beau opened up with all ten guns, any aircraft in its direct line of fire stood little chance of surviving.' It had 'to be treated with some respect in the air', proved 'exceptionally rugged', and although it initially suffered from engine problems, once these were solved its reliability and performance was impressive.[43]

Although enviable, the Beaufighter's performance as a night fighter was surpassed by that of the versatile twin-engine de Havilland Mosquito, or wooden wonder. Various marks served during the war, and it was also employed as a two-seat bomber, fighter-bomber and photographic reconnaissance aircraft. Air Commodore John Ellacombe completed a conversion course on the Mosquito in July 1943, and saw action with 487 Squadron after D-Day. He found it was 'very nice. A lovely aeroplane, I mean it wasn't as tight manoeuvring [as the Hurricane] but it was a good, stable aeroplane with plenty of fuel.'[44]

Originally designed as a replacement interceptor fighter to the Hurricane, the Hawker Typhoon suffered from developmental problems, particularly with the engine and airframe. Another challenge was that it proved awkward when trying to ditch at sea, even in calm water, as the 'big scoop radiator under the nose' tended to swiftly drag an aircraft down before a pilot had time to escape.[45] It was powered by a Napier Sabre engine, generating over 2,000 h.p., giving a top speed of over 370 mph. However, as a pilot with 198 Squadron recalled, while 'there was plenty of power … it dropped off rapidly at higher altitudes'.[46] Owing to its speed, the Typhoon was used to counter tip-and-run raids by Focke-Wulf 190s on British coastal towns, plus sweeps over the Continent. During such actions from 'July to September 1942, the loss from engine or structural failure of at least one aircraft per sortie occurred.'[47]

Yet the Typhoon achieved a formidable reputation as a ground-attack aircraft with 2nd TAF. The Mk IB was equipped with four wing-mounted 20mm cannons, and carried up to eight 60lb rocket projectiles or two 1,000lb bombs on underwing racks. Notably, ahead of D-Day, Typhoons operating as fighter-bombers armed with bombs, rockets and cannons almost continuously interdicted German communications, which had a significant impact on the outcome of the fighting. According to Group Captain Desmond Scott, the commander of 123 Wing, during the battle for Normandy, Typhoons would 'change the whole concept of close-support operations' and ensure 'Hitler's prized panzer divisions were no longer the undisputed victors of the Blitzkreig days'.[48]

Given the Typhoon had limited success as an interceptor, Hawker drew on designs dating from the early 1940s to produce the Tempest. The Mk V Tempest entered service in April 1944, and a specialist wing was formed in 85 Group, commanded by Wing Commander R.P. Beaumont. Again, it was powerful, with a Napier Sabre IIA engine and maximum speed of over 400 mph. After VE-Day, Tony Tooth was selected to work as a ferry pilot delivering a wide variety of aircraft from factories or storage. One job included helping remove a Tempest from an airfield that was closing down, and it might have ended in disaster.

> I had the greatest difficulty getting it started. ... I should point out that aeroplane engines are not like cars; they needed a degree of skill which some people never acquired. When I taxied out to the runway the engine was smoking quite a lot, but as the Sabre engine always did I did not worry unduly. My confidence was misplaced. Halfway down the runway there was one hell of a big bang and the most enormous cloud of white smoke erupted from the exhaust. I immediately throttled back and luckily stopped before reaching the end of the runway. If it had happened only seconds later I would have been over either the town of Silloth or over the sea. Not a nice prospect. The engine would actually have disintegrated.[49]

A variety of American-manufactured fighters were employed by the RAF throughout the war, including the Curtiss P-40 Kittyhawk in North Africa and the Mediterranean, and the P-47 Thunderbolt in South East Asia, both of which were particularly useful as ground-attack aircraft. One that stands out owing to its performance was the P-51 Mustang. Early Mustangs in RAF service had Allison engines and fought in the fighter/reconnaissance role, but later, those fitted with Merlin engines demonstrated an impressive performance. This was especially noticeable at high altitude, and coupled with a high diving speed, made it a formidable fighter. Another significant feature of the Mustang was its inbuilt fuel capacity, giving a combat radius of 400 miles, an impressive feature for a single-engine, single-seat fighter, leading to it serving as a long-range bomber escort.

In 1945, as Squadron Leader Drobinski remembered, 303 (Polish) Squadron re-equipped with Mustangs and served in this role. This included supporting the raid against Berchtesgaden, or Hitler's Eagle Nest, on 25 April that was launched by over 350 aircraft from 1, 5 and 8 Groups from Bomber Command. He found that the Mustang was 'a little bigger plane [compared to the Spitfire], very comfortable inside, there was more room. Not as manoeuvrable as the Spitfire, but more luxurious', and visibility 'was very good'.[50]

Aerial combat

To survive and be a successful fighter pilot required numerous qualities. According to wartime ace Bob Doe, the ability to learn quickly, luck, plus 'flying ability, good eyesight and situational awareness' were vital. Competence at judging speeds and distances, not necessarily easy once airborne, were similarly important. Aerobatics and formation flying formed a strong strand of peacetime RAF training, but didn't necessarily translate well into combat conditions. Many pilots rapidly realised it was safer to 'jink across the sky' rather than fly straight and level for too long because that risked becoming a casualty.[51] As Battle of Britain veteran Geoffrey Wellum recounted, you had to 'remember a simple, straightforward golden rule: Never, but never fly straight and level for more than twenty seconds. If you do, you'll die.'[52]

Potentially faced with their own mortality, fighter pilots had to conquer fear. Hector Bolitho, 43 Squadron's intelligence officer, reckoned many did by adapting 'themselves to it and beat it into a positive part of their character. For their fear and sensibility are one.'[53] One Polish Spitfire pilot found he experienced a form of pre-combat tension, which manifested itself by a 'trembling just above my heel out of my control. But once you start diving the fear is gone, while you use guns or cannon or drop a bomb. … [Later,] you'd get a drink in the mess, play cards with a mate like nothing had happened.'[54]

Fighter pilots also had to contend with the 'deadly weight of fatigue', particularly during the Fall of France in May–June 1940 and during the Battle of Britain, when the Luftwaffe sought to gain aerial supremacy. Hours of duty lasted from first light to last light, a spread of twenty-four hours, with an average of four hours' sleep each night.[55] The tension was exacerbated when a fighter squadron or flight was kept in readiness, prepared to take off rapidly, with pilots waiting in their crew room. Alternatively, pilots might be placed on standby, which entailed sitting in their aircraft, with the engine running, for hours at a stretch, potentially ready for take-off at a moments' notice. Aircraft couldn't always function under this pressure. A Spitfire pilot found their engines could not be kept 'ticking over as they would boil', owing to the position of the radiator away from the slipstream, which prevented efficient cooling for anything 'longer than five minutes'.[56]

Eventually, the order might come to scramble to intercept an enemy bomber formation and/or take on fighters. As a young flying officer with a Hurricane squadron, Paul Richey experienced this in France early in the war.

Sergeant Soper and I were scrambled and we roared off one by one down the flare-path. Johnny [FO Johnny Walker] went first, I followed. After I had cleared the airfield hedge, got my wheels up and checked my instruments, I looked for Johnny's amber formation light, spotted it and climbed up after him. Soon I was tucked in beside him, with Soper on the other side, and we climbed up to our patrol height of 20,000 feet and opened out into battle formation.[57]

It was then that tactics started to become relevant, as aircraft were vectored onto a target or ordered to the area where the enemy was reported. The charismatic commander of a wartime Hurricane squadron, Douglas Bader, stressed that 'He who has the height controls the battle. He who has the sun achieves surprise [i.e. attack out of the sun]. He who gets in close shoots them down.'[58] Broadly speaking, he was echoing First World War fighter experience, plus his own background on biplanes during the interwar years. Another distinguished wartime fighter leader, South African Group Captain 'Sailor' Malan, went into more detail, issuing ten rules for air fighting, copies of which circulated in many squadrons.

1. Wait until you see the whites of his eyes. Fire short bursts of one or two seconds, and only when your sights are definitely 'on'.
2. Whilst shooting think of nothing else. Brace the whole of the body, have both hands on the stick, concentrate on your ring sight.
3. Always keep a sharp look-out. 'Keep your finger out.'
4. Height gives you initiative.
5. Always turn and face the attack.
6. Make your decisions promptly. It is better to act quickly, even though your tactics are not of the best.
7. Never fly straight and level for more than thirty seconds in the combat area.
8. When diving to attack, always leave a proportion of your formation above to act as top guard.
9. INITIATIVE, AGGRESSION, AIR DISCIPLINE, and TEAM WORK are words that mean something in air fighting.
10. Go in quickly – Punch hard – Get Out![59]

Some pilots, including Malan, advised that when tackling an enemy bomber, it was best to hit the fuselage, rather than engines, in order to wound/kill its crew. The reasoning being that this would be demoralising for the bomber's unit if the aircraft succeeded in returning to base. In reality, few pilots had the shooting skill to employ such aggressive tactics. An alternative was offered by leading ace Bob Stanford Tuck, who flew with 92 Squadron during the Battle of Britain, and recommended that pilots attacked in a shallow dive out of the sun and passed through an enemy bomber formation at speed, before pulling up underneath them to launch a close-range attack against their unprotected bellies.[60]

Another distinguished pilot explained how initially, tactical training had been based around the idea that 'dog-fighting was a thing of the past, and rigid air fighting tactics were introduced which, by a series of complicated and time wasting-manoeuvres, aimed at bringing the greatest number of guns to bear against the bombers'.[61] This was understandable given that during the interwar period, strategic thinking had centred on how the British could thwart the expected 'knock-out blow' that would be delivered by German bombers.[62]

The attacks against bombers were enshrined in a series of Fighter Area Attacks. In FAA Number One, for example, a section of fighters were expected to attack a lone enemy bomber, by moving into line astern of it, then each successively attacking from the rear. Contrastingly, in FAA Number Two, a fighter unit would approach bombers from below, the aircraft would then climb up and take turns to fire, so that when one fighter's ammunition was expended it would break off, enabling another to engage.[63] Theoretically, the neatly choreographed FAAs made sense, but in practice they took no account of developments in aerial warfare by 1940, namely that German bombers would be escorted by nimble fighters, and that combat conditions for pilots flying the latest high performance monoplanes were liable to be frenetic and confusing.

Actions during the Battle of Britain in August 1940 demonstrated this. A young Polish pilot recorded completing his first sortie in a Spitfire, intended to familiarise him with the terrain over which he'd be operating.

> After about an hour I started to return to Hornchurch. Suddenly there was an explosion on the ground and I looked up and there was a formation of German bombers dropping bombs. They were at about 12 to 14,000 feet. I was about 5 to 6,000 feet by that time … so I started chasing them with my full throttle, and I was slowly getting up to them but we were both going in the same direction so it was taking a little bit longer, longer than I hoped. They were bombing the airfield. Eventually I came close or thought I was close, but was about 1,000 feet behind and 400 feet below them, but I was ready to get even closer because it's no use wasting ammunition.
>
> Then I took a look at my instruments and I was getting out of petrol because I flew for about an hour on the recce flight, then took a full throttle to keep up with the German bombers and I am practically on zero. I thought 'God I can't get them,' so I decided to press the button and if I hit or not it doesn't matter, provided I am not too slow on speed so it doesn't get into a spin. And I had to stop and come down. Coming down to the airfield at 2,000 feet I see that there were lots of craters [from the Germans' bombing] and I have no petrol to go around. So I had to land straight on … but I landed between the craters and when I touched the ground and got on three points of landing I undid my seat belt and I stood up to see which way to go … and I came back to the dispersal point.[64]

During that same month, a Hurricane pilot with 615 Squadron vividly recounted combat with German bombers, near RAF Kenley.

> I was about 6–7,000 feet up slightly to the west of the aerodrome where we were being attacked. Now, it was cloudy, poor visibility. A string of bombs had just missed us and I looked up and could just see through the haze the Dorniers and they were just on their bombing run to Kenley. So I put my nose straight up, the override on, and opened fire on the leader. And I went on and kept on firing at it. Then I fired at the next fellow, then fell out of the sky and saw some tracers so obviously they'd spotted me. ... And I chased one of the Dorniers, which by this time had gone towards Biggin Hill. ...
>
> Then a Ju88 appeared at an angle and I didn't know if he was going for me, but thought he might be. I was in an ideal position and I gave it a burst, as much as I possibly could, and I obviously killed the pilot and I thought that's the only way to get rid of a German, kill the pilot then he'd have no option. And it went straight into the ground and blew up and still had his bombs on it.[65]

On another occasion, he launched a lead or head-on attack against a formation of German bombers.

> There was a large group of Dorniers coming up from Brighton heading north. I was sent up and attacked them ... so we had practised head-on attacks in 111 Squadron [his former unit] so I thought the only way to get at the Germans was to stop the leaders. If you could get the leader they wouldn't know where to drop their bombs and therefore that was the answer. So I decided I would go head-on. Two other Hurricanes attacked from the other side i.e. the rear ... I went through onto the leader onto the next one and just kept my guns firing all the way through, through the formation.
>
> They were coming up towards Brooklands ... I think 11 German aircraft came down. We were the only people attacking them. Keith and Tony [the other pilots] each claimed one from the back. Now that was proof that a head-on attack onto the leader would've been the answer because their bombing went nowhere.[66]

An alternative was to attack German bombers from behind, not necessarily a bad idea as most types were not as well protected from the rear. Roald Dahl had success with this form of attack against a Junkers 88 that had twin tail guns. He shot it down while flying a Hurricane in Greece, which for an inexperienced pilot was quite an achievement. The Ju 88 sent 'a stream of orange-red bullets' towards him as he manoeuvred to attack. Then:

> by jiggling my plane this way and that I managed to get the starboard engine of the bomber into my reflector sight. I aimed a bit ahead of the engine and pressed the button ... the eight Brownings in the wings all opened up together ... a second later I saw a huge piece of his metal engine engine-cowling the size of a dinner tray go flying up into the air.

The Ju 88 later fell to the ground 'like a leaf', thick, black smoke pouring from its stricken engine.[67]

Beam attacks could also be employed, and tested a fighter pilot's skill. These were 'probably the most effective and certainly the most difficult means of bringing down an enemy machine'. The attacking aircraft:

> would overhaul his target, well out to the side and about 500 feet or so above. When some little way ahead he would bank and turn in, to let the other machine come through his sights almost at right angles, and with a double deflection (twice the diameter of his sights) he would let go in a long burst.[68]

Consequently, a pilot engaged in a beam attack would open fire in front of the enemy's nose, hit him along a flank, where he was vulnerable and had the smallest field of fire, while the fighter presented a small, awkward, moving target for the enemy gunners. If necessary, the pilot could continue by mounting an attack from the rear.

However, German bombers could prove tough nuts to crack, regardless of whether or not they were escorted by fighters, and even if the RAF employed incendiary ammunition or cannon. Typically, Luftwaffe aircrew were well trained, including the air gunners. On 25 May 1942, Air Commodore Brown was flying a Spitfire Mk VB with 616 Squadron based at RAF Wittering, when tasked with intercepting a Dornier Do 217 on a reconnaissance flight over Britain.

> It was very quiet and I and a sergeant pilot as Number Two had been left at readiness, the duty readiness Spitfire pair, when a plot appeared on the board of an enemy aircraft penetrating inland over Lincolnshire flying in and out of layered cloud. We were scrambled up to intercept it and were trying to find it because of the cloud. Old Johnnie [his flight commander and later AVM J.E. 'Johnnie' Johnson] had heard what was going on, so he and his Number Two who hadn't left Wittering came screaming back and got into their Spitfires. So there were four of us trying to find this thing.

I think they saw it pop out of cloud but before they could do anything it popped back in. And suddenly it popped out of the cloud, straight in front of me. I swung round to attack it with guns firing and a succession of great white phosphorous bores linked me into the mid-upper gun section and I was about 150 yards from it, and there was the most terrible 'crash'. And my windscreen quarter panel and hood had been hit and disintegrated, and all the bits came back into me. A whacking great bit of metal hit me in the solar-plexus and knocked my breath out. It smashed my goggles off and my oxygen mask and took out my right eye. So it was a fair amount of mess.

By this time, the enemy aircraft had disappeared into cloud, and I was trying to pull myself together. There isn't really any pain under those circumstances, there's just intense shock. In fact the Spitfire made the decision for me because there was this enormous 'bang'. And I had no idea what other parts of the aircraft had been hit as well. Fortunately, the rest of it was unscathed and I suddenly found that it was flying normally, the engine was running sweetly. So I pulled myself together and was still in cloud at this time. And I couldn't jump out because the hood had been distorted over my head. ... So I just let down and found an airfield right below me.[69]

Despite this injury, he resumed his wartime flying career, briefly as a one-eyed Englishman with 532 (Australian) Squadron, and a night-fighter squadron, before becoming a successful test pilot.

Pre-war drills strongly emphasised formation flying, which practised pilots in control, discipline, precision and teamwork – all deemed important facets of operational flying. Close formation flying enabled large bodies of aircraft, such as a squadron, to penetrate cloud with the minimum risk of scattering or collisions occurring. Air drill was employed, especially when positioning aircraft for attack or defence, when 'battle' or open formations were employed.

In Vic formation, for instance, close formation required a following aircraft's wingtips were 'tucked in' or overlapping between a leading aircraft's wing and tailplane. Paradoxically, it was easier to keep station accurately in close formation than in open or 'battle' formation with spacing increased to 50–100 yards.[70]

Use of air drills led one former RAFVR pilot to state that contemporary 'flying training was superb', but he cautioned that by comparison, 'tactical sense was poor early in the war' because 'tactics were unreal and unrealistic, with no real appreciation of weapons' effectiveness'. They were 'unreal, because not enough attention had been focussed upon tactics and weapons training. The emphasis was on flying.'[71]

The use of the basic 'Vic', or Victor, formation of three aircraft, upon which various formations were based, including those for fighter verses fighter action, was a case in point. It made RAF fighters extremely vulnerable to being 'bounced' by the enemy, as two of the pilots had to spend most of their time concentrating on keeping in formation rather than watching their tails or the sky. Moreover, the inner two had often to throttle back, 'whereas a fighter pilot wanted to leave his controls alone' if possible, and 'keep up full speed in the combat zone'.[72] Wing Commander Gordon Olive, as tactics officer to 65 Squadron during the Phoney War, discovered, 'we were to operate in sections of three. In these we were supposed to shoot at formations, while maintaining formation ourselves. This was very difficult to achieve … we abandoned this idea in favour of a more individualistic attack.'[73]

Unsurprisingly, many units found it necessary to adapt official teachings or develop their own solutions to the tactical challenges faced. In 151 Squadron, instead of relying on the 'Vic' of three formation, Air Commodore Teddy Donaldson introduced a system of pairs, aping that employed by the Luftwaffe. 'Each pilot flew with a wingman protecting him from surprise attacks, allowing the leader to concentrate not on maintaining formation with his wingman, but on navigation and on searching out his enemy.'[74] Another innovation, learned from the French air force, was the adoption of an 'Arse-end Charlie', an aircraft that hung above and behind a formation, often in an open 'Vic', whose pilot's task was 'to protect the formation's tail, which was blind when flying straight, and to prevent surprise attack'. According to Wing Commander Paul Richey, 1 Squadron in France, during 1939–40, usually had two 'Charlies' and they 'proved indispensable … not once during the entire campaign was one of our formations surprised'. Although they were often attacked from above, the system enabled them to see the enemy 'before he was in range and we were never jumped'.[75]

During 1940, the RAF introduced 'weavers' in an effort to counter flaws with the Vic formation, notably blindness to the rear. The idea was for one or two aircraft to 'weave' or fly on a zigzag course, above and to the rear of a squadron, and so form a rearguard. This was costly in terms of fuel consumption. Air Commodore Brown vividly remembered the technique during his wartime operational flying, and had mixed views over its effectiveness.

> Fighter Command adopted a system of 'weavers' with the squadron flying in open combat formation and the chap at the back weaving backwards and forwards at the tail end of the formation to make certain they weren't surprised or bounced from the rear. That was alright up to a point. Normally the chap at the tail end was one of the most inexperienced pilots, so he'd be the chap under the conditions of high

flying combat, fighter versus fighter that was usually the first one to be picked off. And it wasn't until late on in 1941 and probably in Douglas Bader's Wing at Tangmere, that the system of 'finger fours' without the 'weavers' was finally adopted and of course proved to be much more effective.[76]

One of the bitterest controversies over tactics centred on the 'Big Wing' – the idea that, during the Battle of Britain, German bombers should be engaged in strength by massed formations of fighters. This originated in 12 Group, 'where the Air Officer Commanding, the bluff, forceful Air Vice-Marshal Trafford Leigh-Mallory, was strongly critical' of the direction of the battle by Air Vice-Marshal K.R. Park, who commanded 11 Group, which bore the brunt of the fighting. Essentially, 12 Group, covering the less directly threatened area north of 11 Group, was afforded more time in which to ponder tactics. It 'operated a number of squadrons together – usually three, four or five, but once as many as seven – as a mass formation or "wing",' typically forming up in the Duxford area, 'under the inspiring leadership of Squadron Leader Douglas Bader'.[77] At times this achieved significant success against German attacks on London, and there was a belief that operating this way would keep down the RAF's casualty figures.

Contrastingly, 'the size of the fighting unit in 11 Group was conditioned by the time to intercept before the bombing', and was much smaller. Massed formations such as the 'Big Wing' would have taken longer to gain sufficient height, plus 'sixty or seventy packed, climbing fighters could have been seen for miles and would have been sitting ducks for the 109s'.[78] Similarly, a veteran of 11 Group claimed, 'we were very upset about the Bader lot, with the "Big Wing", because they'd never cross the Thames unless they were 30,000 feet up and usually half an hour late.'[79]

The idea that big formations could yield decisive results continued after the Battle of Britain. During sweeps over the Continent that dominated 1941, one Spitfire pilot recalled that they'd form up 'in huge masses of seventy or more fighters and ground our way over the familiar fields of northern France ... so large and cumbersome that we were unable to climb to our best altitudes and had to stooge at heights which could be ten and even fifteen thousand feet below the enemy's fighters' ceiling'.[80] It was anticipated that such large formations would entice the Luftwaffe into launching a comparable response, but this didn't necessarily happen. Instead, the enemy was often content to attack these large formations, using pairs of fighters, in small-scale but nonetheless hard-hitting sorties.

Another challenge was that, especially during the early phases of the war, the standard of aircraft recognition was poor. Battle of Britain fighter ace John Simpson noted how 'Heinkels look quite like Ansons [Avro Anson, a British twin-engine aircraft] from underneath. Several times we have taken Ansons for Heinkels and only just realised in time.'[81] Wing Commander James Sanders, who flew in France in 1940 and in the Battle of Britain, stressed:

> The aircraft recognition was very bad. I was attacked by a squadron of Hurricanes. Now the Hurricane looks like a dolphin in the air, it's got a hump you can't mistake it, and I saw the other lot coming down at me you see. I told Group will you call this squadron off, they're Hurricanes and we're Hurricanes, but they didn't and shot my Number Two down, he was riddled with bullets. Our recognition was appalling but I think the Germans realised even theirs was appalling because they painted their Me 109s with yellow noses so they could recognise one another.[82]

Dogfighting was the ultimate test of a fighter pilot's competence, character, nerve and courage. As with attacking bombers, it could prove frenzied and disorientating, especially for inexperienced pilots. One wartime ace described how 'the whole of air warfare is one of illusion'; at one moment the sky could be clear, then, full of aircraft, before becoming calm again.[83] While serving in North Africa during December 1942, Tony Tooth found that as an inexperienced pilot, he was:

> Wasting a lot of ammunition by firing at a 109 that I am sure was way out of range! At least it was a start! The next day the squadron was jumped by a large gaggle of both 109s and 190s and one hell of a melee ensued, I was completely confused but know I was attacked by a 109 and that I nearly ran into a 190, there appeared to be dozens of aircraft milling around me then suddenly, miraculously, the air was empty, not one plane visible anywhere! That is a characteristic of aerial combat that many pilots have remarked on. I then found myself at 22,000 feet, all alone and over enemy territory and knowing that there were many enemies around, there is only one thing to do under those circumstances, and that is to go home as fast as you can and the best place to do that is right down on the deck, as low as you dare fly. So I duly rolled over on my back and dived vertically to ground level and then flew at high speed all the way home at about 20 feet. The ground crew showed me a bullet hole that had appeared in the engine cowling, luckily it had gone clean thru without hitting anything vital.[84]

In September 1943, he encountered an enemy fighter over Sicily, as the Germans were trying to evacuate troops and equipment. He damaged the 'bandit' but had a hair-raising experience extricating himself from the action.

> I got in a good shot at fairly long range at a Bf 109 which slowed him down considerably and allowed me to catch up, difficult with a 109G as they were

faster than the Spitfire V. When I caught up I found my usual problem, one
cannon not working, so I sat behind him and fired off ammunition in vain.
I then put my thinking cap on and decided that I wasn't in a very invidious
position and it would be better if I cleared off. I was on my own, short of
ammunition and unable to shoot straight, my opponent badly damaged and
probably unable to get home, so I rolled over, dived down to sea level and
set off for home. I had quite a long way to go, over open sea to start with,
then either thru the Messina Strait, not highly recommended as it had one
of the highest concentrations of anti-aircraft guns in the world, or overland
round west of Etna, further, but preferable under the circumstances. First
I had the open sea to cover, and that produced a surprise, as I flew over the
water enormous splashes appeared in front of me and it took a moment for
me to realise what was happening. I was straight off Cap Milazzo where
there was a coast defence battery of eight-inch guns which fired huge shells
and they were trying to drop them in front of me![85]

On 22 June 1941, Squadron Leader Drobinski experienced an archetypal dogfight
situation against a Me 109, during a fighter sweep by 303 (Polish) Squadron's
Spitfires over France.

Until you're able to get the enemy into your gunsight … you keep turning
around, both aircraft are turning and trying to get on each other's tail.
And in the meantime you're losing height because you want to make as
tight turning as possible to get on your enemy's tail, and he does the same.
So practically you have to hang on your propeller and full throttle on 'a
wing and a prayer' as the saying goes.

The Me 109 couldn't hold on as long as me and peeled off. When he
did that I dived down and followed him, and shot him down, and pulled
up to about 2,000 feet. It was a classic dog-fight as far as I was concerned.
But I must tell you I was as wet as I could be with my perspiration,
concentration to not only get one in front of me, but make sure no one's
going to get me from the back. So that was emotionally very nerve-
wracking. I can't say I enjoyed it, but there was satisfaction because he
had the same choice I did.[86]

Many fighter pilots felt similarly, and didn't derive pleasure from killing, although
they were acutely aware of the need to win the war. Others took a detached view,
considering that air warfare was simply a case of kill or be killed. Almost all found
that sometimes operating fighters was an exhilarating experience.

Fighters were needed in a defensive sense, to mount patrols protecting
British air space. As an inexperienced young Hurricane pilot with 253 Squadron,

Air Commodore Brown experienced operations during the latter stages of the Battle of Britain, in November 1940.

> Enemy action was mainly high flying offensive patrols, and the weather itself started to deteriorate. The whole tempo of flying had dropped, so the Squadron had recovered. But it was one of those frustrating periods when the enemy was still penetrating by high flying fighter sweeps, I think in Bf 109Fs which were far superior to the Hurricane Mark 1. So it was always a question of trying to clamber up to them too late and finishing up below the enemy, who in that sense had some form of tactical initiative, in that they could dive down and pick people off here and there in the Hurricane squadrons, and then dive madly all the way back home to France.
>
> Most of the skirmishes I was involved in then were really inconclusive. There was a steady trickle of casualties being shot down or aircraft damaged. And I am sure there were 109s that were damaged and being shot down. But in the main it was similar to the situation that developed in the Pas de Calais in Northern France a couple of years later when we were conducting the high flying fighter sweeps and the combats were taking place at altitude and again frustrating and inconclusive, and the opportunities for shooting people down, and building big scores, really wasn't very great.[87]

Another function of fighters was to serve as coastal convoy escorts, an unglamorous duty, but one that was important if supplies were to reach Britain by sea. John Simpson found these 'dull and very tiring as we fly only a few feet off the water', which required concentration.[88] Kazimierz Budzik discovered these were:

> Rather boring, but even then you had to be on guard because Ju 88s used to come round, and if you're off guard you might get hurt. You couldn't go to sleep, and couldn't get too close to your own ships because they had defences and might take a shot at you.[89]

Fighters had to act as escorts to bombers when, as Wing Commander Sanders put it, 'You stay a reasonable distance, and wait for something to come along, and try and stop him from having a go at it.'[90] A Polish pilot from 308 Squadron remembered how working as bomber escort was an integral part to the combined bomber and fighter sweeps, or Circuses, over France that started occurring regularly by 1941.

> The escorted bombers would go a little bit deeper and different targets and so on. ... When there was a big sweep there were fighters, used to

come one after another one. Then there used to be escort with bombers, and you used to have the close escort, one flight on one side, one on the other one, then another squadron would come right up until you had top-cover. As a close escort, which I've done a lot, you wasn't allowed to go away, but had to stick with the bombers if possible.[91]

Regarding these Circuses, Squadron Leader Drobinski had a slightly different experience, and explained that:

What the RAF did then was try to get up the German fighters to engage them in a fight. ... So we sent a flight of perhaps six Blenheims and 200 fighters. ... Once I got one [a Bf 109] that tried to shoot bomber, a Blenheim, and I intercepted him and shot him down. After the whole expedition had finished, and we had 'Vector Number 1 One', which means coming home. You must remember the Germans that come in a group would attack from the sun to try and get the bombers. But then everyone is dispersed ... everybody is after his own target. And you cannot stay long as long as you want to because of petrol.[92]

Similarly, a pilot with 253 Squadron found that, during Circuses, the:

Germans did not react strongly against just fighters. In order to tempt them into combat, Bomber Command was brought in, mainly with the Blenheims of 2 Group, small formations of Blenheims to act as bait, and then they were replaced by Bostons. At one time in 1940–1941 with Stirlings, but really they started to take a beating and were shot down in ones and twos. Really I don't think Bomber Command were very keen on being the bait for Fighter Command.

My main experience of combat was during those offensive fighter phases and it was a very similar situation to that which had existed at the back end of 1940 over the UK [albeit in reverse] and was as frustrating. High flying fighter against fighter with the Germans understandably I think being unwilling to stop and mix it. So there were fleeting combat opportunities.[93]

Later, while flying a Spitfire VB with 616 Squadron, the same pilot managed to bag a Focke-Wulf 190 fighter during a straight fighter sweep over the Pas de Calais area of Northern France, penetrating as far as St Omer.

I think it was as we were coming back there'd been small German formations pecking away all the time. I didn't see this particular bunch coming down, but somebody else did and screamed 'break!' So my Number Two and I went round in a screaming turn to starboard with a FW 190 shooting at me, but nothing getting enough deflection, so I realised he wasn't going to hit me. And he flashed by underneath to focus attention on my Number Two, so I rolled upside down and there very uncharacteristically this chap had levelled out behind my Number Two, banging away at him, but giving me the opportunity for a pretty good narrow angle deflection shot. So a couple of bursts and I blew his hood off and raked the fuselage around the cockpit, so close you could see the bits flying off. And he rolled upside down and just dived straight away and he didn't get out.[94]

This was an example of a confirmed kill. Confirmation usually came from other pilots in a squadron, analysis of film from cine-gun cameras fitted to aircraft, or eyewitnesses on the ground. Alternatively, 'it became the responsibility of Squadron and Sector Intelligence Officers to assess pilots' claims from the details of combat reports and determine to which category the claim belonged, i.e. destroyed, probably destroyed or damaged.' In the RAF, 'no claims were admissible for aircraft destroyed on the ground' as these fell into the category of ground targets.[95]

Yet another type of fighter sweep were the so-called Rhubarbs, launched by small numbers of fighters. These were 'to destroy enemy machines in the air or on the ground, to shoot up or bomb airfield buildings, ports and communications', within in the overall aim of pining down the Luftwaffe in the West and preventing it from strengthening other theatres.[96] As James Goodson explained, typically, these 'sneak strafing raids' were launched at 'very low level, to avoid being picked up by radar or hit by flak. Presumably the code-name Rhubarb was meant to indicate that you flew so low the propellers clipped the rhubarb.'[97]

Another distinctive feature of Rhubarbs was that they presented pilots with targets of opportunity. Squadron Leader Drobinski recounted one of 15 May 1941, during which six Spitfires from 303 (Polish) Squadron were to:

Go over French airfields and shoot up the planes. And on 15 May I and my Number Two went with the Squadron Commander and his Number Two, and another senior officer and his Number Two, six planes in three twos left the English coast and went on a long flight over France. My target was St Omer. We went into the clouds, about 3 or 4,000 feet to cross the Channel, came out and dived down on a very long flight.

And as I crossed the coast I saw a Ju 52 taxiing across the field, so I wasn't quite sure if it was right or not but said to my Number Two we'll take him on, and he got a series of shots at him, and he turned sharply, probably he was damaged. Then we went to St Omer and couldn't find a great deal because the Messerschmitts were in cement boxes and you couldn't go high because the flak would get you.

In the meantime enemy aircraft appeared, and we saw six Bf 109s above us so we thought wow, so we decide to go back home. On the way back I saw a convoy of six ships going north. They couldn't have been British or French, so I said to my Number Two you take the last one, I'll take the first one. And put whatever ammunition I had left into it. It wasn't too dangerous because flying from the French coast the Germans on the ship thought we must be French or German planes, so they weren't much perturbed until I opened up fire from about 400 yards, and managed to use the captain's bridge as a target. And when I pulled up into the clouds, all hell broke loose and artillery started, shrapnel all over the place, but luckily neither of us was hit. ... When I pulled out of the clouds smoke was coming out of the ship.[98]

Throughout the war, fighter pilots had to deal with technological developments, including the introduction of new Ferranti gyro gunsights fitted to the Mk IX Spitfire. To use these, a pilot had to put his 'eye close to a small aperture and squint through it. Another snag was that you had to hold the aircraft steady in a turn without any sudden manoeuvre for three or four seconds to give the gyro time to settle.'[99] This wasn't necessarily advisable under combat conditions. Yet, once developed, it was deemed effective, notably during the Battle for Normandy during June–August 1944.

As a pilot with 131 Wing, 2nd TAF, Kazimierz Budzik struggled initially to employ the new sight, particularly during an encounter with a Focke-Wulf 190 over Normandy. He reflected:

I was too rough and never allowed gyro time to settle to have the correct reading there. We'd been given new sights with two sections, one that was fixed, and one that was gyro. When you've got a moving target you're supposed to put the middle of the sight on the cockpit and that's supposed to read the correct deflection to hit the target. But what I wasn't told was that to have correct reading you have to allow seconds for a gyro to settle. But when I attacked that FW 190 I didn't allow enough time and I wasn't correct. So switching onto the fixed sight, I hit him because I was very close and then the reason I follow him for a bit was because he was smoking but I hadn't actually seen him hit the ground and I pulled out because I had no ammo left.[100]

Another function of fighters was to counter Hitler's vengeance, or 'V', weapons, launched at Britain from the Continent. Squadrons under Wing Commander

Roland Beaumont accounted for over 630 of the V-1 flying bombs, or doodlebugs. These were pilotless guided bombs carrying a 1,875lb warhead. Many were shot down by Hawker Tempest pilots before they could reach their target. Alternatively, by holding a Tempest close and rigid to a V-1, it was possible for the airflow over the wing of the aircraft to take effect so that 'the wing of the flying-bomb lifted' and 'it heeled over in a dive to earth'. This required skill by the pilot, but obviated the need for the Tempest to actually touch the V-1's wing, which risked blowing them both to pieces.[101]

By summer 1944, Mustang fighters from 316 (Polish) Squadron were similarly engaged in combating the land-launched V-1s, and one of its pilots remembered a sortie when control advised:

> Red Leader, Witchcraft, 5 miles east of Hastings. [Witchcraft was code for a flying bomb.] I was just coming up on the coast when suddenly there was a puff of white smoke ahead, a flare by the Royal Observer Corps, a signal to indicate where the flying-bomb was crossing the coast. Looking down I saw it flying just below me ... I opened the throttle, turned into a shallow dive to gain more speed and quickly took an accurate sighting. It hardly seemed that I had touched the trigger finger before the flying-bomb exploded. The force lifted the Mustang about a thousand feet – just as if somebody had given me a big kick in the arse.[102]

In contrast, the V-2, or A4 rocket, with a 2,150lb warhead, was more difficult to counter, because it travelled at about three times the speed of sound, so couldn't be seen or heard, let alone intercepted by fighters. Instead, the RAF was tasked with mounting air patrols in an effort to prevent these rockets from being launched. Squadron Leader Drobinski explained how this was attempted using aircraft from three squadrons, including Spitfires from 303 (Polish) Squadron.

> Every 20 minutes a section of two sometimes three Spits would take off. We had additional petrol, drop tanks, and it's about 110 miles across the North Sea from RAF Coltishall to the Hague area. Patrol there about 20–23,000 feet, prevent launching of V-2s as the Germans didn't want to disclose their location. As long as visibility/weather was alright, three squadrons could help.[103]

Night fighter experiences

As Squadron Leader Tony Spooner expounded, 'night flying was, and still is, much more hazardous than daytime flying.' Additionally, in wartime, once an enemy raid was confirmed via radar, all lights at airfields in the vicinity were 'doused', plus foggy conditions, often unforecast, made night flying even more perilous.[104]

Early in the war, designated night-fighter squadrons were equipped with either Blenheims, with primitive, unreliable radar sets, or Defiants, without radar. Accordingly, night fighters 'spent their time milling aimlessly about for an hour or so looking for some indication of "bandits", by peering out of their cockpits at the waving beams of the searchlights, the flash of the anti-aircraft guns as they fired and the bomb bursts far below'. Even if they caught a tantalising glimpse of an enemy bomber, they were unlikely to be able to fire at it, before losing it in the dark. Many pilots had to concentrate on their instruments while night flying, and for those that had converted from being day fighter pilots, 'experience of instrument flying was minimal'. Many early night-fighter pilots and their crews were preoccupied with finding their way home, relying on 'primitive radio homing devices', and possibly searchlights, then landing safely on their airfield in darkness.[105]

In September 1940, Wing Commander Sanders was attached to 253 Squadron, while his own 615 Squadron rotated north for a rest. This enabled him to become a 'guinea pig' for experimental night-fighter work, having as a Hurricane pilot already managed to shoot down a Dornier at night.

> I remember one night, it was filthy foggy and all the rest of it. You couldn't fly and Churchill and Dowding had come down to the ops room, where they had a conference. Dowding said something like 'I envisage the night-fighter to take off in thick fog in the middle of the night and he'll be vectored onto the enemy and he'll open fire and he'll come back all due to the airborne facilities we are providing. And they'll never know he's taken off and landed'. And I thought the man's a lunatic to say that a pilot can be expected to do that. I firmly believed the only way would be to get the radar onto the searchlights and that's how we'd get the bombers down.[106]

Eventually, this type of scenario became possible when radar sets became more effective. Group Captain John Cunningham (nicknamed Cat's Eyes Cunningham) achieved fame as a night-fighter ace, and described in a combat report how he and his crew successfully dispatched a raider during 1941.

> Identified E/A [enemy aircraft] as He 111 which was flying just beneath cloud layer and occasionally going through wisps which allowed me to get within 80 yards of E/A and about 20–30 ft. beneath before opening fire. Immediately there was a big white flash in the fuselage centre section and black pieces flew off the fuselage. E/A went into a vertical dive to the

right and about half a minute later the sky all around me was lit up by an enormous orange flash and glow. Bits of E/A were seen to be burning on the ground.[107]

Another form of night-fighter work entailed cat's eyes squadrons that weren't equipped with radar, but instead were vectored onto an enemy aircraft by ground control and expected to achieve visual contact before making a kill. For a period, 308 (Polish) Squadron, equipped with Spitfires, operated like this protecting the Exeter area. One of its pilots, Kazimierz Budzik, remembered:

> We were on stand-by and scrambled near Torquay. I came to a Messerschmitt recce aircraft just over 30,000 feet. Took me sometime, anyhow I'd seen him and must have been about 1,000 yards and I opened fire, and as I was at that height the plane started losing power and I lost that enemy plane, away he went. [This proved too high for him to use his cannon and machine guns effectively.] In anger I pulled off my mask and as I did that I lost consciousness ... and I awoke and was about 9,000 feet, diving towards the sea when I pulled the plane out.[108]

Despite this, he considered that in flying terms, 'anything new was exciting', and recounted that 'before when we were in readiness we had to wear dark goggles and you couldn't see anything until ... you'd get used to them and have to go and fly. And that was a great help.'[109]

As a successful night-fighter navigator, Michael Allen found, by late 1941, a system was evolving to protect Britain whereby a 'Ground Controller – at his GCI station [Ground Control of Interceptions] was to watch a large cathode-ray tube [plan position indicator] and look for blips or radar echoes of the incoming bombers on his screen'. Subsequently, he'd identify which blip denoting a night fighter was best positioned to track the 'bandit', and 'by instructions over VHF radiotelephone direct the fighter to within 2–3 miles of its quarry'. Ideally, the ground controller would attempt to bring the night-fighter as close as possible behind the bomber, otherwise crew relied on their AI (airborne interceptor) onboard radar to bring them into a firing position.[110]

Initially, the RAF employed single-seat aircraft for night fighting, even though these had short endurance and were unable to detect a raider unaided. The Defiant was well-suited in many pilot's opinion, although it still couldn't find a 'bandit' unaided, and was equally as affected as single-seat fighters in poor weather. Wing Commander Sanders became increasingly involved with night-fighter work, and vividly recalled intercepting a German bomber over Retford, Nottinghamshire, while piloting a Defiant in 1941. Unfortunately, confusion arose between him and his gunner, facing backwards in the turret behind him.

I spotted this Heinkel going towards Liverpool, and my gunner was a fellow named Charlie Hill, and he was a butcher. And I told him the aircraft is just there. He says I can't see it, and I reply for goodness sake Charlie I am nearly touching it. I really was. I can't see it. So I said for God's sake put your guns up at eleven o'clock to the left and just fire. He did to his left, not where the aircraft was but in the opposite direction. So I slid away hoping I could keep it in position which I did. He said I can see it. So I said take it easy Charlie and we'll climb up again. Don't open fire until I tell you. We climbed up and Charlie opened fire and this great column of smoke came out of his starboard engine and it was moonlight so I could see. This German, he automatically turned round and started losing height. And I said to Charlie I suggest you bail out and I'll go up to him and knock his tail off because that's the only way we'll get him, he's probably heading back towards Germany. Charlie said oh no, he wasn't going to bail out. So we followed this German for quite a while until I lost sight of him, and apparently the Heinkel did come down near Grimsby.[111]

Another night fighting innovation was the Turbinlite. In theory, it appeared sound, but in practice left a lot to be desired. The system centred on a Boston Havoc fitted with an extremely powerful searchlight (1,400 amps), mounted in the nose, which carried AI radar equipment. These modifications ensured that the weight of the Havoc was such that no armament could be carried. Instead, the Turbinlite aircraft would illuminate an enemy bomber, and an accompanying Hurricane fighter would shoot it down. Having successfully tracked a 'bandit', the Havoc crew would warn the Hurricane pilot that they were to illuminated the enemy, and the enemy would hopefully appear in the searchlight beam. The Hurricane pilot would then 'pull the stick back, get his sights on the enemy bomber, make his attack and shoot the raider down'. Numerous flaws arose on operations. It was found that the Hurricane couldn't always stay with the fast twin-engine Havoc, and in bad weather, it was impossible for these aircraft to work successfully in tandem. Owing to a combination of accidents and its disappointing operational performance, the Turbinlite was abandoned by late 1942.[112]

After his injury, Air Commodore Brown served with a night-fighter squadron using Hurricanes during 1942. The loss of an eye wasn't as much of a drawback as might be supposed, because at night, most 'vision was in the forward segment'. He encountered Turbinlite units, and recalled:

They operated as a normal night-fighter with the AI. They had a searchlight but no guns. The Hurricane flew in formation on the Havoc during the interception phase and at a range of about 2–3,000 yards. The theory was the Havoc would illuminate the enemy aircraft with the searchlight and the Hurricane would then roar ahead and shoot it down. There were two things about that:

First of all there were about nine Turbinlite squadrons formed eventually and they really came on stream when the German air offensive over the UK had petered out, so there were hardly any targets.

Secondly, the Havoc, which was a modified Boston, at certain heights was faster than the Hurricane and so the theory that the Hurricane would then roar ahead and shoot down the target was a bit academic if the Boston was going flat out. In the end only one team of Havoc and Hurricane actually destroyed an enemy aircraft over the Humber.[113]

He became involved in combating what were known as the Baedeker raids, the German bombing of historic British cities, named after the popular guidebook. The RAF attempted to employ similar tactics to those developed by the Luftwaffe during 1943–45 to meet the Allied bomber offensive against the Reich. Namely, night fighters were sent over the target or aimed to infiltrate the enemy's bomber stream, while single-engine daylight fighters acting as cat's eye fighters were stacked up over the target.

I arrived over Norwich during that Baedeker raid, and it was like a miniature Berlin. The place was on fire, but it was so close to the coast that by the time the bulk of the fighter force had been scrambled, and sent to the target most of the enemy were on their way home.[114]

In the later raid against York, he recounted that:

The Squadron had more success then. I think they shot down two or three. I found a twin-engine target, which I chased all the way down the Humber, but didn't dare shoot it because I couldn't tell whether it was an enemy or friendly aircraft. We had been warned that there was a Beaufighter night-fighter squadron in the area, so he got away.[115]

Like the Blenheim, these twin-engine aircraft could easily be mistaken for a German bomber, particularly the Ju 88. However, the rugged, strongly built and heavily armed Beaufighter had great endurance, and proved useful as a night fighter, especially before the Mosquito could be deployed in numbers.

As the war progressed, RAF night fighters, notably those from 100 Bomber Support Group, were tasked not with guarding British skies, but with protecting aircraft from Bomber Command over hostile territory. As part of an ace night-fighter crew, Michael Allen received the DFC and two bars, and reflected:

> The Bomber Support operations were created to cause as much destruction and confusion to the air and ground defences of Germany as possible. The records of over 250 enemy aircraft destroyed in the air – and many more damaged – speak for themselves. And for the Beaufighter and Mosquito crews it was the most satisfying job in the night-fighter business.[116]

Part of this intense effort involved 'Serrate ops', or night-fighter verses night-fighter actions, where Luftwaffe night fighters seeking to shoot down RAF bombers were tracked using onboard radar and hunted down by British night fighters. Navigator Michael Allen and his pilot Air Commodore Harry White recorded the moment when they identified and engaged a Ju 88 over northern France, after it had tried to infiltrate the bomber stream.

> it was a very dark night we flew on – waiting for the E/A to turn into a lighter part of sky … he must surely turn north; this he did, after seven minutes. We were flying just through the tops of 3/10ths thin broken cloud momentarily losing sight of the Ju 88, Harry eventually opened fire from a range of 250 feet and 10 degrees below the E/A and gave it a four-second burst. The Junkers exploded and fell away in two burning pieces, both of which we saw hit the ground – where they continued to burn.[117]

Experiences of ground-attack sorties

Fighter-bombers proved versatile tools, employed for a wide range of tasks. Notably, in many theatres they provided close air support to ground forces, acting like 'flying artillery'. They undertook 'short- and long-range fighter sweeps, deep- and shallow-interdiction missions, escort for light/medium bombers, and anti-shipping strikes'. When employed in ground attack, they possessed a level of tactical flexibility denied to dive-bombers, and used bombs and/or rockets in high-speed, low-level passes that reduced the threat from anti-aircraft fire, or alternatively launched steep-dive attacks. Neither were fighter-bombers restricted to a single target, because an interdiction mission could easily be followed by a close air support strike. This flexibility was a distinct asset, especially as fighter-bombers could readily adapt to changing battlefield situations, and be redirected via radio while in flight. Yet a major drawback was that most contemporary fighter-bombers lacked adequate 'combat radius'. Spitfires employed as fighter-bombers by the Desert Air Force, for example, had to be restricted to operations within the immediate battle area because they lacked the ability to reach more distant targets.[118]

On 17 February 1943, while serving in North Africa, Tony Tooth's 152 Squadron received the surprising news that their Spitfires were to be employed as fighter-bombers.

This caused incredulity as no one had ever heard of Spitfires carrying bombs, in fact I think we became the second unit to try it, the first being one of the Malta squadrons. The idea was to use a dive-bombing technique, but no one had a clue how to go about it, and we could hardly ask the Malta boys, no internet then! The Boss consulted with all the more experienced pilots and came up with the plan that we would go over at 1,000 feet, out of range of the light guns, roll over into a 60 degree dive, aim at the target over the nose, hold it to around 4 or 5,000 feet or until the aircraft started to get unmanageable due to high speed (around 450 mph) then lift the nose to just cover the target, press the bomb release and ease the aircraft out of the dive. This had to be done with great care; too rapid a pull-out would cause the pilot to black out, not to be recommended in the presence of the enemy, or even pull the wings right off the machine.

We were allowed one practice drop in the mountains, without even a proper target, and then we prepared for our first mission in earnest. The great day arrived on April 3rd with our target a farmhouse, reputedly an enemy HQ, near the village of Sidi Nsir. The attack went off without incident, we didn't see any spectacular results, but not long after we got home we were attacked by a force of Fw 190s, eight or nine of which dropped bombs on our airfield without hitting anything, so maybe we had hit something after all![119]

Fighter ace Bob Doe ended his war flying Spitfires in Burma, and his squadron developed similar tactics, while supporting operations against Japanese positions in the formidable jungle and mountainous terrain.

The pilots of 10 Squadron began to climb higher over the target to 6,000 feet and then peel off into a seventy-degree dive, releasing bombs at 3,000 feet. This was followed by a complete circuit and two strafing runs. Pictures were taken and debriefings held of each mission.[120]

Recalling operations in Normandy and North-West Europe during 1944–45, another Spitfire pilot considered: 'The worst thing for a fighter-pilot was air to ground, because you knew you'd be shot at.' Typically, 'ground fire doesn't aim at you. They make a barrage you have to go through it. You never have time to think, you're concentrating so much on the target and aiming.' Even so, 'strafing a German column or truck and seeing the Germans scatter was exciting.'[121] Richard Hough, a Typhoon pilot, found that, regarding flak, 'the German powers of accuracy, speed and sheer volume with their ant-aircraft fire did not diminish by one perceptible degree.'[122]

If the Hurricane 'was all-male, but gentlemanly' and the Spitfire 'essentially a feminine machine, dainty, provocative, not always predictable', the Typhoon was by comparison characterised by its 'uncompromising masculinity'. Taking off in one was, according to a pilot from 195 Squadron, akin to a 'grapple with a low bred all-in wrestler, and the thud of the wheels tucking into the belly ... was like the sound of the bell at the end of the round'.[123]

Yet once its various technical defects were addressed, the Typhoon proved a rugged, versatile and powerful machine, well suited to ground-attack operations. This included tackling V-1 weapon sites on the Cherbourg peninsula, which entailed trying to aim 'a few bombs into narrow slits in the ground, an occupation as difficult as those maddening fairground competitions'.[124] The Belgian Raymond Lallemant flew Typhoons with 609 (West Riding) Squadron in Normandy as part of 2nd TAF. He explained that they tackled German armour during that campaign using 3-inch rockets mounted on underwing racks. These proved inaccurate but powerful weapons.

> Most rockets did end up short of the target due to pilot inexperience, and because of flak. We had to be very low to escape that accurate German flak. That led to fear of collision with obstacles on the ground. Don't think the German tanks were silly enough to park in the middle of a field. They knew all about camouflage. However, the real point was to trace the tanks and kill them before they could run for shelter. When they were [caught] in the open a vertical dive was best.

Alternatively, if armour was hiding, pilots had to fly at low level, 'almost straight and level, holding the aircraft very steady', especially when firing the rockets, and wait for them to 'clear the long launching rails'.[125]

Whatever type of fighter-bomber was employed, close air support missions required some system to control/direct proceedings. Forward Control Posts (FCP) and Visual Control Posts (VCP) were instigated by British forces to direct aircraft from positions with commanding views of the battlefield. These were manned by RAF and army personnel in radio contact with the aircraft, and given code words. ROVER, for example, was the name given to FCPs operating in support of Allied forces in Italy during 1943–45, with ROVER FRANK being a FCP with Eighth Army, specially designated for attacks against German artillery. In Burma, 10 Squadron found that some of its ground-attack operations were directed by a

VCP 'under the call sign of Arcade'. This was 'a combined RAF and Army unit in which the RAF passes by wireless to the aircraft in the air any detailed information about the target they are attacking, when actually watching from the ground the attack of the aircraft taking place, to ensure that the attacks are as effective as possible'.[126]

A distinctive feature of close air support was that it could prove more reliable and accurate than artillery in close proximity to ground troops under fluid battlefield conditions, as occurred in North-West Europe during 1944–45. Related to this was cab rank or Armoured Column Cover in the case of mobile operations. These were methods of providing continuous close air support to ground forces, by maintaining standing patrols of fighter-bombers over the battlefront. Notably, cab rank was first employed in Italy during the assault to clear the line of the Sangro River in November 1943. However, to achieve such a state of continuous air support, although effective, was expensive in terms of the resources required. Wastage occurred as well, because not all aircraft deployed would necessarily be required for close air support. Consequently, despite having aerial superiority by 1944, and large numbers of pilots and aircraft available, it was usually only practicable for the RAF to provide such lavish support for a limited period.[127]

To fly a fighter-bomber was an emotional experience, given the destruction they could unleash against ground targets, and the proximity of pilots to it, especially during strafing attacks. Typhoon pilot Richard Hough found that he 'never actually relished blowing things up and killing people, but a blazing train on a moonlit night outside Lille' was satisfying.[128] Simultaneously, after attacking a German staff car packed with passengers, where he 'could see the cannon strikes dancing along the road like an hysterically fast fuse racing to its point of detonation', causing 'blood and fire', he subsequently found that his 'spirit of aggression had died with those people in the car'.[129]

Chapter 4

At War with Kipper Fleet: Coastal Command[1]

RAF Coastal Command was established in July 1936, and at that time only comprised eight squadrons, handling relatively few aircraft. Yet by late 1941, it had been expanded to six groups, three wings and thirty-three other stations, employing over 55,000 men from the RAF and more than 6,000 women of the WAAF.[2] During the war it operated a wide variety of aircraft, ranging from flying boats to four-engine heavy bombers, but was often under-resourced for the tasks it faced. From April 1942 to April 1943, for example, Coastal Command received a number of ageing Handley Page Hampdens from Bomber Command to press into service as torpedo bombers. During the early years of the war, small numbers of obsolete Armstrong Whitworth Whitley bombers were employed to cover Atlantic sea lanes until better suited aircraft became available, although this didn't prevent some pilots becoming fond of these lumbering machines.

One of the main functions of Coastal Command was protecting merchant shipping, notably by providing convoy escorts. These patrols could be arduous and monotonous, but were essential in ensuring that supplies reached Britain. Linked to this was a concerted anti-submarine campaign, mounted in tandem with the Royal Navy, to counter the grave threat posed by U-boats. This involved a strong element of what Squadron Leader Frank Tilsley described as, spending 'hundreds of hours stooging about in clouds and rain and fog and electrical storms', and some aircrews seldom ever saw the enemy.[3]

Anti-shipping operations were important, as aircrews from Coastal Command attempted to thwart blockade runners and sever enemy supply lines – no easy task. Typically, most anti-shipping sorties entailed hair-raising low-level flying, by aircraft carrying a torpedo or bombs, in the face of fearsome anti-aircraft fire. Later in the war, anti-shipping strikes witnessed aircraft using rockets, which proved highly effective, particularly when a ship was hit and holed below the waterline. Another anti-shipping method involved dropping mines from the air into enemy waters. Often dubbed 'gardening', this was something Coastal Command became involved with, alongside the large-scale mining effort launched by Bomber Command.

Other requirements facing Coastal Command included protecting fishing boats; providing meteorological flights; and undertaking reconnaissance and photographic reconnaissance, primarily to help with protecting convoys and anti-shipping strikes. The Operations Record Book for 220 Squadron based at RAF Thornaby, North Yorkshire, on 3 September 1939, noted:

> 07h 44: Nine [Avro] Ansons took off on search. Object to report enemy aircraft and vessels and their movements. Cruisers and battleships were to be shadowed.

> 11h 15: All aircraft landed. Two tramp steamers and a Swedish cargo boat reported.[4]

Another function of Coastal Command was dealing with magnetic mines dropped by the Luftwaffe in British waters and near Allied ports, which posed a hazard to shipping. One method that proved workable for a time entailed fitting Wellington bombers with a device known as the Directional Wireless Installation (DWI), a 51-foot diameter ring containing an electro-magnetic coil, the magnetic field of which could be used to detonate mines when the aircraft flew low and steadily over a suspected area.[5]

From 1941, all Air Sea Rescue (ASR) operations were co-ordinated by Coastal Command, and provided welcome relief to thousands of aircrew who ditched in the sea. Some crews even mounted 'nickel' sorties, the dropping of propaganda leaflets over enemy territory. As Ted Rayner, a pilot with 220 and 269 Squadrons, recalled, this wasn't universally popular with aircrews. Whereas most willingly went on sorties to perform tasks such as dropping bombs, protecting shipping, or to undertake reconnaissance, and understood the need for these operations, 'to scatter thousands of leaflets (code-named "nickels") over German-held territory in daylight was regarded as akin to delivering a supply of toilet paper.'[6]

Contrastingly, some Coastal Command units were involved in a more offensive capacity, including bombing ports and, when possible, generally harassing German troops in occupied countries. This had something in common with the activities of Bomber Command, such as when Bristol Beaufort aircraft were deployed on a low-level raid against the docks at Nantes, France, on the night of 26/27 October 1941. The city was surrounded by German troops who'd taken several hostages as a reprisal for the killing of the German governor, and the officer leading the sortie recounted:

> We were so low that when we reached the French coast I had to pull up sharply to avoid the sand-dunes. Every time we came to a clump of trees we leap-frogged over them and then went down to almost the ground again. ... It grew darker as we went farther inland and then began the most surprising experience of all. It was as though the whole of that part of France was turning out to welcome us. Every village we went over became a blaze of light. People threw open their doors and came out to watch us skim their chimney-pots. In other places hamlets would

suddenly light up as if the people had torn the blackout down when they heard us coming. ... I remember one house with a courtyard fully lit up. I saw a woman come out of the house, look up at us, wave, and then go back. She switched off the outside lights and then I saw a yellow light from inside stream out as she opened the door. [After dropping their bombs at around 300 feet, Nantes] looked like a city of the dead. Then I began to see white pin-points on the ground and one by one the lights appeared as we raced over the chimney-pots. ... We were at top speed, but even so we could see the doors opening and people coming out. I felt that we had brought some comfort to the people of Nantes.[7]

In going about their duties, aircrew from Coastal Command not only faced the vagaries of the weather, but had to be prepared to counter the enemy air threat as well. German fighters were more nimble than most Coastal Command aircraft. The fearsome, heavily armed, twin-engine Junkers Ju 88 was another distinct menace, and memoirs of Coastal Command personnel tend to resonate with the trepidation that encounters with these aircraft induced. Equally, the long-range Focke-Wulf Fw 200 Kondor, based on the design of a pre-war airliner, was formidable. As Prime Minister Winston Churchill stated:

They could start from Brest or Bordeaux, fly right round the British Island, refuel in Norway, and make the return journey the next day. On their way they would see far below them the very large convoys of forty or fifty ships to which scarcity of escort had forced us to resort, moving inwards or outwards on their voyages. They could attack these convoys, or individual ships, with destructive bombs, or they could signal the positions to which the waiting U-boats should be directed in order to make interceptions.[8]

While many Coastal Command personnel served at bases around Britain, through-out the war others were stationed around the globe in locations as diverse as Iceland, the Azores, Gibraltar and West Africa. Although the contribution and achievements of Coastal Command have tended to be overshadowed by the seemingly more glamorous activities of Fighter Command and Bomber Command, it nonetheless performed a vital role in the ultimate Allied victory, particularly in helping to win the Battle of the Atlantic (c. June 1940 to May 1943). An officer who commanded a Coastal Command squadron in 1940, equipped with Lockheed Hudson aircraft, primarily employed on 'GR' (general reconnaissance), explained:

There is little glamour in our work. It is rather like the northern patrols of the navy – loneliness, monotony, danger of dirty weather. But it is vital work, and the men of my squadron and other squadrons who do similar work include some of the most experienced pilots and navigators in the Royal Air Force. They have hundreds of hours of war flying to their credit, and many of them have been out on more than a hundred long-range operational flights.

They are all grand types, and I should like to make special mention of the sergeant pilots and also of the wireless operators and air gunners, and the ground staff who are an indispensable part of the Squadron.[9]

Given that it was effectively an air force in miniature, engaged on both offensive and defensive tasks under difficult conditions, Coastal Command exhibited its own particular character. One mark of distinction was 'for flying officers to let their cap badges become tarnished. The greener the better; this being a sign of much low flying through sea spray and the hall mark of an old Atlantic hand.'[10] One wartime squadron commander stressed, whereas 'bombers go out on definite sorties. The fighter boys live for an hour or two of intense danger and excitement,' Coastal Command's work 'goes on all the time. It is always flying, always watching, always working over the sea.'[11] Consequently, pilots, and aircrew from navigators through to air gunners had to be highly trained, and capable of conducting lengthy sorties. By Christmas 1939, one RAF officer reckoned 'the aircraft of Coastal Command have flown fully four million miles, on watch and guard over the North Sea and the Atlantic. In other words, in four months, the crews of this Command have covered a distance equal to more than 165 journeys around the Equator.'[12] Therefore, much emphasis was placed on employing what in 1940s parlance were termed 'steady types', or as an official booklet stated, those 'of the phlegmatic turn of mind'.[13]

Equally, morale was important, and closely linked to training. An experienced Sunderland Flying boat skipper who completed numerous anti-submarine patrols explained that although the work was quite different from that he'd previously experienced in Bomber Command, it 'was very rewarding, and a feeling of camaraderie seemed to prevail in every crew'.[14] Another pilot who flew Halifax bombers with Coastal Command emphasised that 'Our crew was a close-knit band of brothers, a team of nine compatible fellows whose total efforts maintained our rating as an enthusiastic unit in the squadron. There was no hint of discord.' Moreover, aside from 'training stooges over the waters of the North Minch', they'd been to a bombing school at Leuchars, near St Andrews, in Fifeshire, and became 'skilled in the latest techniques of missile dropping'.[15]

Convoy protection/escort

Protecting convoys threw up many challenges. Although Coastal Command employed many types of aircraft to do this, the Short Sunderland flying boat was especially well-suited. From bases in the Shetlands, Wales, Northern Ireland and South West England, these could cover huge distances. It was a ten-seat, long-range maritime reconnaissance aircraft that could simultaneously operate as a bomber, capable of hefting 4,960 pounds of bombs, mines, or depth charges. Sunderlands were dubbed 'the flying porcupine' by the Germans, as they bristled with machine guns: ten .303 or 7.7mm machine guns, four fixed forward-firing, two in a bow turret, and four in a tail turret; plus two .50 or 12.7mm machine guns, one on each side of the aircraft.[16]

Crews tended to develop a close affinity to their aircraft, which distinguished flying boat squadrons from other units. As one Sunderland skipper explained, flying was only a part of their job.

> The 'boat' had to be kept clean. ... This was no easy task, as there was always grease and hydraulic oil around on the decks. With a crew of ten and most of their flying gear and sleeping bags on board, plus at least two members living permanently on board, life was usually a bit hectic. The crew did all their own gun-cleaning and maintenance; all the refuelling and checking of batteries, radio and bilges; and not least, keeping the windscreen and turrets clean [from salt spray].[17]

By 1939–40, it was generally accepted that the convoy system was needed to protect the majority of merchant shipping, although some ships still sailed independently. For outward-bound convoys, three major routes proved workable: from Liverpool; from the Thames to the western ocean; and a coastal convoy between the Thames and the Forth. Homeward-bound convoys were scheduled to sail regularly from Gibraltar, Halifax in Nova Scotia, and Freetown in Sierra Leone.[18] For Coastal Command aircrew, achieving a successful rendezvous with the ships they were to escort in the vastness of the ocean wasn't straightforward. Poor weather made operations difficult, as did the need for ships to maintain radio silence so as to avoid detection by the enemy. The experience of one flying boat crew on Christmas Day 1939 provides a case in point. Their task was to:

> Find and protect a convoy which had been assembled at a rendezvous from all parts of the world and which an escort of French warships was bringing along. We knew that the convoy was about twenty hours late, and that it had gone far off the course set for it because of bad weather and threatened submarine attack.
>
> We could only guess the course it was taking. The ships themselves couldn't help us to locate them. They had, of course, to keep wireless silence so that their position might not be betrayed to lurking U-boats.

Our flying boat combed the sea for 550 miles. Then we found the convoy. Rather, it nearly found us! Cloud had become so dense and low that often we could see only the nose of the flying boat and the wing-tip floats. I heard the pilot beside me whistle sharply. 'Blimey!' he said as he lifted the boat suddenly from the height of sixty feet at which we had been flying. In the nick of time he had avoided the masthead of a ship which had appeared beneath the wing. As he climbed to starboard, we saw another mast … then another … then mast after mast. His anxious look gave way to a happy smile. He took his hand from the joy-stick and cocked his thumb. He was over the lost convoy.[19]

Closer to British shores, smaller aircraft with limited endurance, such as de Havilland Tiger and Hornet Moths, and the Avro Anson, protected convoys, especially early in the war. The Anson was a Coastal Command favourite, often known by the sobriquet 'Anson is as Anson does', even though it only had a radius of action of 260 miles. Ted Rayner found that it was relatively 'spacious and comfortable, had no vices, and was robust enough to withstand ill treatment' although the 'substantial undercarriage … had to be cranked-up manually' and similarly, the engines required crank-starting by hand.[20] However, it was reliable and manoeuvrable, characteristics that lent it to convoy protection work near the British Isles. These smaller aircraft also protected coastal convoys sailing up and down the East Coast and in the Channel. 'The practice was for the aircraft to meet the convoy at a chosen rendezvous and then to circle it for several hours before being relieved by another aircraft or by the approach of darkness. Stragglers had constantly to be rounded up.'[21]

In the same way, the Lockheed Hudson – an adaptation of a civilian passenger aircraft – proved useful on convoy escort, even though it was no match for Luftwaffe fighters. It had a maximum endurance of about six hours, and was equipped with an autopilot, known universally as 'George'. This was a novel feature, until 1942, when most bombers were fitted with such devices. 'There were, of course, limits to the manoeuvres which George could sustain, and there were few pilots who could resist the temptation to explore these knob-twirling limits in dive, climb, and turn.'[22]

Ted Rayner flew Hudsons when stationed in Greenland and Iceland. On one sortie he was trying to protect a convoy sailing through 'The Gap' – that stretch of icy water to the south of Greenland that was beyond the limit of air cover from North America and Britain – until the arrival of VLR (Very Long Range) aircraft, notably the B-24 Liberator. He remembered:

En route to one convoy the weather deteriorated. The cloud base remained at 2,000 feet, but the wind strengthened from the northeast, whipping up plumes of spray from the wind-lanes across the turbulent sea. We approached the convoy, flashing the identification code letter on the Aldis lamp, but received no reply; nor could we identify the Senior Naval Officer's vessel. A heavy freezing mist reduced visibility so that we couldn't see the foremost ships in the convoy, and as we passed ahead along the lines we noticed ice floes and even mini-icebergs floating past as the ships plunged slowly forward.[23]

As the war progressed, Coastal Command increasingly deployed its flying boats and other newly acquired aircraft to provide long-distance escorts to convoys, because closer to Britain, Fighter Command was able to provide a fighter umbrella. Typically, the first to meet convoys were the American-manufactured Catalina flying boats, which covered 'many hundreds of miles out in the Atlantic, for the normal duration of their patrol is, in summer eighteen, in winter fourteen hours, and it was possible to remain airborne for considerably more than twenty-four hours'.[24] Behind them flew B-24 Liberators and Sunderland flying boats. These were followed up by Whitley and Wellington bombers, then as the convoy neared its destination, Hudsons and long-range fighter Bristol Blenheims and Beauforts would take over.

As the booklet *Coastal Command (1942)* stated, 'in theory the protection afforded to convoys from the air, once they have reached a certain point, is in daylight continuous and more intense as they near our coasts.'[25] In practice, this wasn't always the case. Poor weather, the need for ships to maintain radio silence, and mechanical faults with aircraft hampered operations. Weariness and the noise of aircraft operating long hours over desolate looking seas were another challenge. This included 'the effect on pilots and crews of the monotony of their task. This monotony results in strain which sometimes has a curious effect on the mind.'[26] The routine nature of Coastal Command work, such as convoy protection and reconnaissance, involved: 'Gazing down at the sea for hours on end [which] could induce a trancelike condition' that 'could well be fatal'.[27]

Friendly fire was another potential worry for aircrews. Naval vessels were notoriously trigger-happy, and standards of aircraft recognition were not necessarily as good as might be supposed. Roy Larkins flew Ansons, conducting maritime reconnaissance and covering convoys sailing between Cape Town and Durban. The aircraft weren't armed but their presence was intended to deter enemy aircraft from attacking shipping. 'On my very first trip I learned not to get too close to a convoy because after weeks at sea the sailors tended to fire first and to consult their identification signal manuals later. At least it proved that I was on "Active Service"!'[28]

During convoy escorts there was the possibility, however remote it may have appeared, that aircrew might encounter opposition, especially from the Luftwaffe.

On 19 December 1939, a Saro London, a flying boat with a crew of six employed early in the war, was engaged on protecting a convoy when it encountered a Heinkel He III.

> The London, though much slower and without the advantage of position, set the starboard engine of the Heinkel on fire. A burst from the German aircraft, however, mortally wounded the British pilot, who, falling inert over the controls, sent the London into a steep dive. The second pilot dragged his captain from the steering column and righted the flying boat just in time to make a landing on heavy seas. The Heinkel, damaged, flew away. The London, after twenty minutes on the water, took off again and completed its patrol.[29]

Despite all the difficulties associated with convoy protection, some Coastal Command personnel relished the task. The much decorated Flight Lieutenant Leslie Baveystock gained considerable experience operating Sunderland flying boats on long-range Atlantic patrols with 201 Squadron. He remarked, 'watching over twenty or thirty ships with hundreds of sailors and tons of precious cargoes, was a great feeling,' and one that was completely different to that he'd experienced on destructive bombing missions as a former member of Bomber Command. 'I never felt bored or tired while guarding a convoy,' and had 'never heard of a convoy being attacked while actually under the protective umbrella of an RAF aircraft'. However, he cautioned that 'the need to be there during daylight hours' was awkward. 'Being wintertime with only about nine hours' daylight meant that our thirteen-hour flights both started and ended with night flying. Fully laden Sunderlands were never too easy to get airborne, and even more difficult in darkness,' plus 'identification of the coast, especially in conditions of low cloud, was always tricky at night.'[30]

Anti-submarine warfare

Inextricably linked with protecting convoys was the war against enemy submarines, or *Unterseeboots* (U-boats). In June 1940, a total of 140 British, Allied and neutral vessels, equating to 585,496 gross tons of shipping, was sunk. U-boats accounted for 284,113 tons of this figure, and by August, Hitler had declared a 'total blockade' of Britain. During 1942, U-boats were responsible for sinking 6,266,215 tons or 1,160 ships, mostly in the North Atlantic.[31] Moreover, German Naval Intelligence (B-Dienst) had successfully penetrated British naval and merchant shipping codes, and used this information to assist U-boat commanders. Together with the use of wireless telegraphy, this enabled Admiral Karl Donitz (Führer der U-Boote) to exercise long-range tactical control of operations during the Battle of the Atlantic. Although, ironically, the very strength of the German system became its greatest weakness, as the 'Y' Service that monitored German radio traffic intercepted communications, and the Enigma ciphers used by the German navy were ultimately successfully decoded at Station 'X' at Bletchley Park, the Government Code and Cypher School. This intelligence, known as Ultra, was then employed to help direct air patrols.[32]

Another key factor that made U-boats so effective was that by 1941, they employed 'wolfpack' tactics, whereby attacks were mounted 'from different directions by several U-boats working together'. Attacks were usually 'made by night, the U-boats operating on the surface at full speed unless detected in the approach. Under these conditions only the destroyers could rapidly overhaul them.'[33] As Coastal Command pilots discovered, dusk was typically intensely nerve-wracking for convoys.

> Once a U-boat had located a convoy, it usually followed it astern during daylight, keeping the tops of the ships' masts in view, while remaining unseen by the ships' lookouts. Then just before dark, having worked out the average course and speed of the convoy, it would race around ahead on the surface, submerge, and wait for the convoy to come into view through its periscope.[34]

Coupled with good intelligence, these tactics were devastating. On 16 March 1943, forty U-boats were directed against convoys HX 229 and SC 122, sparking 'a four-day slaughter' during which twenty-one ships (141,000 tons) 'were sunk for the loss of only a single U-boat'.[35]

Together with naval operations, the aggressive handling of airpower played a significant part in deterring U-boats, if not actually damaging or destroying them. This had been evident by the end of the First World War, but in the early 1940s had to be relearnt. Notably, aircraft were especially suitable for searching a wide expanse of sea. Confident in its own ability to handle U-boats, particularly by using convoys and employing ASDIC or sonar, the Royal Navy initially saw limited need for air support against submarines. According to the Admiralty, RAF Coastal Command would best be employed on maritime reconnaissance, including monitoring German warships that might enter the Atlantic via the North Sea. Broadly speaking, the RAF concurred but maintained responsibility for the training, equipping and administration of Coastal Command.[36] However, ASDIC couldn't detect surface vessels, including U-boats sailing on the surface, and as Prime Minister Churchill highlighted, there was a requirement 'to exploit' the vulnerability to air attack of the surfaced U-boat.[37] Moreover, until the advent of the Schnorkel, U-boats had to surface regularly to recharge their batteries and refresh their air supply. Schnorkels of various types were fitted to U-boats from mid-1943 onwards, enabling them to travel submerged for prolonged periods while still taking on board air from above the surface of the ocean.

Initially, Coastal Command's aircraft were ill-equipped to deal directly with U-boats, but 'scarecrow' patrols operated as a deterrent. From late 1939 until summer 1940, six Coastal Patrol Flights (CPF) covered the British coastline. Equipped mainly with Tiger Moth biplanes, 'armed' only with a signal pistol and homing pigeons, pairs of aircraft would mount patrols over the sea. If they encountered a U-boat on the surface, they were to scare it into submerging, as its crew wouldn't know they lacked weapons. Alternatively, personnel from a CPF might alert naval forces or send for other aircraft when a U-boat was spotted. On 25 January 1940, Flying Officer P.C. Hoyle from No. 1 CPF Dyce (Aberdeen) took off with another aircraft and, an hour into their patrol, spotted an oil slick, possibly from a U-boat, although no kill was confirmed.

> To help the destroyer I repeatedly dived at the head of the oil line, the last dive, in my excitement, being a race for it past the bows of the destroyer. Climbing sharply I turned in time to watch the ship pass its whole length in front of the oil, and then let fly about six depth charges in a pattern. These exploded with fearful crashes a few seconds later. The sea was illuminated deep down and appeared to jerk upwards, causing a spray on the surface.[38]

Roy Larkins served as a sergeant pilot with 61 Air School at George in South Africa, flying Ansons. He recalled that one of their duties was to fly on anti-submarine patrols, when up to five aircraft would fan out over a large area of sea. 'We were so slow that had an enemy submarine been on the surface, it would have heard us coming and been submerged again long before we got there. But this was part of our strategy.' Given that U-boats had to regularly replenish their air supply, 'the longer we kept them submerged, more the advantage swung in our favour.' By constantly forcing U-boats to dive via repeated air patrols, they hoped to eventually force them to remain on the surface for a prolonged period because the air had become so foul. If they sighted a U-boat in such a condition, Roy Larkins and his crew would immediately contact their base, where a Hudson waited 'bombed-up and ready for take-off'. This then 'droned out and was usually quite successful in damaging, if not sinking, the "sitting duck" on the surface'.[39]

The surrender of U-570, a Type VIIC submarine, on 27 August 1941, demonstrated the potency of aircraft against submarines. The U-boat was first spotted by a Hudson from 269 Squadron on patrol from Iceland, which mounted an attack but was unsuccessful. However, its radio reports attracted other aircraft. Another Hudson from that squadron, piloted by Squadron Leader James Herbert Thompson, attacked as U-570 was surfacing, only for it to crash-dive.

> the Hudson launched a salvo of depth-charges. These straddled it squarely as it disappeared beneath the waves. For a few seconds the crew of the aircraft saw only four great plumes of sea and spray; then, as the disturbance subsided they descried on the surface, its nose slightly down, the U-570. Ten or twelve German sailors were on deck. Treated to a burst of the Hudson's guns they scrambled rapidly into the conning-tower, whence they cautiously waved a white article bearing a suspicious resemblance to a dress shirt.[40]

Other aircraft then monitored the surrender. Eventually, U-570 was towed to Iceland under escort. The crew, including the skipper, Korvettenkapitän Hans-Joachim Rahmlow, became prisoners of war. After being salvaged and sailed to Britain, U-570 was taken on strength by the Royal Navy and became HM Submarine *Graph*, serving in home waters until wrecked off Islay. Squadron Leader Thompson was subsequently awarded the DFC, along with his navigator, Flying Officer John Oswald Coleman.[41]

A U-boat was difficult to spot, even when surfaced. According to Air Commodore 'Taffy' Powell, flying anti-submarine patrols over the North Atlantic was no easy task, as navigators were charged with following complicated search patterns 'hour after hour', visibility was often poor in winter, 'and certainly a few whales and pieces of debris got depth-charged in the process of searching for that tell-tale periscope'.[42] Ted Rayner recounted how on one convoy escort patrol from Iceland, halfway to the rendezvous, he and his crew were 'flying at 1,300 feet just below the cloud base' when they 'sighted a lumpen shape lying fore-and-aft to us so that it lacked the confirmation of a distinct conning-tower, in poor visibility three or four miles ahead. It was about to disappear beneath the waves ...' Subsequently, they were able to alert the naval escort via Aldis lamp as to the probable location of a U-boat, and inform a flying boat returning to base, which would alert its squadron's operations room.[43]

There were various telltale signs that could indicate the presence of a submerged U-boat, although these were subtle in the vastness of the ocean. These included what the Official History described as, 'the swirl which betokens a diving submarine'.[44] As the lavatories on U-boats were operated by air pressure, these would similarly release bubbles that could be spotted by aircrew. Another indication was the stench that emerged when a U-boat surfaced and opened a hatch, although this was probably of more use to surface-going vessels than aircraft.

The Schnorkel, used on later models of U-boat, tended to alleviate some of these problems, and technically turned what had until that point been submersibles into genuine submarines.

> When a U-boat wished to charge her batteries with the aid of the *Schnorkel* tube, she was brought to periscope depth and moved ahead on her engines, dead slow. The *Schnorkel* was raised, and the valves connecting it to the normal air intake and to the exhaust pipe of the Diesels opened.

The diesels then powered the U-boat, while simultaneously recharging her batteries, and in the Atlantic this allowed for a speed of around 5 to 7 knots, with the advantage that the U-boat 'showed only a few feet of inconspicuous tubing' rather than her entire superstructure.[45] Yet the Schnorkel tube 'caused a wave or "feather" of water that could be seen in certain conditions, and often showed a hint of smoke discharge'.[46]

Looking for such telltale signs of a U-boat was monotonous.

> To keep an unblinking and vigilant look-out from the turrets and side-windows of a Sunderland or from the blisters of a Catalina flying over what seems an illimitable stretch of sea demands physical and mental endurance of a high order. Sometimes a fishing vessel, British, Spanish, French, Norwegian, Icelandic, is seen; sometimes a raft, more rarely a periscope with a spume of foam about it.[47]

Having sighted a U-boat, three means of countering them were initially available to Coastal Command. An aircraft on an anti-submarine patrol of areas known to be where U-boats operated could, on locating the enemy, choose to attack with bombs or depth charges and/or transmit a signal so other aircraft could be sent to attack and form a 'U-boat strike'. Typically, anti-submarine patrols were flown in a designated area and for a fixed time, depending on the weather, hours of daylight available, and range of the aircraft deployed. A heavy responsibility resisted with the navigator, who had to ensure the aircraft flew within set limits, and returned safely to base. Secondly, aircraft might conduct 'a sweep or special search' for U-boats, similar to that experienced by Roy Larkins above. Finally, when a U-boat was sighted near a convoy, aircraft on convoy escort were often expected to launch an attack. Importantly, signals from aircraft sighting a U-boat were invariably received by other aircraft and naval vessels, so that these too could converge on any suspect.[48]

A semi-official account by an Australian Sunderland flying boat skipper in 1940 vividly described how he and his crew successfully tackled a U-boat. They'd been ordered to search for it after the U-boat had been reported attacking shipping, and ordered to attack if they saw it.

> I sighted a disturbance in the water about five miles away. It looked like a round patch with a wake leading up to it, and I felt pretty sure that it was the enemy submarine. She must have seen me at the very moment I saw her because she did a crash dive. I saw the swirl and prepared to attack it. I turned towards it and carried out a dive at a shallow angle, and released four bombs in a stick. The bombs fell onto the swirl on the surface and overlapped the disturbed water and formed what we call a 'tight pattern' – (much the same as good grouping with a rifle). I then did a circuit with the object of coming back for another attack. ...
>
> By the time I had turned the submarine had completely surfaced and I immediately carried out a second attack. I did the second attack at an angle, slanting across the submarine from the quarter to the bow and dropped another four bombs in a low-level attack. The submarine at the time was still moving forward very slowly under the impulse given by her rush to the surface. Immediately after the second four explosions she swung round violently to starboard and practically stopped.[49]

The U-boat started sinking, and her surviving crew members were picked up by a naval escort vessel that was contacted by the Sunderland.

Bombs weren't necessarily effective against U-boats, even with a direct hit. 'The 250-pounder would have to explode within six feet of the pressure hull to do serious damage, and the 500-pounder at about eight feet.'[50] Consequently, many aircrew, including leading anti-U-boat ace Squadron Leader Terence Bulloch, preferred depth charges, particularly once these used powerful Torpex explosive. These were dropped low, from around 300 feet, and official teaching stressed they needed to land across a U-boat's heading. Yet he reckoned the correct method of attack was:

> to drop the 'stick' of depth-charges more or less in line with the track being made by the enemy below. The wind effect and the aircraft's drift might cause them to fall marginally to one side or the other but, this would not matter overmuch. Also, to counter such incalculable minor errors, he aimed to drop the 'stick' not dead in line, but about 30 degrees away from the U-boat's track.[51]

Even so, U-boats invariably proved tough to deal with. Analysis of the captured U-570 demonstrated how well built the Type VII was. It 'could withstand pressures of up to 14 tons per square inch. This meant that the 250 pound depth-charges being used had to be dropped with almost incredible accuracy for the welded and riveted hull to be ruptured,' plus when an aircraft sighted a U-boat, usually there was limited opportunity for them to attack, and unlike a ship, they couldn't remain in the area for a prolonged period.[52]

The Official History explained that another challenge lay in the inability of the Allies to provide effective air cover over the oceans. So long as air patrols from Newfoundland couldn't meet with those from Iceland and Northern Ireland, and those 'from Gibraltar failed to link up with those from Cornwall', gaps occurred. This ensured that the U-boats were able to take advantage of the lack of air cover in the 'Greenland Gap' in the north, the 'Azores Gap' in the south. However, ideally, carrier-based aircraft or VLR shore-based aircraft from Coastal Command had to close these gaps. To this end, the arrival in late 1942 of a handful of B-24 Liberator Mk Is with 120 Squadron, with an operational range of 2,400 miles, was an asset. That squadron also flew a number of Liberator Mk IIs (range 1,800 miles) and Mk IIIs (range 1,680 miles), plus Coastal Command fielded Catalina and Sunderland flying boats, both of which had ranges in excess of 1,000 miles.[53]

The Liberators, supplied by America, were significantly modified to conduct low-level operations with Coastal Command, rather than acting as conventional bombers. Squadron Leader Tony Spooner described how one major addition was the installation of ASV (Air-to-Surface Vessel) radar, which 'required the plane to be festooned with additional aerials: along the plane's spine, under its wings and on its sides. The ASV scanner itself was fitted to "look" forward in an unsightly bulge under the nose.' This aroused much comment at 120 Squadron's base, leading to the rumour spreading amongst gullible locals that the aircraft manufacturers hadn't remembered to leave room for the pilot's feet, so the bulge was to accommodate these.[54]

Initial models of ASV radar were of limited effectiveness and range, more useful for picking up convoys than U-boats. Invariably, the radar operator's position was wherever there was 'room to spare in the aircraft – in some types the radar operator had to sit on the lid of the Elsan chemical toilet, which he had to leave if anyone wanted it for its original purpose.'[55] After capturing a Hudson aircraft equipped with ASV radar, the Germans were able to furnish U-boats with a successful countermeasure, a receiver known as the Metox 600, after its French manufacturer. It had a range of 40 miles, giving U-boats ample time to detect an aircraft and submerge before it approached.[56] Squadron Leader Spooner observed that another drawback with early ASV was that it was shrouded in secrecy and non-commissioned aircrew tasked with operating it had minimal training, and when flying over the sea it was difficult to gather useful information owing 'to the clutter that filled the tiny viewing screen given back by echoes from the large waves and heavy rollers'.[57] To watch the 'fuzz oscillating in a continuous manner' was 'a great strain on the eyes', and required 'intelligent interpretation and extreme watchfulness' if the operator was to accurately detect 'blips' denoting a possible submarine.[58]

By 1943, ASV MK III centimetric wavelength radar equipment was available. It was a distinct improvement over earlier models, and similar to H2S that was employed by Bomber Command. Flight Lieutenant Leslie Baveystock found ASV Mk III 'consisted of two rotating scanners, one under each wing, outboard of the engines. They were synchronised to sweep 360 degrees around the aircraft' and when a radar beam struck a solid object such as a surfaced U-boat, these 'bounced back and showed up on the PPI tube in the aircraft. It was also able to show the coastline around us – an altogether revolutionary piece of equipment.' So long as the sea wasn't too rough, they 'could even count the number of ships in a convoy'.[59]

Baveystock, with his Sunderland crew, sunk two U-boats during 1944: U-995 on 7 June and U-107 on 18 August. Radar played a part in this, especially against U-995, when shortly before midnight, Flight Sergeant Dennis South, operating the radar, picked up a strong contact 9 miles away. The alarm klaxon sounded and the depth charges were run out, while power to the engines was increased. The aircraft came down to 300 feet and the blip remained steady, and for a time they baited the U-boat, tracking it by dropping flares and monitoring it on radar, until launching a successful depth charge attack. Having reached their PLE (Prudent Limit of Endurance), the crew retuned to base.[60]

Although radar could pick up U-boats at night, it couldn't actually help aircrew to identify them visually. A solution was offered in the form of flares and the Leigh Light, deployed in tandem with radar. Named after its inventor, Squadron Leader H. de V. Leigh, a First World War veteran working at Coastal Command Headquarters, this was a powerful and reliable searchlight. During 1941–42, these were fitted to a small number of Catalinas and Wellington bombers for trials. On 4 June 1942, Leigh Light Wellingtons patrolling the Bay of Biscay at night illuminated a number of ASV contacts, including an Italian submarine that was heavily damaged. Ultimately, this ensured that enemy submarines could no longer expect to use the cover of darkness to recharge their batteries, and had to proceed submerged both by day and night when sailing in the Bay of Biscay to and from their French bases.[61]

Squadron Leader Spooner and his Wellington crew employed the system with Coastal Command. 'The Leigh Light was supposed to be switched on at one mile or even at three-quarters of a mile, but experience had taught us that the chances of its beam immediately picking up the target and so blinding their gunners was so remote that in practice this admirable theory fell down.' Instead, they carried out one successful attack, when in error they'd switched on their light at 2 miles from their target. They then steered down the U-boast's 'line of fire confident' that they 'were still outside lethal range'. Subsequently, 'the firing ceased as their gunners fumbled furiously to replace ammunition drums with fresh ones' while blinded by 'two million-candlepower shining into their eyes', and 'we were never hit once'.[62]

By mid-1943, in the Bay of Biscay, instead of submerging, U-boats were being ordered stay on the surface and fight it out with aircraft when attacked. Consequently, 'the Bay' became a brutal campaign for Coastal Command, not only due to the battle against the U-boats, but because Ju 88 fighters from KG 40 were tasked with roaming the area in an effort to shoot down anti-submarine aircraft. The ultimate success of the campaign was one of the factors responsible for creating the conditions necessary for D-Day in June 1944. During the fighting in 'the Bay', U-boats appeared with enlarged gun platforms, and additional ones carrying either one 37mm or, more often, one quadruple 20mm anti-aircraft gun. These were deadly against single, low-flying attacking aircraft, as all their fire was directed against that one target. One countermeasure was for aircraft to stay out of range, and call upon the nearest surface submarine hunter group, whose appearance would force the U-boat to dive, so it could be attacked with depth charges.[63]

The experience of Flying Officer Bob Sweeny (224 Squadron) and his Liberator crew illustrated the dangers when faced by a U-boat employing anti-aircraft tactics over the Bay of Biscay. Having spotted the U-boat, they made a direct attack with depth charges. His wireless operator, Flight Sergeant E. Cheek, recorded:

> During the run-up we were under heavy and sustained fire from the U-boat, the starboard outer engine was hit and seized. We were just able to see that our attack had been successful, but our immediate concern was our own predicament. At this time we were flying at about 15 to 20 feet, apparently unable to gain height and Bob ordered me to commence the radio distress procedure. ... [Having contacted 19 Group HQ at Plymouth] I now had a nasty suspicion that my planned 21st birthday party instead of a riotous party with the 'boys' would, at best, comprise a few Horlicks tablets in a heaving rubber dingy.[64]

As the war progressed, improved designs of U-boats entered service, including the Type XXI, which in 1945 was the most advanced submarine in the world, capable of unlimited travel submerged as its diesel engines drew in fresh air via the special Schnorkel. The Germans introduced the acoustic torpedo, 'which, when fired, homed in on the noise of a ship's propellers. As soon as its listening apparatus picked this up, it altered course and made straight for this most vital spot.'[65] The Allies produced the Mk 24 mine, dubbed 'Wandering Annie' by crews in 224 Squadron, which was 'actually an acoustic torpedo which was designed to follow the U-boat's engine noise after submerging and home on it'.[66] Other systems for detecting submerged U-boats, based on American designs, were the radio sonobuoy and the magnetic anomaly detector, or MAD, equipment, which became increasingly important after the war.

Another innovation, successfully employed by Coastal Command, was the use of rocket projectiles (RPs), which comprised 25lb solid shot, and when released at the correct speed and dive angle had spectacular ballistic qualities. As Squadron Leader Bulloch found, these could be devastating, as after entering the sea they 'would descend to approximately 25–30 feet depth, then level off – travel horizontally a distance, and then re-emerge from the sea. The head would penetrate the pressure hull of a U-boat and come out the other side.' The correct technique was to employ 'a 20 degree dive with cruise power set' and then fire the RPs. 'Thankfully we were equipped with a special radio altimeter and on the pull out were less than 100 feet above sea level.'[67]

Anti-shipping operations

Strikes against shipping were typically difficult and dangerous, entailing extremely low-level flying, to avoid detection and if possible maintain an element of surprise. One RAF officer stressed:

> The whole essence of a successful, shipping 'strike' is surprise. ... The attacking aircraft has to come in very close and very low. ... It is in this position, however, for only a few seconds, and we rely on catching the gunner on board when he is lighting a surreptitious cigarette, talking to a pal, or perhaps blowing on cold fingers ...[68]

A pilot from 407 Squadron, when bombing enemy shipping, flew 'so low to attack that he struck a mast and hung one of the bomb-doors thereon', while another from 455 Squadron Royal Australian Air Force returned from attacking shipping off 'the Dutch coast with several feet of mast attached to his aircraft'.[69]

Consequently, sorties against enemy shipping were risky, particularly in daylight. Between April 1940 and March 1943, Coastal Command 'made 3,700 direct attacks' on enemy shipping. It 'sank 107 vessels (155,076 tons) and lost 648 aircraft – just over six aircraft for each vessel sunk'.[70] However, by the summer of 1941, squadrons from Coastal Command undertook 'regular offensive reconnaissance along the enemy coastline' from Stadlandet in Norway to Lorient in France. This was accompanied by photographic reconnaissance (PRU) Spitfires taking photographs, notably of ports, while Beaufort and Hudson aircraft, 'in free-lance patrols at irregular intervals, were scouring the Channel and North Sea. And Blenheims from Number 2 Group, escorted within range by Fighter Command, were attacking targets at sea rather than on shore.'[71]

The Blenheim Mk IV was powered by two Bristol Mercury radial engines, generating a top speed of 266 mph, and could carry up to 1,000 pounds of bombs internally and 320 pounds externally. It was armed with five .303 machine guns, one firing forward mounted in the port wing, two in a power-operated dorsal turret, and two beneath the nose remotely operated and fired aft. Many aircrews considered it 'a great aircraft' owing to its high performance, but as one pilot cautioned, 'there were no margins when an engine cut at the critical point of the take-off with a bomb load on board'.[72] One unit that was equipped with Blenheims was 114 Squadron, on loan from Bomber Command to No. 18 Group, Coastal Command in 1941, and tasked with convoy escorts, anti-submarine and anti-shipping patrols. Personnel were trained to employ high-level attacks, but of greater significance to Coastal Command was the training 114 Squadron had put into low-level bombing. One of its pilots, R.E. Gillman, explained, 'it was much more exciting and certainly more accurate' than high-level bombing. Rather than rely on a bomb sight, the pilot used a button on the control column to release the bombs, and the idea was 'to come in at sea-level and at right angles, letting the bombs go like torpedoes and then climbing over the ship'.[73] This exposed aircraft to murderous anti-aircraft fire, so jinking and yawing was necessary, before lining up on the target.

Most merchantmen were armed, and the enemy frequently used convoys rather than allow ships to sail alone as inviting targets. These deployed heavily armed flak ships, acting as a screen against bombers and torpedo bombers. Naval vessels were sometimes deployed to protect convoys, and capable of providing significant anti-aircraft fire. Floatplanes escorting convoys similarly alerted coastal Luftwaffe fighter bases to the presence of hostile aircraft. As an RAF officer emphasised, by late 1940, 'the German ships can only creep along their own coastline, or that of countries which they have occupied, slipping along close inshore under cover of their land batteries and fighter aerodromes, escorted by flak-ships.'[74]

On a sortie near the Frisian Islands, crews from 114 Squadron attacked one convoy escorted by destroyers.

> The decks throughout their length sparkled with the flashes of the multiple cannon and the bass chorus of the bigger guns belched flame and smoke like a series of obscene eruptions. The sea before us was splattered with the impact of shrapnel and the sky was pock-marked with the black puffs of shell bursts.[75]

Given the extremely stressful nature of anti-shipping work, LMF was an issue. South African Flight Lieutenant Ronnie Selley served with 220 Squadron before dying in a flying accident in March 1941. He recorded during one anti-shipping operation:

> the machine was jumping around and an anti-aircraft shell blew the side of my aeroplane in and left a hole so big that you could get through it

easily, none of my crew were hurt but one of them lost his nerve, and we have had to take him off flying.[76]

Another challenge was determining the correct fuse setting for bombs so they didn't explode on impact, damaging the aircraft delivering them. An official booklet explained what occurred when a ship carrying a large number of depth charges was hit off La Rochelle, France, by a single 250lb bomb dropped from 400 feet without a delay fuse. 'The bomb detonated all the charges and blew the ship to pieces. The aircraft returned riddled with bits of its target.'[77] Accordingly, it became general practice to use delayed-action bombs on such sorties. New Zealander James Sanders served two tours with Coastal Command, primarily conducting daylight reconnaissance patrols and night bombing. He observed that normally, eleven-second-delay fused bombs were deployed on anti-shipping strikes, and these could be released close to a ship in daylight, 'followed by a smart pull-up to clear the masts and rigging and the inevitable anti-aircraft balloon flying above the vessel'.[78]

Alternatively, shipping was attacked by night. On 29/30 October 1941, a noteworthy anti-shipping operation occurred at Aalesund, Norway, when enemy ships in the harbour and nearby fjords were bombed by Hudsons from 220 Squadron, which had flown from the North of Scotland. It went down in Coastal Command folklore as 'the Aalesund strike' and seven ships were sunk. According to one pilot:

> There was a lot of flak coming up as I came over the target. I could see one ship burning, with smoke pouring from it. The ground was covered with snow and I had the whole target in silhouette. I flew round pretty low for a bit, then climbed up to get a better view and choose my target, keeping out of range of the flak. I saw a second ship hit and it soon became an inferno of flames. We could actually see the plates red-hot, I saw four other aircraft attack shipping in the harbour. They were flying very low, and the flak was streaming down on them from batteries in the hills – green, white, red, yellow. A lot of it was going straight onto the enemy's ships.
>
> I had by then chosen my target – the biggest ship in the harbour, about 5,000/6,000 tons. I approached from the North, about five miles away, my engines throttled right back. I came down to about 5,000 feet, by which time I was nearly over the ship, and dived straight onto it. I dropped my bombs at about 2,000 feet. I did my own bomb aiming. Directly the bombs were gone I pulled up over the town. I was then down to about 1,000 feet, still throttled back; then I opened up fully and went off. There was a lot of flak coming up at us. Some of it came pretty

close, but we couldn't actually hear it. The gunner definitely silenced two flak positions.[79]

Another pilot, Ted Rayner, highlighted why the Aalesund operation was so successful.

A moonlight strike at optimum strength such as this depended for success on a number of factors: a full, or almost-full moon at the right time of night and of month, shining from an appropriate place in the sky; precise and speedy information of the disposition of the enemy convoy sneaking along the Norwegian coast and fjords, provided by agents and their equally brave radio operators, or by photo-reconnaissance aircraft, or indeed by a previous Squadron patrol; a lull in other operations for a few preceding days to allow maximum strength to be deployed in the strike, and a careful plan of attack to create maximum impact in minimum time to avoid confusion in the air, but to create it among the ships.[80]

As indicated, enemy vessels were detected by a variety of means, including 'Rovers', or air patrols, 'given a roving commission to attack any suitable shipping target which may present itself'.[81] These were usually instigated by squadron or station commanders in keeping with the general policy of their group, and for aircrews offered a potentially exciting break from the monotony of convoy or anti-submarine patrols. According to an officer who flew Beauforts with 22 Squadron during 1940–41, two types of Rover were evolved. 'Moonlight Rovers' entailed aircraft being 'sent out on moonlit nights with complete freedom to fly anywhere over a large area of coastline searching for enemy ships. Torpedoes were used as well as bombs, and ships continued to be found and sunk.' Contrastingly, 'Daylight Rovers' sought to harness cloudy conditions to protect aircraft from fighters while they searched for and attacked enemy ships. 'Ideal conditions were given by a cloud-base of about three hundred feet accompanied by limited visibility of three or four miles, and even slight rain.'[82]

Consequently, the Rover was 'a clear-cut game with well-defined rules of conduct for the safety of aircraft, a game which must have been tantalizing to the enemy, who could never know quite when aircraft might descend on his shipping or his shore'.[83] As the Germans strengthened their defences, Rovers had to be modified in light of intelligence, and so as to take advantage of suitable weather conditions. Typically, aircraft would fly low over water searching for ships, because that way they were difficult to see and hear, or detect by radar. According to a pilot who experienced several Rovers, they represented 'the most demanding operation in individual effort, the most satisfying in achievement, the most thrilling in action'.[84]

An alternative method of attacking enemy shipping by night, which emerged by 1944, involved chandelier flares and radar to locate and illuminate a target. As James Sanders, who completed a tour with Halifax-equipped 502 Squadron, explained, 'The technique was to home in on the marine target by the aid of radar, drop our flares to illuminate the quarry, make a fast turn and then run in for a bomb-drop,' often using 500lb bombs with air-burst pistols fused to explode at wave-top height.[85] However, the method had drawbacks, as by illuminating the target, bombers alerted enemy ships to their presence, and both they and their escorting flak ships tended to throw-up significant fire, plus this could attract roaming German night fighters.

Later, their bombers were repainted black, rather than standard white Coastal Command camouflage, rendering them less conspicuous. Additionally, crews were encouraged to rely on radio altimeters that bounced signals off the ground or sea, and measured the distance via impulses, allowing aircrews to adopt very low-flying techniques, which dispensed with the need for flares. Off Scandinavia, aircrew from 502 Squadron found that 'at a cruising height of only two hundred feet they could capture a pretty clear radar sighting at a distance of twelve miles and home their aircraft onto the "blip" without any trouble'.[86] Approaching the target, they'd climb to 1,200 feet, from where it was safe to bomb. The 'pilot, the navigator-bomb aimer and the radar operator' worked 'as a precision team' who'd make the bomb run, then descend back to the safety of 200 feet.[87] This lessened the chance of being picked up by enemy scanners, because these were better at locating high-flying aircraft, and ensured bombers were less vulnerable to night fighters, which favoured attacking head-on or from below.

Torpedoes were another method of attacking shipping, and could prove devastating when they exploded below the waterline. Yet unlike bombs, torpedoes had to be well aimed and carefully dropped to stand any chance of being effective. There was a danger that they'd disintegrate if an aircraft was travelling too high or too fast. One pilot cautioned:

> A torpedo must be dropped well within a thousand yards of the target if it is to have any chance of scoring a hit, but at this distance, particularly from an aircraft attacking under fire, a ship looks uncomfortably close at the dropping height of 60 feet, and over-estimation of a range is a general fault. Not only must range be judged carefully, but the target's speed must be estimated and correctly allowed for when taking aim.[88]

Torpedoes had to enter the water at the correct angle, and if released too close to a target, risked travelling underneath it. 'For a torpedo to have a reasonable chance of a hit, the target should not be less than two hundred feet long, a length achieved by ships of about 5,000 tons.' Obtaining an element of surprise was beneficial, and aircrews weren't to linger during an attack, to stand any chance of avoiding anti-aircraft fire. Simultaneously, they needed to manoeuvre into a position from which to take aim. Owing to such difficulties, thorough training in deploying torpedoes was essential. Yet, despite practice, the bravery and determination of aircrews, many sorties still missed their targets. A pilot from 22 Squadron vividly remembered the agonising occasion when, during a torpedo strike, he thought he'd hit a vessel off the French coast, only to be mistaken.

> Suddenly, a great water spout rose into the air, and I thought we had hit it, but it was not at the target, but just short of it; the torpedo had hit a sandbank or submerged wreck and exploded prematurely. ... Smoke hung in the breathless summer air like a grey canopy above the tanker, gun muzzles smoked and spat tongues of flame, the sky around us was still daubed with vanishing smudges of black smoke, but nothing happened; we had missed again.[89]

During late September 1940, the RAF launched a daring attack against heavily defended German shipping moored in Cherbourg harbour. Notably, this was one of the first occasions when a torpedo attack was mounted at night. Torpedo-carrying Beauforts targeted the ships, while, crucially, Blenheims bombed the target to divert the enemy's anti-aircraft defences. One of the Beaufort pilots recorded his experience, including the moment he released his torpedo.

> I was so close that I could actually see them and I watched a German gunner, one of a crew of three manning a Bofors gun, trying to depress the barrel, which moved slowly downwards as he turned the handles. He could not get it sufficiently depressed and the flak passed above our heads. It was bright red tracer and most of it hit the fort at the end of the other breakwater on the far side of the entrance. At the same moment I saw a large ship winking with red lights, from which I judged that there were troops on board firing at us with machine guns and rifles.
>
> I dropped the torpedo in perfect conditions, for I was flying at the right speed and at the right height. Half a second after I had dropped it five searchlights opened up and caught me in their beams. I pulled back the stick and put on a lot of left rudder and cleared out. The trouble about a torpedo attack is that when you have released the torpedo you have to fly on the same course for a short time to make quite sure it has, in fact, left the aircraft. I remember counting one and two and three and forcing myself not to count too fast. Then we were away.[90]

Although a purpose-designed torpedo bomber, the Beaufort was used for a wide variety of tasks by Coastal Command, including bombing and minelaying. With a crew of four, and top speed of 260 mph, the twin-engine Beaufort wasn't the easiest of aircraft to master. A Polish pilot who encountered it warned, 'the Beaufort, a deadly thing it was, there, were quite a few crashes. You had to be really correct with it but we'd had a lot of practice because we'd started before the war.'[91] Wing Commander Patrick Gibbs's crew preferred the Mk II Beaufort with Pratt and Witney rather than Taurus engines. It was 'faster and handled more smoothly than its predecessor' and had a 'device by which they could be persuaded to give an extremely high "boost" for a short time; this seemed to ... have a special application to meetings with single-seaters! [i.e. enemy fighters].'[92]

As indicated, anything that could assist the torpedo bombers was generally welcomed. Wing Commander Gibbs recounted that, at times in the Mediterranean, empty beer bottles thrown from aircraft so that their 'whistling' might be mistaken for bombs could distract German gunners. Alternatively, on some routes in the Mediterranean, dusk or dawn attacks were contemplated as a means of catching the enemy unawares. Both were problematic. 'At dusk the targets were at extreme range,' and aircraft returning from sorties risked running out of fuel, and with limited wireless/radio to help, there was an increased risk of pilots being unable to return to base. At dawn, formation flying was virtually impossible, 'and aircraft operating singly would have little chance of hitting their target with the one torpedo they carried, while the enemy could easily concentrate on a single attacker' the same volume of fire that would be experienced during a combined attack when it 'would be spread between several aircraft'. Limited time was available to search for targets, and enemy fighters operating from North Africa could reach target areas shortly after daybreak.[93]

Despite the challenges associated with it, so long as a torpedo was delivered with skill and accuracy so that it hit below the waterline, it would invariably lead to a sinking. Yet for all that, it 'was essentially a one-shot weapon – a distinctly hit-or-miss armament which left no room for immediate repeat performance'.[94] Bombs weren't so effective, even with a direct hit, but unlike a torpedo, they could readily be deployed against other targets, if no shipping was found. Alternatively, as Squadron Leader Spooner stressed, when encountering shipping in calm water, the idea was to fly low and level and release bombs early so they 'would skip or bounce on the surface of the sea', ensuring that 'fatal underwater hits' could be achieved.[95]

In late 1942, Coastal Command's anti-shipping capability was enhanced by the arrival of the versatile, powerful, two-seat Bristol Beaufighter Mk VI, which was able to carry a variety of weapons and equipment. The Mk VIC, or 'Torbeau', could carry and launch the standard manufactured American or British torpedo. Equally, owing to its strength, speed and endurance, the Beaufighter proved invaluable when deploying its 'combined cannons, machine guns, rockets and bombs to cut a deadly swathe through any merchant convoys encountered'.[96] During late 1942, purpose-built Strike Wings were established around Beaufighter squadrons, each with different models of the aircraft whose characteristics complemented one another. The first at North Coates, Lincolnshire, comprised the following Beaufighter squadrons: 143 (fighter versions), 236 (fighter-bombers) and 254 (Torbeaus). The idea was for a Strike Wing to operate a formation of self-protected attack aircraft, with long range, which could tackle any worthwhile targets found sailing in British waters. Other Strike Wings followed, including one established at Wick, Scotland, which initially comprised Nos. 144 and 404 Squadrons, and the 'Banff Strike Wing', because from that Scottish location it was specifically designated to target the Norwegian coastline.

By April 1943, some Beaufighters were armed with 3-inch rocket projectiles mounted under their wings. These were particularly useful in flak suppression, and proved fearsome against maritime targets. A pilot with 143 Squadron outlined tactics that were evolved by the 'North Coates Wing', including the use of RPs:

> The Method of operation was a sea-level trip to the target area, then up to about 3,000 feet and close ranks on sighting, attack in quick succession in the following order – anti-flak aircraft with cannons and machine guns; rockets if carried or further cannons and mg; finally torpedoes. The secret of success was in good position and accurate timing, so that each attack was followed immediately by the next. With practice and experience the time taken in actually attacking was, I suppose, remarkably short, but the concentration of fire in such a brief period must have been quite dreadful at the receiving end.[97]

Attacking shipping off Norway was complicated by the terrain, as most merchant captains knew how to hug the rocky coastline, or moor near to the cliff faces of fjords to obtain protection from the air. This made vessels harder to locate, and heightened the risks entailed with low-level flying. One Beaufighter pilot provided a vivid account of the difficulties he faced, and explained that you had to:

> Approach any ship moored alongside a cliff ideally from the land side and then pass out over the mouth of the fjord towards the open sea if surprise was to be maintained. This method often meant skipping over a bloody steep mini-mountain first, instantly dive into the fjord, line up and fire within seconds, then bank like hell to avoid spreading oneself all over the cliff sides. We usually made such attacks – when possible – in very close single file, which often meant having to fly through a hail of rock splinters and ricocheting cannon shells and bullets fired by the Beaufighter immediately in front.[98]

Another aircraft deployed in the anti-shipping role was the de Havilland Mosquito, which by the end of the war replaced most of Coastal Command's Beaufighters. Initially, these performed invaluably as reconnaissance/escort aircraft, such as when 333 (Norwegian) PR Squadron from the 'Banff Strike Wing' located targets for Beaufighters. However, it became increasingly possible to employ both types of aircraft on combined strikes. On 14 September 1944, Mosquitoes from 235 and 248 Squadrons accompanied Beaufighters from 144 and 404 Squadrons on an armed reconnaissance in Norwegian waters, destroying four vessels and damaging their escorts.

Like the Beaufighter, the Mosquito proved a highly versatile aircraft that enhanced the capabilities of Coastal Command. The standard version employed was the Mk VI, which could carry 2,000 pounds of bombs, and was adapted to employ RPs mounted on under-wing racks. In October 1943, a few Mosquito FB Mk XVIIIs were issued to 248 Squadron, then stationed at Predannack, which incorporated a 3.7-inch anti-aircraft gun. This led to the development of twenty-five Mosquitoes being fitted with a 6-pounder (57mm) gun instead of the usual four 20mm cannon in the nose. Known as the Tsetse, these were specifically intended for anti-shipping/anti-U-boat strikes.[99] As Des Curtis, a navigator who flew the Tsetse explained, essentially:

> you had a wooden aircraft and this twelve foot long piece of artillery was bolted onto the main spar of the aircraft, slightly off centre in a longitudinal sense. ... We carried twenty-four rounds of ammunition which were fired singly by the pilot, automatically re-loaded. It made a hell of a bang when it went off and initially the flame from the explosion shot out 130 feet in front of the aircraft.[100]

Warships presented another target for anti-shipping operations, and with their heavy armour and anti-aircraft defences, could be formidable, regardless of whether attacked in port or open waters. Most were liable to be escorted by numbers of smaller destroyers, which contributed to the anti-aircraft screen. During 1941, the German battlecruisers *Scharnhorst*, *Gneisenau* and *Prinz Eugen* were attacked no less than sixty-three times by Coastal Command. In early 1942, further attacks occurred against these heavily defended targets while in dry dock, and during the 'Channel Dash', when, daringly in daylight they sought to sail from Brest, through the Straits of Dover, and into German waters. All attempts to sink them failed and resulted in heavy losses. Sergeant Pilot P.A.C. McDermott and his navigator, Sergeant J.S. Boucher, from 144 Squadron, were among those aircrew involved.

> The Hampden broke cloud again at 900 feet above sea-level and I picked out the target about half-a-mile ahead. To make a proper run up under

such conditions would have been impossible if one was to survive to complete the task. I leaned over my bomb-sight and pressed the 'tit'. For a few fleeting moments I could see the German gunners, frantically firing at us. They seemed so close that I felt myself to be before a firing squad. The pilot opened up the throttle and we roared up into the cloud again at 180 mph, too soon even to see our bombs burst. The sudden upward movement threw me back into my seat, and a second later there was a yellow flash as a shell exploded, shattering the Perspex nose of my cabin and driving me backwards under the floor of the pilot's cockpit. Stunned for a moment, I tried to open my eyes but the pain was too great. I felt the wet blood on my face. The cold blast of air, now passing through the gaping hole in the nose, had blown all my maps and my log through the pilot's cockpit window. I crawled back through the fuselage to where the wireless-operator was sitting, and plugged in his 'inter-comm' gear. We were relatively safe now that we were in cloud again and leaving the coast behind us. A rough mental calculation enabled me to give the pilot a course for the Lizard ...[101]

The *Prinz Eugen* was attacked again on 17 May 1942, off the southern tip of Norway, having already been damaged by the Royal Navy submarine *Trident*. As she steamed southwards towards Germany for repairs, Hudsons and Beaufort torpedo bombers attacked, escorted by Beaufighters and Blenheims. The operation:

was pressed home with the greatest determination in the teeth of heavy anti-aircraft and fighter opposition. The Beaufighters, sweeping ahead, raked the decks of the German vessels with cannon and machine-gun fire, while the Hudsons and torpedo bombers went into attack. In this action the rear gunner of one of the Beauforts beat off a series of attacks by enemy fighters lasting 35 minutes, though one of his guns had jammed and he himself had been wounded in the face, hands, legs and head. Five enemy fighters were shot down, and we lost nine aircraft.[102]

Rather than direct attacks against shipping, minelaying offered a less costly means of damaging the enemy. For the period April 1940 to March 1943, about 16,000 mines were laid and accounted for 369 vessels (361,821 tons) at a cost of 329 aircraft. Consequently, mining was costing less than one aircraft per ship, whereas to sink one ship during that same period resulted in the loss of six aircraft. The significance of such statistics wasn't lost on Air Chief Marshal Sir Arthur Harris who, as the Commander-in-Chief of Bomber Command, enthusiastically supported minelaying, together with the effort made by Coastal Command. He realised that it compelled the enemy to divert more resources into anti-minelaying devices and shipbuilding for repairs or replacements, and increase the numbers of naval personnel engaged in minesweeping. It also added to the strain on the enemy's other communications.[103]

The A Mk I–IV was the standard sea mine used throughout much of the war. It contained about 750 pounds of explosive and was designed to survive being dropped from an aircraft flying at 200 mph at heights of between 100 feet and 15,000 feet. A later model, the Mk V, was smaller and incorporated less explosive, and was principally intended as a magnetic mine.[104] Aircraft involved in minelaying could 'make their way into narrow roadsteads, shallow channels and even into harbours where no surface vessel could possibly penetrate in the face of enemy defences'.[105] Accuracy was vital, and required excellent navigation. This was so mines could be placed exactly where required, by night, and so they were laid in accordance with those areas designated under international law. As a Canadian pilot expounded, 'we're each given a pinpoint on the chart and that pinpoint is where we've got to plant our mines – or bring them back.'[106]

According to the same pilot, another 'advantage of minelaying by air is the speed with which a minefield can be sown. On one occasion there was an urgent need for a certain enemy channel six hundred miles away from our base to be mined without delay. We received the order at 6 o'clock one evening. By midnight that minefield had been laid.'[107] The actual process of 'gardening' tended to work as follows:

> The mine is stowed away inside the bomb compartment and enclosed by folding doors in the underside of the fuselage. There's a parachute attached to the mine and as the bomb doors are opened and the mine falls clear, this parachute automatically opens. It checks the rate of fall so that the mechanism of the mine won't be damaged by too violent a contact with the water. The mine doesn't make much of a splash as it goes in and it drags its parachute down after it to the sea bottom, where it stays put until a ship passes overhead and sets it in action.[108]

Yet minelaying wasn't a benign activity. As a member of 217 Squadron discovered: 'Gardening trips were as nerve-racking as any, for they were flown at wave-top height at night. … We were dropping sea mines or "cucumbers" usually in an area known as "Jellyfish" in the Goulet de Brest.' Additionally, sometimes there was 'a lack of visibility, sea mist etc., or a burst of fire from a guardian flak-ship from out of the murk – and the adrenalin could flow quite smartly!'[109]

Air Sea Rescue (ASR)

By the end of the war, thousands of British, American and Allied aircrew had reason to be thankful to the Air Sea Rescue organisation established to cover

British waters, along with at least 500 enemy airmen saved from a watery grave. In overseas theatres, including the Mediterranean and Far East, ASR operations saved over 3,000 aircrew plus a number of other Service personnel and civilians. A member of 294 Squadron, recalling service in North Africa, noted how under Wing Commander R.G. Walker DFC, they were 'part of Middle East Coastal Command ... equipped with Wellingtons and Walrus aircraft used for search and recovery, taking in the desert as well as the sea'.[110] Those aircrew that survived a ditching were subsequently eligible to become members of the Goldfish Club, established in November 1942 by Lieutenant Colonel F. Baden-Powell Weil, the managing director of a company that produced dinghies and other rescue equipment. This offered recognition and support to those who'd suffered a harrowing ordeal at sea.[111]

Clearly there was a humanitarian incentive in saving lives at sea, including those of enemy personnel. A pilot from 276 Squadron, flying a Spitfire Mk II, adapted to carry smoke floats and an inflatable dinghy, vividly remembered an incident after D-Day in July 1944, when he and another pilot sighted a number of dinghies in the Channel. A Walrus amphibious aircraft was directed to the area, and when it landed, much to the crew's surprise, the occupants of the dinghies were an entire U-boat crew, totalling forty-six men.

> The senior German officer was taken aboard the Walrus and gave the bemused crew a couple of bottles of wine as souvenirs. We saw no reason why his 46 should not be added to the Squadron total of successful rescues![112]

Individual aircrew's circumstances causing them to crash or bail out varied, but it was extremely heartening for them to know that there was a reasonable chance they'd be rescued on ditching in the drink. As Air Commodore Graham Pitchfork astutely remarks, crucially, the ASR organisation also existed for 'the recovery of trained manpower for the furtherance of the war effort'.[113] The Battle of Britain, during which much aerial combat occurred close to home over the Channel, and the strategic bombing offensive against Germany spurred on the need for an improved ASR set-up. During 1940–42, numerous advances were made, particularly in instructing aircrew how to safely ditch and extricate themselves from a land-based aircraft forced to land into the sea; how to maintain the life of ditched aircrew once they'd abandoned their aircraft; and how to locate ditched aircrew and recover them.

In 1941, overall responsibility for ASR operations passed to Coastal Command, but numerous other agencies were involved in rescues. Around Britain this included: 'The Post Office Radio Stations, the Royal Observer Corps, the Coastguards, the Royal National Lifeboat Institution, the Merchant Navy and even amateur wireless enthusiasts'.[114] Additionally, the Royal Navy (RN) had smaller craft that could be deployed as part of the ASR effort, while the RAF possessed maritime craft, notably high-speed launches (HSLs) that could be employed to help recover ditched aircrew. Although initially few in number, by 1944, over thirty RAF units were operating HSLs on ASR duties around the British coast alone. This included several of the 63-foot type manufactured by the British Power Boat Company, known as 'Whalebacks' owing to their distinctive curved hulls and humped cabins. These were manoeuvrable, highly seaworthy, and possessed a purpose-designed sickbay. As the war progressed, their armament was increased, making them better suited to the tasks they faced.

After joining the RAF in March 1941, H.J. Field from Hastings, Sussex, was passed medically fit to train as aircrew and posted to Blackpool. Here he was surprised to find that his PTI was none other than Corporal Stanley Matthews, the famous footballer. Bored of the routine, he volunteered for 'Motor Boat Crew'. Eventually, he underwent an arduous course to qualify as a coxswain, and served on motor launches at numerous British bases and in West Africa. He became coxswain of HSL No. 192, and recalled rescues he was involved with while serving on that craft.

> After a while we moved to the North Sea, so as to operate from Lowestoft and Gorleston. We were kept very busy with the American Air Force who flew over that area. One in particular was on 26 July 1943, when a Flying Fortress from the 94th Bombardment Group had landed in the sea off Holland, and was called 'Destiny Tot'. 192 was despatched to find them, and after three and a half hours steaming, we found the plane still afloat, and the crew sitting on top of the fuselage. I put the bow of 192 between the wing strut and body and they all got onto the boat, and not even a wet foot. Went astern, and a few minutes later the tail came up and down she went. So it was back to base with 10 very grateful American flyers. I still get a Christmas card from the captain of the plane.[115]

Of course, not all rescues turned out as smoothly, and crews of HSLs often faced tragic circumstances as part of ASR work.

> We used to chat to the planes on the VHF wireless. The fighters were 'little friends', and bombers were 'big friends'. On one occasion we were talking to one of our own British bombers who had been badly shot up, and begged them to 'ditch', as you could see the damage. The reply was: 'We've got it so far and can see the coast,' when it just exploded, and we had four young men to pick up. One more sad day, but at least we could bring them home to be buried in England.[116]

A group of RAF personnel eagerly inspect the remains of a Junkers Ju 88 shot down near St Osyth, Essex, in September 1940. (Author's collection)

Airmen from 38 Squadron in their full-length flying suits, flying boots, and parachute harnesses. NCO Navigator Reggie Wainwright stands at the back left wearing a field service cap. (Charlie Wainwright)

Reggie Wainwright (third from left) and his Wellington crew from 38 Squadron. They served in Europe before moving to the Middle East in November 1940. (Charlie Wainwright)

The WAAF made a major contribution towards the war effort. Maise Goulty was granted an emergency commission in April 1944, and promoted section officer the following November. (Author's collection)

A WAAF band parades in Brussels shortly after the Allied liberation of Europe from Nazi occupation, 1945. (Alastair Fraser)

Sport was a major part of Service life, even in wartime. Here, the winning team from 2 Group, Brussels, 7-a-side tournament pose for the camera in May 1945. (Alastair Fraser)

Harry Blee on passing out as a flight engineer from RAF St Athan. After serving in the Far East, he was granted a permanent commission, and served until 1975. (Simon Blee)

Flight Lieutenant Anthony Goulty, photographed at the end of the war while serving with Number 7 IAU in the Far East, sporting the medal ribbon of the Burma Star. (Author's collection)

With 358 Squadron, Harry Blee (flight engineer, second from right) regularly flew Liberators with Chris Headley (skipper, far right), and Jack Tubb (navigator/side-gunner, third from right), India 1944. (Simon Blee)

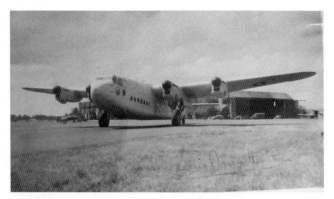

Reggie Wainwright served as navigator aboard this Avro York, regularly used to ferry Earl Mountbatten (Supreme Commander South-East Asia, 1943–46), who has signed the photograph. (Charlie Wainwright)

The Mosquito, affectionately dubbed the 'Mossie', was one of the most successful and versatile of all the aircraft employed by the RAF during the war. (Author's collection)

A fine view of a Sunderland flying boat: *'C' for Charlie*, registration SZ268, moored in a Norwegian fjord. The Sunderland proved especially useful in anti-submarine work. (Robert Goulty)

On 21 March 1945, Mosquitoes from RAF 2nd TAF, escorted by Mustangs, launched a daring low-level strike against the Gestapo archives in Shell House, Copenhagen – marked here by an 'X'. (Alastair Fraser)

The Short Sunderland flying boat was dubbed the 'flying porcupine' by the Germans owing to its heavy armament. Landing and taking off from water could be tricky and required great skill. (Robert Goulty)

Air Sea Rescue operations helped recover trained aircrew so that they could continue the war effort. Here a Supermarine Walrus is greeted by an airman who's ended up 'in the drink'. (Author's collection)

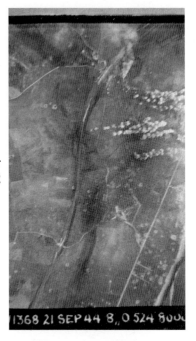

An attack on German gun positions near Boulogne by RAF Bostons and Mitchells from 2 Group, 2 September 1944. (Alastair Fraser)

This photograph of the harbour at Kiel was taken on VE-Day by a Mitchell bomber from 139 Wing. (Alastair Fraser)

Cologne, as viewed from an RAF Mitchell on 8 May 1945 (VE-Day). The massive destruction caused by aerial bombardment is clearly evident. (Alastair Fraser)

This shot of Kiel was taken from a Mitchell bomber flown by Flight Lieutenant John Smith-Carrington (139 Wing). Note the effectiveness of the camouflage in breaking up the outline of the ship in the centre of the photograph. (Alastair Fraser)

Bomb damage at Kiel, May 1945. This provides a graphic illustration of the level of destruction caused by RAF Bomber Command's policy of area bombing against German cities. (Alastair Fraser)

The wider resources of the RN and RAF could potentially be used to assist rescue efforts. Mike Henry, an air gunner with Bomber Command, recounted how his aircraft was used on 2 June 1942 after a heavy raid against Cologne, 'on a three-hour air-sea-rescue operation. We searched a section of the North Sea for dinghies.' During his service he completed further searches like this, and each was counted as 'half an operation' towards the completion of his tour.[117]

Importantly, specially designated ASR squadrons were established by the RAF in 1941. Initially, 275 to 278 Squadrons were largely dependent on ageing Westland Lysanders and the Supermarine Walrus, an amphibian, described by a former senior RAF officer as an 'ugly but extremely effective' aircraft.[118] H.J. Field commented how the Walrus:

> had only one engine, a pusher type [i.e. propeller facing to the rear], and a particular drawback was they would put down in any sea to pick up aircrew, but in the case of bomber crews, they would pile them on board, and obviously couldn't take off, so taxied towards England. And then we'd go and bring the lot back and tow the old Walrus astern. Usually they had burnt the engine out. There was always rivalry between us, but as long as the crews go home, that was the main thing.[119]

As spares for Lysanders became hard to obtain, Boulton Paul Defiants were converted to the ASR role, no longer being needed as night fighters. Later, improved aircraft became available including the Sea Otter, an amphibian biplane designed by Supermarine, and notably, refurbished Spitfires. 'With eight machine guns,' these 'could search and fight back if intercepted. Everyone felt a lot easier in mind.'[120] Contrastingly, in late 1944 when 279 Squadron re-equipped with Vickers Warwicks, 'effectively an enlarged version of the Wellington', the move wasn't universally popular, despite their ability to carry significant amounts of rescue gear. American aircrew who were diverted to RAF Thornaby, where the Squadron was based, observed a Warwick, 'just not believing that the RAF actually flew canvas-covered trelliswork framed airplanes in combat'.[121]

While flying on ASR duties with 276 Squadron, Nick Berryman discovered it proved possible to fly vastly different types of aircraft, even in one day. 'I flew the Spitfires and Walruses ... No two aircraft could be less alike, and their role just as different. I enjoyed the challenge.'[122] Nos. 275 to 278 Squadrons supported Fighter Command on searches up to 40 miles from the coast. Typically, individual flights would cover a particular area, rather than personnel operate together as an entire squadron. Longer-range ASR sorties were mounted by other units, including 279 Squadron, initially employing Hudsons and Ansons. Regarding the American manufactured Lockheed Hudsons, an officer noted: 'The first two "kites", A279 & B279 are called "Queen of the Air" & "Flying Pig" respectively. You wouldn't believe the difference possible in flying characteristics in two machines that are identical down to the last rivet.'[123]

The obsolescent nature of aircraft employed on ASR work was a shock to the uninitiated. When Nick Berryman was posted on operations, he hoped to fly the Hawker Typhoon, having completed his flying training on the Hawker Hurricane. However, on joining 'A' Flight 276 Air Sea Rescue Squadron at RAF Warmwell near Dorchester, he was taken aback as, 'in front of the hanger, bearing a 276 Squadron noticeboard, stood three Boulton & Paul Defiants and two Supermarine amphibian Walruses. "Hell," I thought. "What's all this?"'[124] He soon discovered life could be hectic. 'As an ASR pilot I never knew when the next call would come. It was a "watch on stop on" job, as we were not over established with Defiant pilots and there was always an Immediate and a Thirty Minute Readiness available.'[125]

As soon as a distress signal was received from an aircraft, it was supposed to be communicated to the nearest Area Combined Headquarters who, in turn, informed the controller of the group in whose area the aircraft was reported, thus initiating the search process. The group controller would then inform the nearest Coastal Command airfield, so a reconnaissance aircraft could be sent to search for dinghies. Simultaneously, RAF or naval craft would be alerted, and directed to the area by the reconnaissance aircraft. Clearly, communication – especially by radio/wireless – was vital. An official publication on ASR stressed:

> The crews of all aircraft have been instructed if in trouble to send out the SOS signal as early as possible, and to continue to do so at frequent intervals, giving their position at the same time. The object of this procedure is to obtain a line of bearings which will simplify the search conducted by the aircraft, and also make it possible to obtain a cross-check on its position by means of radiolocation.
>
> This rescue procedure may sound somewhat complicated: but in practice, under most conditions, it is quick and effective.[126]

Sometimes, SOS signals weren't sent or received. Alternatively, the radio set in an aircraft might have been damaged, in which case it was only possible to mount a search once it was confirmed by its base as overdue. One way around this problem was to employ carrier pigeons for emergency communication, although these couldn't fly in poor visibility, at night, or when wet. It wasn't until 1942 that a watertight pigeon container was issued for bombers, and a year later, the use of pigeons was largely phased out because distances covered on operations increased beyond 'pigeon range'. Nonetheless, at least one spectacular pigeon-based rescue occurred in Europe, when Winkie, a bird from a loft in Dundee, was employed by the crew of a Beaufort that had ditched after one of their engines blew up while returning from a sortie to look for the *Scharnhorst* and *Gneisenau* in Norwegian waters. The crew were desperately trying to stave off the effects of exposure in their dinghy when they released Winkie.

> the Operations Room received a telephone call from a civilian pigeon-fancier reporting that one of his pigeons, which he had lent the Royal Air Force, had just returned, wet and covered with oil. He gave its code number, from which the station identified it as one of the pigeons carried by the Beaufort for which search was being made. No message was attached to the bird, but the station navigator, assisted by the civilian owner of the pigeon, worked out the bird's probable cruising speed and thus obtained cross-check on the distance from land from the spot at which it had been released. The calculation thus made was transmitted to the searching aircraft, which found the crew within twenty minutes. They were subsequently picked up by two launches converging on the spot from bases seventy-five miles apart. The pigeon had crossed about hundred miles of sea.[127]

Problems arose if the position given for the dinghy was inaccurate, or it had drifted by the time a search was launched. Poor weather was another challenge, and it is difficult not to overemphasise the impact it had on ASR work. According to a wartime booklet:

> In bright sunshine and a calm sea a dinghy can only be seen from a short distance, but in other conditions, and if the clouds come down and fog drapes the surface of the water, to spot it becomes almost impossible. In a storm, with white caps cresting the waves, the dinghy may be practically indistinguishable from the blown spume.[128]

Each rescue followed a similar pattern, although simultaneously was characterised by specific challenges, such as the weather. In all, speed was of the essence, and could mean the difference between saving lives or potentially the grisly task of recovering dead bodies from the sea.

Landing on the surface of the sea was a frightening experience. The crew of a Liberator shot down by a Ju 88 over the Bay of Biscay found:

> the aircraft immediately sank and we went down with it – twenty feet under water – completely dark. The terrific impact with the water had broken its back and almost ours as well: like hitting a brick wall at a hundred miles per hour. It was far too dark to see anything… No one can realise the horrible feeling it gives one, to be jammed in an aircraft under water and slowly drowning.

Although they struggled free, and found a dingy, only three of the nine-man crew survived the ordeal.[129] However, there was a difference between ditching a large aircraft such as a bomber, compared with something smaller. Bombers often remained afloat long enough for the crew to climb aboard dinghies, whereas fighters sunk swiftly owing to the weight of their engines. Consequently, fighter pilots often chose to bail out rather than risk becoming trapped and drowned in their aircraft.

Pilot Officer Tadeusz Turek, a Pole serving with 609 Squadron, had a narrow escape when his Typhoon (JP 745) was shot down by anti-aircraft fire over the Channel in late September 1943.

> I aligned the aircraft and saw below me the speeding waves coming closer with every second. There was a sudden and great impact, like hitting a wall. I saw in that moment the ASI [Air Speed Indicator] reading 150 mph. I hit my head [not helped by having had the head cushion removed from his armour plate] and in that instant all I could see was a red glow of flames – everywhere.

When he regained consciousness he was neck-deep in water, and felt paralysed, and feared he was going to drown. In a moment of inspiration, he suddenly thought about his forthcoming wedding. Quickly, he 'grabbed the release harness and was free. I wasted no time in paddling, and looking back I saw the tail of my Typhoon just vanishing.'[130]

In contrast, a Lancaster from 106 Squadron, based at Syerston, Notting-hamshire, made a 'perfect ditching' that same month, enabling the crew to escape with most of their equipment, as it remained afloat for several hours. It was piloted by Squadron Leader Howroyd, and had been attacked several times by a night fighter during a sortie against Berlin, which killed the rear gunner and bomb aimer, and damaged the aircraft's electrical instruments, including compass and radio. Unaware of the compass failure, the crew flew off course and as they crossed the Dutch coast, only forty minutes' fuel remained. Knowing they couldn't possibly reach home, the crew braced themselves for a ditching. Howroyd had to be lashed to his seat as his harness had been shot away. 'As the Lancaster descended through 1,000 feet all the engines cut out and an engineless ditching seemed inevitable, but at only 10 feet off the sea the engineer managed to switch over to tanks containing a few more gallons of fuel.' This enabled Howroyd to execute a perfect landing, and 'the crew felt hardly any shock on impacting the water'.[131]

To assist ditched aircrew, several aids became available. Close to British shores numerous rescue floats and buoys were moored, offering aircrew relief from the shock of landing in the sea, if they could reach them. These were equipped with food, signalling apparatus, and first aid kits. However, given that many aircraft ditched further from home, life jackets were important. When inflated, the 'Mae West', nicknamed after the buxom film star, could keep an airman afloat for several hours, especially if he remained on his back. Having suffered problems when trying to switch over his fuel supply from the auxiliary tank to the main tanks, Group Captain W.G.G. Duncan Smith was compelled to ditch his Spitfire in the Mediterranean. Fortunately, his number two had transmitted distress signals, ensuring a good fix was plotted. Lacking a dinghy, he spent hours alternating between swimming and floating on his back buoyed by his 'Mae West'. He recalled, 'the hot sun blazed down from a deep blue sky, burning my skin with its relentless intensity.' Eventually, he was dragged aboard a Walrus as it came under fire from enemy fighters.

> As eager hands were reaching to drag me on board the amphibian, I heard several loud explosions, followed by a stinging blow across the back of my neck that spun me round in the water. ... I tried to get to my feet but instead pitched forward onto my face. ... When I came to, I found myself covered in a blanket. A man was grinning at me and trying to force brandy between my chattering teeth.[132]

It was better if ditched aircrew made use of dinghies, as this improved their chances of survival, and several types were manufactured. By 1940, heavy bombers were employing a version of the 'H' type dinghy, stowed in a special compartment, and 'when the aircraft came to rest on the water, the sea activated an immersion switch, which actuated the carbon-dioxide bottle that automatically inflated the dinghy'. The design was relatively stable, and it became standard practice that modified versions were supplied on all multi-seat aircraft. Fighter pilots had initially to rely on their 'Mae West' to keep them afloat if they ditched or bailed out over water. However, by late 1940, they were officially encouraged to bail out, rather than ditch, and a dinghy that could fit into the confined space of a fighter's cockpit became an urgent requirement.

The 'K' type 'was a boat-shaped dinghy packed in a valise attached to either the parachute harness or the Mae West' and was rapidly improved with the addition of 'paddles, a telescopic mast, emergency rations and a flag to draw attention'. The type proved so successful that they were issued to crews of multi-seat aircraft (excluding heavy bombers and trainers). The ability to sail a dinghy was deemed important, especially in winter, and it improved aircrew's chances of resistance to exposure if they had to concentrate on sailing towards friendly waters. This led to the 'K' type being modified with a protective hood and apron, and studier mast and sail. A 'Q' type multi-seat dingy was similarly developed to replace the 'H' type, which incorporated a mast and sails, radio with kite aerial, and basic navigational charts. Dinghies also contained first aid kits, emergency rations and packets of fluorescein, a chemical that dyed seawater greenish yellow and was visible from the air.[133]

With the issue of dinghies, the attendant dingy drill became important, and varied depending on the aircraft flown. It was practised, but even so, there was nothing quite like facing the reality of a ditching. Every member of crew had to appreciate their specific duties before, during and after a ditching. For example, the wireless/radio operator was:

> responsible for taking with him the Very light pistols, destroying the secret papers, and stowing in the dinghy the carrier pigeons and distress signals. The rear gunner will throw out the dinghy valise with the help of the second pilot. He must be the first man on board the dinghy, and if it inflates in an inverted position he must jump into the sea and right it.[134]

During the war, three RAF stations concerned with ASR operations notably developed their own forms of life-saving kit that could be air-dropped to ditched aircrew. The Thornaby Bag, named after RAF Thornaby, a Coastal Command station on the east coast of Yorkshire, was a canvas bag constructed from readily available components containing items such as first aid equipment, rations and cigarettes. It was of limited effectiveness as it tended to burst on impact but represented a step in the right direction. The Bircham Barrel, after RAF Bircham Newton in Norfolk, another Coastal Command base, was produced from readily available materials and designed to fit the bomb racks on searching aircraft. It proved more successful and durable, eventually being fitted to a wide range of aircraft. Finally, there was Lindholme Gear, developed by the station commander at RAF Lindholme in South Yorkshire, which consisted of a number of containers linked by floating ropes, containing a large, sturdy dinghy, food, water, protective clothing, and signalling equipment. These could be hauled in by ditched aircrew, and the system proved extremely useful.[135]

Effort went into developing suitable wireless/radio sets for dinghies and equipment for marine craft so they could home in on transmissions from dinghies. The ASV oscillator proved valuable as an alternative to the dinghy wireless, despite appearing late in the war. Known as 'Walter', it emitted 'automatic distress signals capable of being detected on the searching aircraft's ASV radar set that produced a clear, unmistakable image on the radar screen'.[136] Another important innovation, pioneered by 279 Squadron, was the airborne lifeboat. Appearing in 1943, it was dropped from a Hudson (later a Warwick) by parachute to assist the rescue of a ditched aircrew in their dinghy. These were well equipped with survival aids, navigational and signalling/communications gear, plus water and rations.[137]

Squadron Leader Howroyd and his surviving Lancaster crewmembers owed their lives to much of the above technology. They'd ditched 130 miles north-east of

Bircham Newton, and Hudsons from 279 searched the area, eventually obtaining fixes on the still floating Lancaster and nearby dinghy, which were passed back to base. Lindholme Gear was dropped before two more Hudsons arrived to take over the operation. One, piloted by Warrant Officer Passlow, dropped an airborne lifeboat to the survivors, and they were able to transfer to this from their dinghy. Unfortunately, the parachute lines snarled its propellers so the engines wouldn't start. They hoisted the sail but made little progress, before other Hudsons directed maritime craft to the lifeboat, and the survivors were subsequently landed safely at Immingham.[138]

Chapter 5

Service with Ferry/Transport Command

Another less well-publicised, but nonetheless important, aspect of the war in the air was the role performed by Ferry Command, later reorganised as RAF Transport Command. Lord Beaverbrook, as Prime Minister Winston Churchill's influential Minister of Aircraft Production, formulated plans in mid-1940 to fly American-manufactured bombers to Britain to supply the RAF. This was before the Japanese attack on Pearl Harbor had occurred, when America was still technically a neutral country but willing to help her allies. By VE-Day, about 10,000 military aircraft had been successfully ferried across the Atlantic from North America to Britain. This figure included an array of American-built aircraft, including over 600 Lockheed Hudsons. Other types included the Lockheed Ventura, Boeing B-17 Flying Fortress, Consolidated B-24 Liberator, North American B-25 Mitchell, Martin B-26 Marauder, and Consolidated PBY Catalina flying boats. Notably, the Liberator and Catalina proved particularly useful to Coastal Command in the war against the U-boats.

The set-up posed many challenges, not least initially owing to America's neutrality. As Air Commodore 'Taffy' Powell (Senior Air Officer to Air Chief Marshal Sir Frederick Bowhill, the AOC Ferry Command) remarked, in relation to the B-17, 'foreign personnel from the RAF were not allowed to take any active part in flying or operating' these aircraft, so there was 'little training, some familiarisation, but lots of bonhomie'. The six aircraft of the initial batch 'proceeded to cross the United States via Wright Field, Dayton, where they were camouflaged and RAF roundels added', before being diverted to Floyd Bennett Field, Long Island, a USN station. This caused a commotion amongst the local civilian population, who didn't recognise the strange-looking aircraft, but eventually they were flown on to Britain.[1]

Regardless of the aircraft type to be flown, another significant issue facing the ferry organisation was the weather. Flying across the North Atlantic in winter was extremely daunting, even to well-trained pilots. As Canadian ferry pilot Don McVicar explained, the weather potentially provided a huge obstacle to anyone contemplating this journey by air in winter. 'Towering ice-filled clouds' could literally 'dump an aircraft into the sea', but desperate times called for desperate measures.[2] Pre-war experience of weather forecasting in the Atlantic proved invaluable, especially as a meteorological office established by the Canadian

Department of Transport in 1935 to handle Atlantic traffic was made available to the ferry organisation. In particular, forecasters had to predict the probable altitude when icing would occur, and pilots were instructed to 'fly over the top'. An aircraft's de-icing equipment and the provision of oxygen for the crew were important in such conditions. Forecasters had to 'indicate winds – their probable velocity and direction – for headwinds may add hours to the flying time', and information was constructed from 'reports made by aircraft at terminal points, by survey from those points, and by study of world-wide weather movements'.[3] Even when it was spring in Britain, 'aircraft were being serviced, and despatched from Montreal and Gander in fifty sometimes sixty degrees of frost'.[4]

Another natural phenomenon encountered by ferry crews (and other wartime aircrew) was 'St Elmo's Fire', caused by a build-up of static electricity around an aircraft. While it wasn't usually physically damaging, it could be extremely unnerving. Don McVicar reported that 'it scared us out of our wits' when he and his crew encountered a 'display' during one trans-Atlantic flight, when their aircraft was already suffering problems.

> Purple, orange and white balls formed on the windshield. Then the propellers became circular sheets of varying colour. The balls rolled over our heads and off the wings. Inside the cockpit, two small spheres of intense blue roamed aimlessly around and then headed through the fuselage and disappeared into the tower where Baker [his flight engineer] beat them out of his small window to the accompaniment of furious oaths.[5]

Initially, Canadian Pacific Air Services was ordered to assemble crews and prepare to deliver twenty-one Lockheed Hudson aircraft fitted with long-range petrol tanks. The first seven of these crossed the Atlantic under the command of D.C.T. Bennett, the Australian long-distance flight record holder, who later became an air vice-marshal and leader of the wartime Pathfinder Force. The flight left Gander, Newfoundland, on 10 November 1940, and six aircraft arrived safely in Aldergrove, Northern Ireland, while the remaining one landed safely elsewhere. They attempted to fly in formation, although later on, aircraft being ferried across the Atlantic often flew individually. Navigation was largely down to Bennett, who recalled that three-quarters of the way over they ran into a front earlier and higher than expected. Having attempted to climb over it and failed, the aircraft faced dense cloud and had to separate.

> I had no particular worry about the navigational side of the flight for the other aircraft. The icing, however, was fairly severe, particularly as I endeavoured to climb over the front, and was still in the 'thick' at 22,000

feet. I only hoped the others had sufficient knowledge of icing and that their de-icing facilities worked satisfactorily.[6]

From these relatively humble origins, the organisation was expanded to become ATFERO, or Atlantic Ferrying Organization, and then, on 20 July 1941, it became RAF Ferry Command under Air Chief Marshal Sir Frederick Bowhill, the former Commander-in-Chief of Coastal Command. It retained its distinctive character with a mixture of civilian and military personnel, and according to an official booklet, these 'continued to work together both in the air and upon the ground'.[7] Air Commodore Powell asserted that there was no problem in a military organisation subsuming what had been an overtly civilian set-up. 'I think it remained a healthy organisation because the RAF, in spite of the clout of an Air Chief Marshal, did not come in and change everything.' Some moves may even have been morale-boosting, such as the adoption by all personnel in mid-1941 of RAF type insignia, including 'cap badges, wings and half-wings, which were worn with chrome buttons on dark-blue winter uniforms and khaki in the summer', plus RAF style stripes were issued for 'senior captains, co-pilots and other aircrew'. Consequently, personnel became 'reasonably sure of officer status being given to those who got into strange situations or became prisoners of war'.[8]

Several key personnel, such as pilot/navigators, wireless operators and flight engineers, came from civilian airlines, including Trans-Canada Airlines (later Air Canada), and the British Overseas Airways Corporation (BOAC), created in 1939. For example, Jock Cunningham was an ex-BOAC wireless operator who had 'responded to an army reserve commitment and when the ferry call came was teaching army signallers at Catterick in Yorkshire. His talents shone through in the war. He retired as a Wing Commander to become co-founder of a modest electronic business named Racal.'[9]

Pilots were recruited from a variety of sources. According to Don McVicar, 'it was a truly cosmopolitan gathering of talent'.[10] Many came from countries overrun by the Nazis, including Belgians, Czechs, Free French, Norwegians and Poles. These served alongside Australian, British, Canadian, New Zealand and South African personnel, and there was even a Cuban. Additionally, there were what Squadron Leader Tony Spooner dubbed 'American mercenaries'. These men had a variety of experience to draw upon, but according to him were largely 'in it for dollars and "kicks"'. By 'British standards' they were 'absurdly highly paid and soon became a law unto themselves'.[11] Not all personnel proved acceptable. One navigator, who joined the organisation direct from civilian life, opened the cockpit window on his side of the aircraft and stuck his hand into the icy blast. 'He apparently thought that as his fingers were extremely cold the procedure for recovery was to put them out into a minus 40 degree Centigrade, 170 knot breeze.'[12] Unsurprisingly, he was swiftly rejected and sent back homewards to California.

Dorval Airport in Montreal became a major hub on the North American side and a receiver of land-based aircraft from American factories, while Prestwick, on the west coast of Scotland, was the main point of arrival in Britain. From there, male or female pilots from the Air Transport Auxiliary would usually take over and deliver specific aircraft to where they were required. Air Commodore Powell explained that, in 1941, 'the Ferry Command parish' encompassed the 'north Atlantic ... made up of the land plane route through Gander and the Catalina route via Bermuda to the Clyde. Within a year we were also on the south Atlantic when the swing of battle in North Africa made it essential for aircraft reinforcements to be made more directly.'[13] A further impression of the various North Atlantic routes can be gained from an official booklet, which stated:

> Nine hundred and fifty miles nearer to Britain [from Dorval] is the Newfoundland base at Gander, from which direct landplane flights go to Britain and where seaplanes for Bermuda can take off from Gander Lake. Eight hundred and twenty miles north-east from Montreal is Labrador airfield, from which medium bombers or aircraft with limited range can take off for the American bases in Greenland or fly the 1,550-mile trip to the British staging post established at Reykjavik, Iceland. Outbound aircraft from Gander also use Iceland on occasion – a trip of 1,620 miles as against the direct hop of 2,000 miles. ... Seaplanes reach British hands at Elizabeth City, an American base on the mainland of North Carolina. From there these are ferried either to Bermuda or to Newfoundland. Their ultimate destination is also Scotland – a 3,400-mile trip from Bermuda.[14]

Under Bennett, a system was evolved that made use of RAF navigators undergoing training in Canada. Consequently, while most pilots remained with the ferry organisation on a permanent basis, these navigators completed one trip only. Lacking 'practical operational experience', they were first trained on two long flights by a captain (pilot) who was also responsible for the serviceability of his aircraft. Both 'then went up to Gander, which was a further navigational trip for the youngster behind him, and they set off across the Atlantic'.[15] Ferry crews required numerous skills, and these were similar to those favoured by Coastal Command. Ideally, they had to 'be steady, assured very patient, and capable of sitting for long hours methodically carrying out the job'. There were also 'special characteristics which have to be developed. They must be "jacks of all trades", ready to cope with unforeseen circumstances in outlandish places. They must understand loading problems in various types of aircraft. They must be tactful, and able to handle passengers.'[16]

Proud Ulsterman Squadron Leader Terrance Bulloch, who became a leading anti-U-boat ace with Coastal Command, spent part of his war service as an

Atlantic ferry pilot. According to his biographer, the experience heightened his skill at navigation and 'interest in meteorology and it confirmed the good opinion he held about American-built aircraft', all characteristics that were to be useful to him during his later wartime flying career.[17]

During his tenure, Bennett recounted that there were no serious navigational failures, so the system appeared to work well. Yet navigation could be fraught with difficulties. A veteran ferry pilot recounted the challenges he faced when taking over the navigator's role while trying to deliver a Catalina flying boat via the 'Atlantic bridge'. Over the Greenland coast, 'I tried to pinpoint our position. Not an easy job. All fjords look alike.' Subsequently, 'the northern lights were staging their ghostly dance across the sky,' something that to the casual observer might have been beautiful and entertaining, but 'to a navigator they were a headache. At best he would have trouble seeing his stars through their ever changing bands of light. At worst he would lose any chance of astro [astro-navigation].' In freezing conditions, with ice building up on the aircraft outside and frost on the inside, he relied 'on a dead-reckoning course over the most hostile of lands with no allowance for an unknown wind'.[18]

Unsurprisingly, crashes occurred, and were often 'of a major nature'. The weather and human error were significant causes of these accidents. In one case, confusion between Flying Control and the pilot of an aircraft resulted in tragedy. Australian pilot Ken Garden, ferrying a B-24 from Canada, was approaching the British coast when his position was misidentified and he was instructed 'to descend on a particular heading and this took him into the side of the Mull of Kintyre'.[19] All aboard the aircraft were killed.

Onboard conditions were another issue, and even American-manufactured aircraft weren't necessarily regarded as comfortable by aircrew. Trans-Atlantic flights were typically arduous undertakings, made all the more difficult by adverse weather. According to one pilot, 'the heaters provided in the B-24 either blew up with violent heat or completely failed to function.'[20] Another discovered that the automatic pilot in the B-24 didn't always work, giving crews no respite, plus at higher altitudes (over 10,000 feet), they had to don oxygen masks that were 'poorly designed ... which cut into my face, especially the bridge of my nose. I hated the constriction, and the smell of the brittle rubber made me feel sick.'[21] On the Catalina, 'the pilots' seats were massive and uncomfortable, and the control column could have been used to steer a battleship.' The aircraft was also extremely noisy as there was no insulation, so crew were advised to wear earplugs.[22]

For ferry pilots, each aircraft type tended to exhibit particular characteristics or foibles. The Hudson was a 'stubby converted airliner with its distinctive twin rudders almost touching the floor', modified as a stop-gap measure to serve as a light twin-engine bomber with the RAF, until better designs entered service. One instructor reckoned it was an 'honest aircraft' with good single-engine performance, but simultaneously cautioned: 'Handle it like a thoroughbred and it would treat you just fine. Abuse it and it would bite back.'[23] This was because it possessed wicked characteristics, including 'an ability to drop a wing if bounced and quite a nasty stall if one was so stupid as to get too slow'.[24] According to Don McVicar, it 'had killed many men, who had forgotten their pre-take-off cockpit drill', especially in relation to 'the elevator trim tab setting' used on landing to help bring the tail down. Despite this, it proved 'a great aircraft to fly', particularly 'at light weights'.[25] Contrastingly, he didn't favour Ventura, a 'big, awkward beast' that 'was a sort of elongated, over-powered' version of the Hudson.[26]

Typically, pilots completed at least five trips on twin-engine types, before being tasked with ferrying a large four-engine B-17 or B-24. One found that when compared with the B-24, the B-17's 'controls were feather-light, but I could see the big vertical fin and rudder, combined with a tail-wheel, could be a real handful in a cross-wind'.[27] However, once he'd become accustomed to the heavy controls on the B-24, 'he learned to like the ugly black monster'.[28] The B-25 Mitchell, a twin-engine medium bomber, proved even better, and was 'a dream to fly'.[29] It was 'a tricycled [landing] gear bomber, powered with Wright 1750 horsepower engines that pulled it through the air at speeds that were more than 100 miles per hour faster than our Hudsons'. With a beautifully laid out cockpit, it made many ferry pilots desperate to fly one when it first appeared.[30]

While the Catalina flying boat was arguably less glamourous than a B-17 or B-25, and not necessarily the most comfortable, many ferry crews admired it for its durability. The same couldn't be said of the twin-engine B-26 Marauder, dubbed the 'Widow Maker', which suffered from numerous design flaws, including a questionable ability to fly on one engine owing to lack of adequate rudder or rudder trim tab, and an awkward fuel selector/transfer system – a concern for any pilot expected to fly long distances. When Don McVicar first encountered one, he recalled, the short (65-foot) wing looked troublesome, as did the large Curtiss Electric four-blade props that hung close to the ground. 'If you made a hard landing it was quite conceivable that a blade would touch and come flying through the fuselage,' narrowly missing the pilot, if he was lucky.[31]

Despite the difficulties that ferry crews encountered, they completed flights of notable endurance, sometimes setting records. Terrance Bulloch brought one of the first B-17 Flying Fortresses to Britain, after intensive training on that type with 30th Air Bombardment Squadron USAAF, even including instruction on the much vaunted Norden bombsight, then still shrouded in secrecy. With favourable winds at higher altitudes, he and Ian Patterson, his co-pilot, took their B-17 'up to 30,000 feet, a high average speed was maintained and the 1,832 nautical miles (2,110 miles) to their destination in Scotland were covered in 8.40 hours at an average speed of 245 mph. It established a trans-Atlantic record which was to stand for a long while.'[32]

Usually, trans-Atlantic flights took longer, even when non-stop. A B-24 Liberator piloted by Captain S.T.B. Cripps DFC took 12 hours 51 minutes to fly non-stop from Montreal to Britain, while a Catalina flying boat flown from Bermuda to Britain by Captain R.E. Perlick completed its journey in 19 hours and 50 minutes.[33]

Having ferried an aircraft to Britain, pilots and other aircrew had to be transported back to North America if they were to continue their vital work. Two options were available. They could either make the return journey by sea or fly across the Atlantic, once a return ferry service was operational. Converted B-24 Liberators provided this return ferry service. Typically, conditions aboard these were primitive, their armament being stripped out, and bomb bay doors sealed up. A vivid description of these makeshift arrangements is provided by Air Commodore Powell:

> The bomb bay itself then had a wooden floor fitted and another wooden floor went in the tail behind the entry point, which was underneath the fuselage. A fairly simple passenger oxygen system was fitted with up to 20 individual masks but the provision of adequate heat defeated us for a long time mainly because of sealing difficulties. Sleeping bags, pillows and rugs made up the luxury fittings but I must say that the sleeping bags of that era did not compare with the wind-proof, light weight products of today. All passengers had full flying kit: sidcot suits [full-body flying suits that remained in use with the RAF into the 1950s], overboots, gloves and leather helmets.[34]

These Liberators were draughty and extremely noisy, owing to the proximity of the passengers to the exhausts for the four large underwing engines. According to one experienced ferry pilot, who experienced several return flights:

> The bomb bay reminded me of a torture cell where you can't stand up straight or stretch out at full length. All stretching of sinews and muscles had to be done on the bias, so to speak. In order to pack in the maximum number of bodies we alternated head to feet. That meant a big pair of stinking flight boots on either side to keep you company. Sardines have it better.[35]

Poor weather and human error again caused horrific accidents. One B-24, having taken off from Prestwick, flew into cloud and smashed straight into the Isle of Arran. All on board were lost. When another crash killed a number of American 'mercenary' pilots, others responded by mounting a 'strike', which temporarily suspended the service.

By comparison, travelling by sea was slower, and convoys risked falling prey to U-boats. On a voyage aboard the *Tetela*, 'an ex-banana boat ... built for neither speed nor comfort', Terrance Bulloch recalled they were attacked by a Fw Condor, a long-range German bomber/transport aircraft, and progress proved 'painfully slow'. The *Tetela* had a maximum speed of around 9 knots and in 1941, there were few naval vessels available to mount an effective convoy system, plus to avoid U-boats, they'd been tasked with maintaining a northerly route via the Minches.[36]

In addition to the North Atlantic, a ferry/supply route was established in the South Atlantic, which became increasingly important as the focus of the war shifted from Europe towards the Middle East and Mediterranean. This witnessed thousands of pounds worth of freight and large numbers of aircraft, notably light bombers, being delivered from west to east.

> The mainstay of this traffic, carrying to Africa so much freight and many passengers, including the returning delivery crews, is a fleet of Liberators which run a scheduled service back and forth from Florida and the Bahamas to the Gold Coast, a distance of over 3,000 miles.[37]

The trading post of Takoradi on the Gold Coast played a major role in supporting the supply network across the South Atlantic. Here a major base was built by the RAF, eventually requiring around 7,000 men to work efficiently, an effort that proved invaluable during the North African campaign. It was 'an air-oasis upon that tropical coast, surrounded by the palm trees and rank vegetation of the bush, by mosquito-breeding swamps and pools, and hazy, shark-infested sea'.[38] Aircraft, especially single-seat fighters such as the Hawker Hurricane and American-manufactured Curtiss Tomahawk, were shipped in crates to Takoradi then reassembled. Subsequently, they were flown to Cairo, Egypt, in stages via Lagos, Kano, Maiduguri, Fort Lamy (held by Free French forces), Geneina and Khartoum. This entailed a gruelling five-day journey, with ferry pilots 'flying over hundreds of miles of thick forest or great patches of emptiness with only the faint trace of a wadi or an outcrop of rock for landmarks, where engine trouble or a navigational mistake could end in a lonely death'.[39]

Aircraft even launched an 'ammunition lift' to resupply ground forces at El Alamein during the campaign in North Africa, which helped turn the course of the war, although this stretched 'the limits of non-operational' status conferred upon Ferry Command.[40] As the war progressed, new routes were opened up for ferrying aircraft owing to the changing ground situation. This was particularly evident when flying aircraft from Britain to India and on to the Far East once the Germans collapsed in Italy. From October 1943 until August 1945, Wing Commander Harry Blee served as a flight engineer with a Heavy Conversion Unit that was reformed as 358 Squadron at Jessore, east of Calcutta. It was equipped with Liberator bombers, largely engaged on 'special operations' mounting supply drops to dissident tribes and British Army officers fighting the Japanese behind the lines in Burma and Indo-China (Vietnam). He recounted that once:

> They kicked the Germans out of Italy – that was the key to the whole thing – that meant you could go through the narrow gap in the Mediterranean, and they were out of North Africa, so you could go through the Mediterranean on to Africa and off to India, which previously was not possible. That changed the ball game. The result was they could fly aircraft that route as well. When that happened they decided that any conversion work done could be done in the UK and crews fly their own aircraft straight out to India. The HCU was disbanded and converted into 358 Squadron. We went up to Jessore and operated from there instead of Bangalore.[41]

On 11 March 1943, RAF Transport Command was established by parliamentary proclamation to deal with the 'increased number of transport squadrons' and 'control their operations throughout the world'.[42] Effectively, it incorporated the organisation that existed under Ferry Command, and bore responsibility for 'operation of all Service Air Lines, Service Air Movements of freight and personnel, and Overseas and Inter-continental delivery of aircraft by operational ferry air routes'.[43] As the war progressed, Transport Command became increasingly involved in assisting military operations. In July 1943, it supported Operation Husky, the Allied invasion of Sicily, and later that year was earmarked to support Operation Accolade, an amphibious assault to capture Rhodes and the Dodecanese islands that had been abandoned in light of German opposition and because of the situation on the Italian front, where an assault on Anzio was planned.

During June 1944, Transport Command helped spearhead Operation Overlord (D-Day), the Allied invasion of Europe, when rugged, reliable Dakota transport aircraft from 46 Group – the European Transport Group – dropped airborne units and supplies, and towed gliders. Having survived flying Beauforts in the Mediterranean, and served in Britain as a navigational instructor, E.F. Carlisle-Brown was posted to 271 Squadron at Down Ampney, near Swindon, in April 1944, shortly before D-Day.

> Our duties on Transport Command Dakota aircraft were the dropping of army parachutists and supplies into the battle area landing ground (zone), the towing of airborne infantry in Horsa gliders to the battle landing ground (zone) and then at a later date on the return trip to Down Ampney, transporting the wounded men back from Normandy in France to the Down Ampney hospital. Prior to this the Squadron carried out

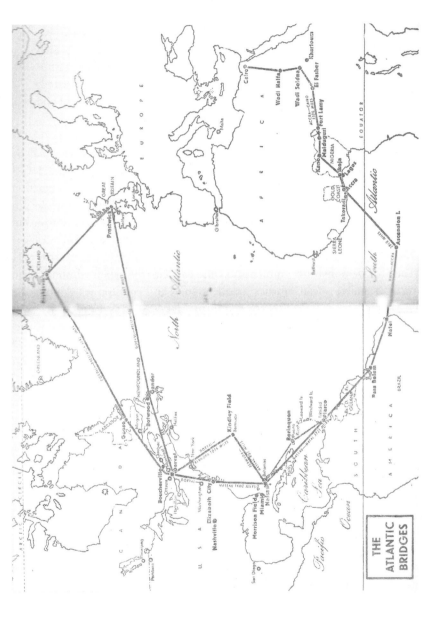

A map showing the various Atlantic ferry routes established during the war – as outlined in Chapter 5. (Atlantic Bridge: HMSO, 1945)

many training flights over England as great accuracy was required in map reading and dropping troops at the correct point. Because of my previous experience I became second pilot/map reader, using one inch to the mile Ordnance Survey maps. Navigation was easier than in the Mediterranean theatre of war as we had the benefit of radar 'Gee' navigation apparatus and charts which gave figure co-ordinates on the radar screen which were transferred to lattice Mercator charts, giving accurate fixes within a couple of miles; also radar 'Rebecca' and 'Eureka' equipment assisted; 'Rebecca' sending out a signal from the dropping zone (DZ) and the aircraft homing on to it with 'Eureka', the receiving set in the aircraft.[44]

As indicated, casualty evacuation was another important function performed by transport aircraft, particularly the Dakota, a militarised version of the DC-3 airliner. Shortly after D-Day, the RAF established a Casualty Air Evacuation Centre to receive casualties, treat and sort them at the end of their journey by air. This was in addition to the seaborne evacuation of casualties from the invasion beaches. Crucial to this effort were WAAF medical orderlies, who landed close to the Normandy battlefront and dealt with casualties while they were airborne. They had to demonstrate immense skill, particularly when dealing with awkward cases such as head injuries, tracheotomies and colostomies. Among the first WAAF medical orderlies to see action in June 1944 was Leading Aircraft Woman (LACW) Edna Birbeck from Wellingborough, Northamptonshire. She recalled:

> The flights to the Continent were approved by the Air Ministry and soon operated on a regular basis. We nurses carried large flasks of tea with us on the aircraft, which was most acceptable by the wounded. We also had our pannier of medical supplies. The initial flights to France were all to emergency airfields, lacking any facilities, but later as the front progressed fully equipped airfields were used. The nature of the Dakota freight carried outbound – ammunition, petrol, general war supplies etc. – prevented the aircraft carrying the Red Cross insignia. Quite often we had to night stop, or carry supplies from one base to another, often visiting several before we eventually picked up a load of casualties.[45]

Transport Command went on to support airborne operations extensively during Operation Market Garden in September 1944, the ill-fated attempt to seize key bridges in Holland that would enable an invasion route to be established into Northern Germany, and again in March 1945, during Operation Varsity, the Allied effort to bounce the Rhine. For pilots and aircrews from Transport Command, sorties to Arnhem often proved horrendous owing to the amount of opposition encountered. Years later, one Dakota pilot recounted that he narrowly escaped being shot down over Holland owing to an excellently executed act of flak suppression by accompanying fighters.

> we were towing gliders at full throttle at 90 miles an hour, and the outstanding thing of my first experience of this sort of nasty anti-aircraft fire, because we were in daylight you see, was going up the Scheldt there before turning north to Arnhem. ... We were just a couple of miles apart. That is all and suddenly there was anti-aircraft fire on the aircraft in front of me and I thought oh well, my turn next, and out of the blue came a couple of Typhoons armed with rockets ... and they just blew the whole gun battery down there, was blown to pieces. ... So I thought well, thank you very much, and then went on to Arnhem.[46]

During the bitter fighting at Arnhem, Flight Lieutenant David Lord DFC, a Dakota pilot with 271 Squadron, attempted to resupply 1st Airborne Division, and flew low, as air supply drops were conducted at 600–700 feet. The anti-aircraft fire was intense, and his aircraft was hit twice. Realising that two of the supply containers were still on board, he commenced another run, even though his starboard wing risked collapsing. Having ordered his crew to bail out, he died at the controls as the plane crashed attempting a second supply run, and was awarded a posthumous Victorian Cross. Part of his citation explained that by 'returning to the drop zone a second time and, finally, remaining at the controls to give his crew a chance to escape', he had 'displayed supreme valour and self-sacrifice. There could be no finer example of sustained courage and determination by a transport pilot on air supply operations.'[47]

In the Far East, what became Troop Carrier Command performed a major role in supporting operations in that theatre. The experience of No. 177 Wing, initially comprising 62, 117 and 194 Squadrons, in Burma, provides a case in point. Originally trained to carry 50th (Indian) Parachute Brigade, each of the Wing's aircraft carried a pilot and navigator, plus two wireless operator/air gunners (Wop/AG) who doubled up as 'jumpmasters'. The brigade initially assisted the Long Range Penetration Groups (Chindits), pioneered by Major General Orde Wingate, before more widely meeting the supply requirements of 14th Army. In eight months of operations it transported 36,102 tons of animals, stores and equipment, 31,217 troops, and evacuated 23,898 casualties, while suffering sixty-one personnel killed, and four wounded.[48]

Once the Japanese had surrendered on 14 August 1945, Transport Command was required to employ its aircraft to help repatriate large numbers of British Service personnel, including former Far East prisoners of war, or FEPOWs, who'd endured a harrowing experience at the hands of the Japanese. Having completed a tour with Bomber Command, Flight Lieutenant Brian Sibree was posted to 187 Squadron, operating Dakotas with Transport Command, as the war in Europe entered its final stages. He became involved in the 'Trooping to India' programme, it being faster to fly reinforcements to the Far East rather than rely on troopships. After VJ-Day, the programme was scaled back, but his squadron continued to fly back and forth to India until May 1946.

> We still flew troops out there for various duties, and brought back tour expired people, those who were needing medical treatment and the POWs from the infamous Japanese camps. The ones we flew back were the fittest and I can only ask: 'What were the other poor chaps like?' having seen the fittest. When crossing the English Channel, we invited as many as we could cope with, to come up to the cockpit and see the White Cliffs of Dover as we flew in. Their faces told it all. Even so, I don't think any of us realised at that time, just how bad it had really been for them. I hope we gave them something good to remember, for once.[49]

Rupert Cooling was another of those pilots employed with Transport Command late in war. This was after surviving two operational tours on Wellingtons, one with Bomber Command in Europe, the other in North Africa/Mediterranean during 1940–43. There followed a period flying Blenheims and Avro Ansons in Britain. These were employed to drop smoke bombs and explosive charges, in an effort to simulate battlefield conditions for troops training ahead of D-Day. Like many who joined Transport Command, he hoped it would enable him to forge a career in civil aviation after the war. He experienced handling the famous Douglas C-47 Skytrain, or Dakota, as it was known to the British. This proved awkward because of his physical stature. Another type he encountered was the twin-engine Vickers Warwick. Although conceived as a bomber, it arrived too late, so some were deployed as RAF transport aircraft. It was bedevilled by technical issues, especially relating to the engines. Ultimately, Cooling hoped to fly the Avro York, a large four-engine passenger/cargo transport aircraft, based around components of the Lancaster, which entered service towards the end of the war. In mid-1944, he:

> went down to Crosby-on-Eden where they had Dakotas. And I did two weeks of the ground course and the Wing Commander (Flying) said to me 'Can you get into a Dakota?' And I said 'I don't know. I've never tried.' And he said, 'right, we better try you first of all.' So they put me in a Dakota and instead of having the stick between your knees it comes up and cranks over. When my feet were on the rudder bar although straight and level was fine, I couldn't push the stick forward to get the tail up, and I couldn't get the stick back to bring the tail down for landing. So they

sent me down to Bramcote [Nottinghamshire] and I did another OTU on Wellingtons believe it or not, and was posted to Warwicks at RAF Blackbushe [Hampshire].

Warwicks – They were very nice aircraft, only problem was they had French Pratt & Whitney engines. The tale was that the French had ordered these engines [from America] before the fall of France. When France collapsed the British said 'oh we'll have them' and brought them back to this country. No one knew what to do with them and someone said 'well let's try them in a Warwick. We had a lot of engine trouble, back-firing and missing and so forth. Once I had to do a forced landing at Niece and I was there for about four days while they decided what to do about it, and they decided they couldn't do anything about it. So I left the aircraft there and came home as a passenger in a Dakota. Then I was hoping that I would be posted to Yorks to four-engined stuff. And the RAF said 'the Japanese have packed in. We're not going to start teaching you how to fly Yorks, you wouldn't finish the course before your demob.'[50]

Like their counterparts in other Commands, personnel from Ferry / Transport Command and Troop Carrier Command were equally capable of dedicated, brave service, even if their role perhaps appeared less glamourous than that of aircrew engaged on direct combat sorties. The following awards were received by personnel from No. 177 Wing during its war in Burma: twenty-three Distinguished Flying Crosses; one Bar to the DFC; one British Empire Medal (BEM); one Distinguished Flying Medal; plus six American Distinguished Flying Crosses.[51]

Having completed a tour on Wellingtons as an NCO navigator with 38 Squadron, Reggie Wainwright was posted to 24 Squadron during September 1941. For the next two years he served as a navigator, mainly on the Lockheed Hudson, flying around Britain, to Iceland, intensively in the Mediterranean, and between locations in Britain and the Mediterranean. In January 1943, by which time he'd been promoted to warrant officer, he received the Air Force Medal (AFM) for his role in helping to resupply Malta. During 1941–43, the island of Malta, which held a strategic position in the Mediterranean, was besieged by the Germans and Italians, who at one time dropped a greater weight of bombs on its airfields than Coventry had received in the infamous raid of October 1940. According to Wing Commander Patrick Gibbs, who served there commanding a torpedo bomber unit, the blockade was strict but not total. Transport aircraft were able to bring in supplies from Gibraltar and Egypt under cover of darkness, and then take off with passengers, usually civilians desperate to flee Malta.

The transports landed about midnight, unloaded their cargo, which usually consisted of Spitfire spares, and after taking on board just sufficient petrol to reach their destination, left again within the hour, the service operating with the matter of fact regularity of a peacetime airline.[52]

Reggie Wainwright's AFM citation gives a clear indication of what conditions were like for aircrew mounting this much-needed resupply effort, which helped keep Malta in the war and prevented it from falling to the Axis powers.

Ferry Command
902557 Sergeant R. Wainwright, No. 24 Squadron, 44 Group

This N.C.O. has been employed as a navigator of an unarmed and overloaded aircraft operating the shuttle between Gibraltar and Malta for the conveyance of aircraft spares to Malta. In the midst of intense enemy air operations and despite the bad weather and the difficulty of making night landings at Malta without knowing whether the runways were obstructed or cratered, Flight Sergeant Wainwright completed 299 flying hours in 7 weeks. During one period he flew 79 hours in 10 days.

The excellence of this Flight Sergeant's navigation contributed much to the success achieved.[53]

After a period spent training under the auspices of the Central Navigation School in Britain during late 1943, Reggie Wainwright converted to the Avro York, often flying under Squadron Leader Jack Matthews. In mid-1944, he was posted to the communications squadron with South East Asia Command (SEAC), and his aircraft often employed as the personnel transport of Lord Louis Mountbatten, Supreme Allied Commander South-East Asia (1943–46). By the end of the war in August 1945, he'd amassed considerable flying/navigational experience, as reflected by his log book. He recorded the following flying times: a grand total of 1,750.60 hours by day and 1,150.20 hours by night, much of which had been acquired with Ferry Command, or Transport Command as it became, and was to serve him well post-war when he embarked on a career in civil aviation.[54]

During 1945–46, ferry operations were gradually run down, although not before a concerted effort had been made to support the largely American operations in the Pacific theatre. Overall, Transport Command had played a significant role in the war. However, with the reduction of the armed forces post-war, it was dramatically downsized, so that by mid-1946, only about 540 aircraft were at its disposal worldwide. Coupled with this, the ending of Lend-Lease ceased the supply of American-manufactured aircraft, such as the Liberator and Dakota, which had proved invaluable in RAF wartime service. Most of the Liberators were returned to America, while the Dakota soldiered on with the RAF for several years, and notably was employed during the Berlin airlift in 1948 and in supporting counter-insurgency operations during the Malayan Emergency. Another challenge that rapidly emerged during the aftermath of the war was that with demobilisation, like other branches of the RAF, Transport Command lost large numbers of key personnel, including aircrews and maintenance/ground staff.

Chapter 6

Ground Crews and Other Non-Flying Personnel

Much attention has been devoted to the aircraft of the wartime RAF and the men who flew them. This accent on man and machine is understandable, especially given the heroic efforts of Fighter and Bomber Commands. Yet, to get aircrews airborne required a host of non-flying, ground-based support services, which although seemingly less glamorous to the public, were essential to the success of operational units. For every member of aircrew there were about seven ground-based personnel with various trades whose primary task was to keep them flying. The RAF ran its own apprentice school and drew upon personnel with experience of civilian industries who volunteered or were conscripted. As the war progressed, increasing numbers of trades were opened up to the WAAF, and so women also became involved with aspects of aircraft maintenance.

At officer level were numerous positions not directly involved on operational flying but provided invaluable support, covering areas such as engineering, intelligence, signals, and meteorology. Many airmen and WAAFs never went near an aircraft during their service, but instead were confined to a host of domestic, clerical and administrative duties at training centres and other establishments that contributed towards the overall smooth running of the wartime RAF.

Many such duties were carried out by what in RAF slang were known as 'erks', that is, airmen or airwomen below the rank of corporal. According to wartime instrument repairer, or 'basher', Ted Mawdsley, the term erk was 'a corruption of "airk", which is shortened from aircraftman', the lowest rank in the air force.[1] Although technically applying to all airmen and airwomen, erk became synonymous with ground crews specifically concerned with the maintenance/servicing of aircraft. This was essential, but often overlooked. Although not all ground crew would've recognised the analogy, some likened themselves to the artillery, as effectively, they thought that by readying an aircraft for take-off, they were 'firing a long range gun (albeit with a man in the missile!)'.[2]

On enlistment, airmen and airwomen were assigned to one of 300 trades within the trade structure employed by the RAF. Eric Marsden joined the RAFVR before the war, and was called up in 1939 as a trainee fitter. He remembered that there were five main trade groups. These reflected the degree of technical skill and standard expected, i.e. whether a person was a top fitter or lacked mechanical or technical training. The most skilled tradesmen were mustered in Group 1, and a Fitter 1 was classed as a comprehensive trade able to work on engines and airframes, and to reach the rank of sergeant, a man normally had to be a Fitter 1. In contrast, Fitter 2 was a single trade specialising either in engines, air frames or instruments. Group 2 incorporated flight mechanic (air frames), flight mechanic (engines), armourers, electricians, and instrument bashers, and Groups 3 and 4 were ancillary trades such as clerks and station HQ personnel. The lowest grade, Group 5, comprised new recruits and aircraft hands general duties (ACH/GD) tasked with unskilled work. A further Group M concerned mainly medical personnel, such as dental and nursing orderlies.[3]

The experiences of ground crews, or 'erks'

Many members of ground crews served throughout the war on stations at home and overseas, and thus accumulated six or seven years' service in a variety of settings by the time they demobilised. The experience of Leslie Baker provides a case in point. Having qualified as a fitter, he was posted to 58 Squadron at RAF Linton-on-Ouse, Yorkshire, on 2 August 1940, where he worked on Whitley Mk V bombers. By June 1941, he'd been promoted to corporal and posted to Fighter Command. He served as ground crew with 1455 Flight, equipped with Douglas Boston 'Havocs', fitted with the Turbinlite system, which proved of limited effectiveness in night-fighter work. Then, in April 1942, he volunteered for what was described as 'A Dangerous Task'. This entailed undergoing training with the Commandos, as 'apparently, three small "Commando Units" were to be formed, to go in with the assault troops [during amphibious landings], and to service aircraft as soon as landing fields could be found.' Subsequently, he served with 3203 Commando in North Africa, during the invasions of Sicily and Italy, including Salerno, spending considerable time on advanced airstrips near the front lines. During December 1943, he contracted yellow jaundice, and on recovering was posted to a maintenance unit (MU) near Naples, before ending his war in Italy and Greece with 12 Squadron, Desert Air Force. On demobilisation in January 1946, he'd served six and a half years with the RAF, over half of which was spent overseas.[4]

Work could be extremely demanding, even though ground crews didn't necessarily come under fire. When Harry Old was posted to RAF Debden, a key airfield in Essex, in late 1939, the operational tempo was high.

> We were averaging out at about seven or eight scrambles a day. The rest
> of the time we used to eat and sleep in the hangar because we were a day
> and night fighter squadron with Blenheims and Hurricanes. We just did

not get away. We never even got our clothes off! We were allowed twenty minutes to go and get a bath, a wash and a shave, and that was it, per day.[5]

Eric Marsden recounted the hectic period he experienced during the summer of 1940, by which time he'd been posted as a flight mechanic to 145 Squadron at RAF Tangmere, Sussex. An essential aspect of the ground crews' work with that squadron was developing practices that reduced turnaround times required to service aircraft. A system was evolved whereby it proved possible to service a Hurricane and have it flying again within eight minutes.

> Everyone in the Flight should learn to do everything. So that we already took for granted for example that mechanic (airframe) and mechanic (engine) would do interchangeably quite a bit regarding re-fuelling, changing oxygen bottles, things of that order. ... We had to learn at least three-quarters of rearming, so that if our aircraft came in for the petrol bowser or the oil, we immediately set to, opened up the panels on the wings, the gun bay panel on the wings and opened up the guns and took out the empty or partially used ammunition tanks and put these by the aircraft, and the armourers by this time would have done their job and come down the whole of the flight line dishing out new ammunition tanks. We picked these loaded ammunition tanks up, put them into place, laid the belts of ammunition into place, and then opened the breach of the gun and left it like that. Meanwhile, myself, or the rigger would have opened up the side panel on the starboard side of the aircraft behind the pilot and taken out the oxygen bottle. Even if it had only been partially used, it came out and we put a new one in for each flight. Because with fighter aircraft oxygen is used from take-off, simply because the rate of climb is such that within a minute you can be in need of it. Armourers then cocked the guns and made sure everything was OK and worked down the line, while fitters etc. closed the panels.[6]

Such a level of efficiency required teamwork, and was reliant on having well-trained, disciplined individuals. When he was called up, Eric Marsden initially served with 83 Squadron at RAF Scampton, Lincolnshire, equipped with Hampden bombers, and was classed as a Fitter 2E U/T, or Fitter Group 2 Engines Under/Training. Consequently, he wasn't 'allowed to sign for anything but was allowed to work and assist, and assigned to a ground crew' tasked with such duties as mounting daily inspections of aircraft, refuelling, taking off cowlings and checking engines. Essentially, he was performing the 'work of a flight mechanic albeit he was U/T'.[7] However, trade training tended to be relatively thorough, even though under wartime conditions courses and syllabuses were condensed accordingly. On commencing his training as an instrument basher at an RAF training establishment at Melksham, Wiltshire, Albert Bennett 'discovered that contrary to the general tales circulating at that time [1939–40] that recruits were being given all the wrong jobs in the service to that in which they had been involved in "civvy street"; on this course there were in the main office machine engineers and watch repairers, quite appropriate for dealing with the servicing and repair of aircraft instruments.'[8]

Having left his wife, young children and family's drapery firm in London, Peter Jago embarked on becoming an aero-engine fitter. 'We were told that what the normal apprentices used to take four years on we did in about eight months!'[9] In December 1939, Leslie Baker was posted to a RAF School of Technical Training at Hednesford, Staffordshire. He qualified as a Fitter 2A with a rank of aircraftman first class (AC1), and found it ran:

> a very extensive course of aeronautical engineering ... covered all aspects of aircraft construction, hydraulic engineering [British manufactured aircraft were operated by hydraulics as opposed to being electrically operated], repair and maintenance, theory of flight, aerodynamics, metallurgy and workshop practice etc. Each section of the course had practical and written examinations. It was approximately an eight months' course, six days per week with the seventh day either doing guard duties or the occasional day off![10]

Notably, after the outbreak of war, the RAF continued with its Aircraft Apprentice-ship scheme for boys aged 15½ to 17. Most trades were catered for at RAF Halton, near Aylesbury, while apprentices in the wireless/radio trade went to RAF Cranwell, Lincolnshire. It served as the basis for producing a great many regular RAF personnel, many of whom went on to serve post-war. According to one former apprentice, 'discipline was strict at Halton', they were viewed as 'little sods', and 'had to be kept in line'.[11] Wing Commander Harry Blee commenced his air force career as an apprentice at Halton on 5 March 1940, and fondly recalled the conditions he faced as a teenager fresh from a farming family in Cornwall:

> What had been a three-year training course was shaved down to two years one month or something. The result of that was in April 1942 I passed out as an Airframe Fitter.
>
> Half of it was in the school sitting behind a desk, mechanics, physics, maths etc. And the other half was in the workshop. And the workshop was quite different from apprentices in civil life. In civil life apprentices are productive in some sort of work, even if it's just brewing the tea. But in the Services it was entirely instructional. In other words it was 50 percent

classroom sitting behind a desk doing theories, and the other half was practical when you actually did test jobs and made pieces of kit, riveting, soldering, welding, brazing, you name it, we did it.

Yes, the workshops at Halton were brilliant, and contained all the usual nonsenses of course. We were actually wearing hob-nail boots in 1940, and of course the habits of the 1930s still existed, and we had hob-nail boots, and in the workshop when we got round to the welding and brazing and so on we put on these shoes and the boots were left beside the bench. You can guess what's coming ... some wag would weld somebody's boot and no one would notice till pack-up time. So those were the sort of games people got up to, it was all good.

The whole system was operated like a boarding school. We had NCOs in charge of our barrack blocks, twenty to a room, and they looked out to make sure the food side of things, all that were in good working order. There was still plenty of sport going on, in the summertime you know, evening cricket matches twenty overs etc. And I must say it was brilliant. ... A fair proportion were grammar school boys, those sorts of people but they didn't have to be. And there was an entrance exam and anybody, from wherever without any secondary education could get by if they happened to be sharp lads. And there was a completely mixed bag, including quite a few people who came from pretty poor backgrounds from places such as Liverpool, Manchester etc. In that sense, looking back on it now, it was a very useful social achievement, although that had nothing to do with it really. ... It raked in lots of people who would have found it hard to make headway outside in civil life. They got proper organised domestic support, food, clothing, all that sort of stuff. All they had to do was get to work, do their training and it was super.

There was no nonsense and we had NCOs in the domestic side of things, and a lot of NCOs and officers technical people in the workshops. Once you were in the workshops it was a technical issue then, and you were in the classroom or the workshop. Outside of that it was the conventional discipline. And there were people who didn't take kindly to it. ... There were times when you could go out and that meant going past the Guard Room gate. And in those days you'd still be in uniform and one of the police corporals would be on duty keeping tabs on what you looked like. And if you looked like a tramp, you wouldn't go out, you needed shiny buttons all that sort of stuff. ... They operated a system called defaulters and if you were on some sort of minor punishment you'd be put on the jankers. And that meant you had to get up in the morning in your shiny clothes and shiny buttons and be down at the Guard Room to be inspected by the Duty Corporal at 6.30 am, lunchtime, and at least twice in the evening, which ruined your complete day. It was a marvellous system and it ground the most recalcitrant bod down in the end.

I had no problem. I accepted the rules as 99 percent of us did and I did what I was told. It's a bit like school if you obey the rules life is simple. A lesson from Halton days and it applied to the rest of my service was: If there are rules, there's usually a reason for them and you might as well observe them, and if you do life is easier and if you don't it's damn tedious.[12]

However, some NCO instructors weren't particularly pleasant characters. After serving at RAF Scampton, Eric Marsden was posted on a six-month long flight mechanic course at 5 School of Technical Training, RAF Locking. The flight sergeant in charge of his wing was a decorated veteran of the Royal Flying Corps, and 'near illiterate'. '[O]n pay parades we never heard him get past 'E', calling out the initial letters and then he'd pack it in and let the corporal do it.' He proved 'a fairly nasty tempered individual, spiteful. What we didn't know until later was that he was running a swindle. He was selling weekend passes and he was also selling immunity to guard duties.' As lowly airmen under training there was a limit to what Eric Marsden and his comrades could do, as they were 'in the hands of the Orderly Room etc. ... But there was this enormous resentment because we were convinced we were being hard-done by.'[13]

Having completed their training, most erks were posted to an operational squadron. On posting to 145 Squadron at RAF Tangmere, Bertram Hughes was greeted 'with total indifference'. He was:

given some overalls and a few basic tools and sent to 'B' Flight ... the NCOs were neither friendly nor unfriendly. They were clever, scruffy, cynical, superior – and utter 'piss-tanks'. They were, in fact, typical regular airmen. Their bland indifference to the vicissitudes of service life in wartime, and their absolute professionalism somehow warmed one towards them, however, and a certain grudging admiration for their competence grew into an odd friendship.[14]

Another erk, Len Bower from Leeds, served as a fitter on bombers, and found that life at RAF Binbrook, Lincolnshire, was a culture shock, because he encountered:

unfamiliar dialects, vocabularies and turns of phrase. My ears had to expand, and quite quickly in the case of barked orders from senior NCOs, to take in the variations of lilt and modulation, monotone and grittiness from the foreign fields of Land's End or Lossiemouth, Llanelli and Lowestoft.

I remained Yorkshire, but broadened into Britishness. This educative mix broke down much of the class awareness with which we entered into service life; the grammar school boy; the elementary school leaver at fourteen; and the public school pupil, now worked together on an egalitarian basis, their proportions accurately reflecting the national statistics. Some were already married, some had been students or apprentices, most had left employment of some kind in city or countryside, commerce or industry.[15]

When dealing with aircrew, he discovered that 'somehow rank differences were blurred in the inter-dependability of the relationship with ground crew'. Yet apart from aircrew, most erks generally saw little of officers, who at RAF Binbrook remained something of a 'race apart'.[16]

As a humble instrument basher, Ted Mawdsley recounted how aircrew were 'revered' by ground crews at RAF Elsham Wolds, Lincolnshire, where he served with Bomber Command. It was pretty much an unwritten rule, being etched into their collective consciousness, that you 'NEVER LET THE AIR-CREWS DOWN'.[17] They were only too well aware of the casualties suffered by bomber crews. On watching Lancasters take off on sorties, he experienced a range of emotions. There was a sense of guilt that he wasn't joining them as, like several ground crew, he'd volunteered for aircrew but in his case was rejected on medical grounds (colour blindness). Yet soon this feeling was tempered by the practical thought: 'Rather them than me!'[18]

In fighter squadrons there was a similar level of deference or admiration demonstrated towards pilots by ground crews. One Spitfire pilot engaged in the relief of Malta commented that with his unit's ground crews, 'you could see they felt like a football crowd'.[19] Eric Marsden, who'd experienced the Battle of Britain with 'A' Flight 145 Squadron, remarked:

> We were all very well aware that we weren't going up to get shot at. The relationship between most of us ground crew, certainly with regard to the pilots, was enormous respect, something even akin to love. ... I suppose we were ashamed because we could do little more than get them ready and send them out to die.[20]

Alternatively, as Bertram Hughes found, within a fighter squadron ground crew were faced with three distinct sorts of pilot. Firstly, there were 'those who genuinely wanted to fly' and fight, and who 'irrespective of specific instructions, came to grips with the enemy at every opportunity'. On the ground, such individuals tended to behave coolly and aloofly. Secondly, and by far the largest group, were those 'who did a good job, obeyed instructions meticulously, never sought trouble, but dealt with it efficiently when they met it, and provided the solid background against which the stars were permitted to shine'. Finally, there were 'playboys, who never flew without their silk scarves, would have chosen another career but for the "brevet", and much preferred landing to taking off!'[21]

Being intimately connected with pilots and aircrews, ground crews were acutely aware of the dangers and pressures that flyers routinely faced. This included what officialdom branded as cowardly behaviour, or Lacking Moral Fibre, when a pilot or member of aircrew appeared to lack the appetite for operations. Although it could be difficult to describe specific symptoms, it was often obvious to ground crew when a pilot seemed unable to cope. One fitter felt:

> you could look a man in the face, and in some cases you were aware he'd had enough, and in other cases you knew he was going to be dead soon. … I wouldn't call it LMF. People who are going out time after time, and putting their lives at considerable risk can't be expected to go on forever. And you can't expect all men to be equal because they aren't. … And so people have their breaking points.[22]

More commonly associated with bomber crews, LMF wasn't unheard of among fighter pilots either, as the case of a Hurricane pilot in 145 Squadron demonstrated. One of the ground crew recorded:

> On a few occasions he came back from flights complaining of faults, overheating or one thing and another. Claiming that there were problems which when the aircraft was ground run and checked out afterwards, didn't show up. And then he made a glorious hash of things on a scramble. Instead of taking off with the Flight, he had the propeller in course pitch and simply ploughed straight across the field and through the hedge. He was posted away after that.[23]

Ground crews tended to reject 'spit-and-polish type bull for its own sake' as they reckoned it impinged upon their primary function of looking after aircraft. Yet, as one veteran stressed, that didn't mean we weren't prepared 'to be reminded from time to time, that we were a military establishment'.[24] Many were happy to stay with the units to which they were posted, experiencing a strong sense of comradeship. Consequently, many erks lacked personal ambition, although promotion might occur once their efficiency was recognised and they passed the various trade boards. At RAF Binbrook, one airman noted:

> Everybody worked hard with an equal aim, the efficiency of the Squadron, the maximum serviceability of aircraft. There seemed to be an absence of any kind of competitive spirit between all the ground staff

with whom I came into contact, in the sense of the opportunist seeking personal advantage, or the bright boy aiming for promotion. Airmen helped each other for the sake of the job in hand.[25]

Depending on their trade, erks would usually be assigned to a specific aircraft or expected to look after a small number of aircraft. From February until May 1941, Len Bower served as a fitter with 149 Squadron at RAF Mildenhall, Suffolk, equipped with Wellingtons.

My aircraft was 'U' for Uncle, on a lonely dispersal point at the far end of the airfield, by a silver birch wood with a Nissen hut nearby. I helped out with other aircraft when necessary. In that Nissen hut we thawed out, spent nights either guarding the aircraft (it was never unguarded), or waiting for it to return from some operation, or later any food that arrived by van. … We worked at night as often as we did by day, and every day being the same, we often forgot what day it was.[26]

Ted Mawdsley commented that 'engine and airframe bods' were probably 'more possessive about their charges than anyone else because they were, mainly, "one-kite" men, responsible for a single aircraft', whereas other trades, such as instrument bashers, had normally to work on two or more aircraft. Despite this, they could experience a 'sense of ownership', and become attached to a particular aircraft and its crew.[27] In fighter squadrons, ground crew were normally responsible for specific aircraft. In 145 Squadron, Bertram Hughes was assigned to a Hurricane piloted by 'Jean Offenberg, an escapee from Belgium', who tragically perished in a flying accident with another squadron.[28]

The daily inspection (DI) loomed large in the routine of many ground crews. As members of 103 Squadron discovered: 'It was the job of every "trade" out on the Flights to carry out a daily inspection of those parts of the aeroplane [Lancasters] for which we were responsible – and accountable – and to remedy any faults or to repair any damage reported or discovered, that was within our means.' Significant repairs such as an engine change would done by the Servicing Flight, or the 'hanger boys', away from the dispersals.[29] One such hangar boy was Len Bower, who described how, at RAF Binbrook:

My work was carried out exclusively in the hangers, in 'Servicing Flight'; as a fitter I was qualified to carry out more detailed technical maintenance of aircraft. After 40 hours of flight, a '40 hour inspection' was carried out, followed in due course (if the aircraft had not been lost) by an '80 hour', of more dismantling and scrutiny, and so in further 40 hour stages, to a 'major inspection', which was rather rare. The inspections were referred to as 40, 40 star, 40 two star and so on, each level of inspection laid down in detail in inspection manuals.[30]

Every check or piece of work/repair had to be signed for. Form 700 was the official RAF form/document that tradesmen signed after carrying out an inspection or work, and it declared that to the best of his knowledge the parts of an aircraft that he was responsible for were safe and in good working order. It was countersigned by the pilot on receipt of the aircraft, who'd normally check matters by mounting air and/or ground tests before he accepted an aircraft.

However, as one instrument basher explained, on a busy airfield such as RAF Elsham Wolds, despite the routine nature of maintenance work, for ground crews there wasn't any such thing as a typical day. 'Operations could be scheduled and then scrubbed – even at the last moment. Stand-downs could be ordered in the midst of intense activity. ... Incidents and mishaps on the drome could disrupt the numerous routines that were being pursued in the various areas of activity.'[31] Even the weather could hinder proceedings, and it was notoriously unpredictable in Northern Europe.

Initially, few women from the WAAF were engaged directly in aircraft maintenance and servicing. There were around 700 in June 1940, but by late 1944, this figure had peaked at over 17,000. These women were employed in trades, such as flight mechanics, fitters, electricians and instrument repairers, and shared many of the responsibilities of their male counterparts.[32] Yet initially, they weren't necessarily welcomed by airmen and male NCOs. One WAAF remarked it felt as if 'the men would have preferred we made the tea'.[33] Despite this, some found they were treated kindly by male colleagues and NCOs, so that as the war progressed, these women were more accepted.

Early on, conditions were different for WAAFs, with jobs being split into sections, whereas their male counterparts would be expected to deal with an entire task. The role of sparking plug tester (SPT), for example, became a designated trade solely in the WAAF, as it was the only part of a fitter's training able to be separated from the rest of the trade. According to one historian of the WAAF, 'the men preferred to tackle the whole engine', including dealing with spark plugs, whereas women preferred 'one-process to multiple jobs in mechanical trades'.[34] There were also genuine concerns about the level of scientific education attained by most women during the period. Conversely, it was felt that mechanical jobs in workshops 'only required an adaptation of skill in the descendants of generations of patient delicate-fingered females who had devoted long hours to cross-stitch, petit-point or invisible mending', plus the work wasn't necessarily that physically demanding, as cranes could lift engines out of aircraft.[35]

Trixie Irving worked as an SPT at Leuchars, servicing Coastal Command aircraft. She recalled:

> after an aircraft engine change, when the spark plugs came out of the aircraft, they had to be washed and cleaned in high octane petrol ... checked for faults and the electrode at the end of the plug had to re-set to 12–15,000th of an inch, so that the spark would cross the gap and so ignite the engine.[36]

Another woman who completed training in a technical trade was Hilda Bell. As a Flight Mechanic (Engines) she was stationed at RAF Holmsley South, Hampshire, a former bomber station that later in the war was used by transport units.

> We got aircraft ready for quite a number of things – VIP trips to Italy, and Mr. Churchill and Mr. Eden's planes ready for the trip to Yalta. I worked on the York [Avro York transport aircraft] on which Mr. Churchill's pilot perfected his flying. He did landings and circuits and bumps, as well as trying out anything that might happen, so that he would know what to do![37]

Non-flying duties

At officer and other rank level, a wealth of non-flying or ground-based duties were required to be performed within the wartime RAF. Many didn't have that much directly to do with aircraft, but were still important. These ranged from administrative/clerical work to more active concerns, such as bomb disposal and airfield defence. WAAF personnel were needed in a host of ground-based trades, many perhaps seemingly unglamorous, but which had a role to play in the war effort, and maintaining the morale and efficiency of the Service.

According to Group Captain Hugh Verity, 'A huge amount of timely intelligence was essential to victory in World War Two' and came from the 'complimentary efforts of independent sources: signals intelligence, air photography and patriotic people on the ground'.[38] Having attended Oxbridge in the early 1940s, Anthony Goulty was granted an emergency commission in the RAFVR in May 1944, and like many young men of his generation, aspired to join aircrew. However, he was barred from flying on medical grounds, and after training in Britain, including a course at Bletchley Park (the government's Code and Cypher School), he was posted to an inter-Service signals intelligence unit near

Delhi, India. Housed in a former school building, this was known by the 'bland and innocuously sounding title: Wireless Experimental Centre'.

I was trained for, and then engaged in cryptography in reading Japanese radio signals. I'll try and give you an idea of how this worked. Typically, the Japanese had a code book, in which words were represented by groups of numbers – usually in threes sometimes fours according to how complicated the subject matter – and then these numbers were encrypted by being added to figures from a random number table. The sender and receiver, of course, had to be using the same random number table to encipher and decipher messages. The random number tables were changed frequently – but not frequently enough! Suppose the same tables were in use throughout an Air Command for a week. Our airmen wireless operators were taking down all the messages, which were sent out in Morse as groups of numbers – this was called our 'Y' Service. These messages came through to us, and were then fed through Hollerith machines which produced cards with punched holes representing the sequences of numbers. Other machines then sorted the cards, so as to identify similar sequences, and where these occurred, it was a fair assumption that part of the underlying text was the same, and enciphered on the same tables. Officers were trained in the language and cryptography, then put these sequences together, and paid special attention to the groups before and after the coding sequence, and calculated the 'differences' between preceding and subsequent groups. By making guesses and inferences, one soon became familiar with significant 'diffs', as we called them. For example, weather is important in air signals, so you might get say 2474 as the basic code for 'fair' and 5741 as the basic code for 'cloudy'. The diff between these would be 7733 – no 'carrying' in cryptography! So whenever you find that diff in two messages, e.g. 2986 in one and 5253 in another – on alignment from the coinciding sequence, it is a very laborious process, one needed a great many coinciding sequences –'depths', they were called: and sometimes the operators hadn't got the groups down correctly, so we had what we called 'corrupt depths' to contend with.[39]

While signals intelligence (Sigint) was vitally important, especially when the enemy generated large volumes of wireless/radio traffic that could be monitored and deciphered, other forms of intelligence work were equally required. At the 'coalface' within most operational units were trained intelligence officers (IO) and their teams, tasked with briefing aircrew ahead of sorties, and gathering information from previous missions. Former schoolmaster F.R. Chappell served as a squadron and wing IO in the Western Desert with 205 Group. Briefings entailed providing information to some 120 aircrew in front of senior officers, including intelligence in the form of maps, a description of the target, its importance, and the target's defences. These were tense affairs, as most IOs were only too well aware that they could be dealing with men for whom 'this might be their own final briefing'. Last-minute information might even have to be handed to aircrew by intelligence staff, especially if there were any late changes to the target, which added to the apprehension felt by all concerned. Returning bomber crews then had to be 'interrogated', photographs of raids studied, and an operational summary (OPSUM) produced for each sortie and communicated to Group HQ.[40]

Inescapably linked with intelligence, and other aspects of the RAF, was the role of signals/communications, something that involved large numbers of WAAF personnel. As an 18-year-old, Rita Symons was stationed at Bomber Command HQ, High Wycombe, where:

> tele-printing was the most secretive means of communication. ... You would type on a machine here and it would come out elsewhere. Raids would be planned at headquarters and we would send out – some of it in code – signals to all the different Bomber Command stations, planning what they were to do.[41]

Subsequently, signals would be received telling HQ what had happened, and all this information had to be processed. Jack Ambler trained as a wireless operator in Blackpool, prior to training in direction finding (DF: the measurement of the direction in which a received signal was transmitted). His entire war was spent at RAF stations in Lincolnshire and East Anglia, initially at RAF Scampton, a few miles north of Lincoln. He vividly remembered conditions at his remote post, located on the edge of the airfield, which was manned twenty-four hours a day.

> The radio cabin was a strongly built wooden structure, surrounded by a brick wall and four vertical masts, each fitted with a lightening arrestor. Due to the sensitivity of the DF aerials, the local farmer was instructed not to approach within 220 yards with any machinery, without giving notice. The operating range was about 500–800 miles.
>
> Inside the cabin was a large and well maintained radio set, a big dial instrument marked in degrees 0–360, called a Goniometer (Greek angle measurer); two telephones; a small telephone switchboard; the Morse key; a list of secret codes; two alternative electrical supplies; a large map of Europe on the wall behind the operator; and a Sten gun, which like the fire extinguisher, we hoped we would never need to use. Everything

was perfectly and strictly maintained and regularly checked and logged. One telephone was a direct link to the Airfield Controller.[42]

As the war progressed, radio was similarly vital in assisting mobile units with tactical air forces handling tasks such as aircraft control. By 1944, mobile radar units also formed part of 2nd TAF's establishment in North-West Europe. Among the personnel involved was Stanley Wright, who despite poor eyesight had worked his way from being an aircraftman during 1939–40 to becoming an NCO and competent radar operator/controller by 1943. Ahead of D-Day, he was posted to Church Fenton, where he:

> learnt to be a mobile controller, became a Combined Operations sergeant instead of an ordinary sergeant, learnt to drive all sorts of lorries/trucks and things. And in the fullness of time came down to Salisbury Plain and went to Normandy via Beaulieu, with the Americans. … If you can imagine the difficulties of putting radar sets into lorries and carting them across rough ground – God knows how it worked – but it did, beautifully.

Subsequently, he acted as a mobile controller of fighter-bombers, including covering the Guards Armoured Division's advance towards Arnhem. After being recalled to Britain, he retrained on the Type 70 Centimetric Radar Set, and served in Holland during the Rhine crossing and on into Germany in 1945.[43]

Leslie Baker underwent extremely tough training, both physically and mentally, because RAF Commando units were expected to secure and operate airfields close to the front line. In April 1942, this involved a period at the Commando Training Centre at Inveraray on Loch Fyne, Scotland, where those who didn't meet the standard were rapidly posted elsewhere. Aboard HMT *Ettrick*:

> We practised getting into assault craft in 'Battle Order' via the inevitable cargo nets, often in the middle of the night – quite a performance! During the days that followed we were engaged in: drills, forced route marches, bayonet practice, battle courses, weapons training, self-defence and unarmed combat, swimming, compass and map reading, and physical training.[44]

A related area was airfield defence in Britain and the Middle East. It wasn't until February 1942 that there was a designated unit – the RAF Regiment – charged with maintaining airfield security and protecting them from ground attack. Prior to this, ground gunners, with a distinctive 'GG' badge on their sleeve, manned light anti-aircraft guns, while the army provided heavier support. Yet, early on, many RAF personnel were inadequately prepared for airfield defence. According to one airman, when there was an invasion scare at his station in 1940, personnel were ordered to disperse.

> Our total camp armament comprised two rifles and a hundred rounds
> of ammunition. One rifle and a bandolier of fifty rounds was kept in the
> guardroom, and the aerodrome guard had the other one. They used to
> walk round, one man carrying the rifle, one carrying the ammunition,
> so that was our total defence armament![45]

Various RAF personnel were sometimes tasked with guarding airfields in addition to their other duties, even once the RAF Regiment was established. An armourer at RAF Uxbridge recounted that one of his main duties 'was to issue rifles and one clip of ammo to the guard of about 20 or so unlucky airmen and collect them in the morning at the station armoury, a two-storey building behind the duty Pilot tower'.[46] Similarly, a member of the Accounts Section at RAF Staverton, Gloucestershire, in November 1942, discovered personnel had to partake in 'security patrols', covering the perimeter of the airfield.

> For this purpose we were provided with a bicycle, a very powerful torch,
> a .303 rifle and bayonet ...we were allowed to carry the rifle loaded with
> a full magazine and "one up the spout" when challenging any suspicious
> intruder.[47]

An overlooked activity was that of bomb disposal. The RAF employed mobile squads for dealing with incidents. Personnel trained for this risky task were characterised by a special type of courage, and relied on good discipline, patience and teamwork. While a member of the ARP, 44-year-old A.E. Haarer underwent limited bomb disposal training under the auspices of the Royal Engineers. Subsequently, he responded to a call for volunteers to join the RAF, and become specially commissioned for what flying boys termed chair-polishing jobs. After basic training, he was posted on a number of courses, including one at Melksham, Wiltshire, which 'gave us a good grounding on bombs and fuses, on how they acted, on safety precautions, and on some methods of bomb disposal such as the use of special machines to cut out discs of metal by remote control'. Trainees worked diligently, well aware that their safety, and that of their men, depended on 'their ability to recognise one fuse from another and how it operated'.[48]

Eventually, Haarer was promoted to squadron leader and posted to command No. 14 Bomb Disposal Squad at RAF Digby, Lincolnshire. He recalled:

> We not only had to deal with enemy explosive material dropped on
> Air Force property, but all our own and American bombs and pyrotechnics

dropped in civilian areas. There happened to be a good many of these on account of damaged aircraft trying to get back, and accidents to loaded aircraft. Quite a lot of our own material was as dangerous for us to handle as some of the worst enemy bombs.[49]

This included rendering safe devices, such as smoke or flame floats dropped as markers, cannon shells, anti-aircraft rockets, various types of cartridges, and even signalling flares. Many discovered that knowledge of mines was equally important, particularly:

> the horrible G-type mine which could be used as a bomb on land or as a mine in the sea; it had delayed action and anti-handling devices. These rendered them sensitive to light on account of photo-electric cells, to the slightest noise because of acoustic devices, and sensitive to metal because of magnetic influences so that a man who carried a bunch of keys might detonate the vile thing.[50]

Another facet of their work entailed studying anything new found in an enemy aircraft after it was made safe. This ensured intelligence reports multiplied to the extent that a bomb disposal unit's spare time was occupied with absorbing a wealth of technical detail upon which its safety and security depended.

In contrast, many men, including Henry Brown from Ruskington, Lincolnshire, were required to fill administrative positions. Having qualified as a chartered auctioneer and estate agent, he volunteered for the RAF in 1941, and worked with pay and accounts. He enjoyed the challenge of learning 'a system of single entry book-keeping which was probably unique to the services, and completely different to the double entry system which I had been taught in my civilian business life'.[51] Later, he was posted to RAF Lyness, on Hoy in the Orkneys, and allocated a pay ledger covering corporals and lower ranks in alphabetical order of surname A to L. 'Office hours were 8 am to 6 pm with a one hour break for lunch. Sunday we worked from 9 am to 1 pm. There were no days off except by special permission under exceptional circumstances.' Seven days' leave was granted every two months, plus two days' 'travelling time'.[52]

His work became more dramatic when he volunteered as a 'floating pay bob'. For two or three days a fortnight this involved accompanying an officer aboard a requisitioned fishing vessel, collecting cash from the bank in Kirkwall, and sailing to various instillations, including balloon sites on small islands and trawlers, to hold pay parades. Sailing had its dangers, including when transferring from the boat to a trawler. His predecessor had broken his leg and ribs while doing this. During his time at RAF Lyness, he was also involved in guard duties, and served as a member of a Lewis gun team on airfield defence exercises in conjunction with the Black Watch. It was during one of these that he fell, injuring his arm, leading to him becoming medically downgraded. In February 1942, he passed his final trade test and was promoted to LAC (Leading Aircraftman), and having refused a commission, ended his war at RAF Spitalgate, Lincolnshire, before being medically discharged.

By late 1942, substantial numbers of WAAF personnel handled administrative matters. Jackie Poulton worked as Clerk (General Duties), and outlined the variety of forms that she regularly contended with:

Form:	575	Shoe Repair Label
	292	Result of Course
	413	Railway Warrant
	Appendix B	Application for Commission (WAAF)
	1020A	Application for Commission (RAF)
	381	Record of Leave (Officers)
	252	Charge Form
	295	Leave and Pass Form
	1394	Certificate of Discharge
	1672	Railway Warrant and Leave Form
	1755	Burial Certificate
	RB 12 & 8	Ration Cards[53]

The provision of food/rations was essential, and by 1945, WAAFs accounted for around 61 per cent of all cooks in the Service. One, Dorothea Barrie, provides an indication of their working conditions, and the volume of foodstuffs routinely handled. A large kitchen serving an RAF camp consumed about a ton of potatoes per day, plus on flying stations, sandwiches had to be made for aircrew on operations. Work normally was arranged into three shifts:

> starting about 4.30 am one day then the following day from 8 am until 7 pm (when we did the cleaning and preparation of vegetables) ... The night shift was from 7 pm till 4.30 am, and on more difficult camps there were sometimes only two shifts of 12 hours each.[54]

Another role performed by women that is perhaps overlooked was as MT (Motor Transport) drivers, there being around 15,000 in the WAAF by 1943. They were expected to drive a wide variety of vehicles, up to 3 tons, often with little or no training. For those who wanted to drive, it was potentially an exciting prospect. As an MT driver, Phyllis Cove had an experience that readily illustrates the contribution of women to the war in the air. She'd been detailed to pick up a ferry pilot and go to the officers' mess. 'After a few moments, the door to the aircraft opened and out stepped a slim, petite blonde. I expected a strapping man!'[55] The woman in question was a member of the Air Transport Auxiliary tasked with delivering a variety of aircraft.

Yet another important ground-based aspect of the RAF that contributed towards its operational efficiency was the role performed by its medical services. As a teenager, too young for military service, Morton Charlton from Hexham, Northumberland, became involved with the men's detachment of his local British Red Cross branch. Activities included assisting with the transportation of wounded troops, who'd been evacuated from Dunkirk, to an emergency hospital. He was at the receiving end, carrying stretchers to where patients could be assessed, before being sent to the relevant department. In March 1941, he enlisted with the RAF's medical branch with the help of the Red Cross. After being inducted into the Service, he trained at the Medical Training Establishment and Depot (MTE & D) at RAF Halton, where owing to his previous experience he was able to pass out as a nursing Orderly, rather than as a lower grade medical orderly.

His first posting was to RAF Hospital Rauceby, near Sleaford, Lincolnshire, a former peacetime mental hospital given over to military use. Work included treating severe burns injuries. For these:

> we used a special oiled skin bag for treating the arms. This elongated bag fastened above the elbow and had two openings to allow irrigation, one near the elbow and one near the wrist. Into the bag we introduced a solution of sodium hypochlorite, more commonly known by its brand name 'Milton'. This had the action of bleaching the damaged tissue and cleansing the wounds of any pustular discharge.

Additionally, facial burns required dressings, and 'this was done by applying gauze swabs soaked in saline solution, and these were left in position until the next renewal period.'[56]

Airfield conditions

To an extent, all airfields were characterised by their geographical location in Britain. At RAF Kirknewton, Scotland, this seemed amiss. 'It stood on the top of a hill with a convex contour, resembling an upturned bowl. Thus the middle of the runway was considerably higher than the ends,' plus at one end was woodland, and a steep hill at the other, which led to numerous crash-landings.[57] RAF Acklington in North-East England was intended as a training station, but on the outbreak of war was transferred to Fighter Command, and assumed importance as one of the few fighter bases in that region. It was situated on the fringe of the Northumberland and Durham coalfield, largely surrounded by farmland, and tasked with defending the industrial areas on the Tyne and Tees that were a target for the Luftwaffe.[58] Likewise, the Bomber Command station at Binbrook was situated on a high plateau about 12 miles south-west of Grimsby in north Lincolnshire, with the village of Binbrook nestling below it.[59]

According to Squadron Leader Haarer, RAF stations were akin to 'large villages ... with their clustered offices, workshops, barracks, messes and large hangers'.[60] This was especially true of all those airfields developed during the 1930s and 1940s in Yorkshire, Lincolnshire and East Anglia to support the strategic bombing of Germany. The design of RAF stations was another factor that influenced their character. Lawrence Wheatley spent time at RAF Hemswell, Lincolnshire, and RAF West Raynham, Norfolk, both pre-war stations with a standard layout: 'four hangars in shallow semicircle and the watch-office (control tower nowadays) in the middle. Most of the accommodation was wooden huts but new barrack blocks had been built round a new square.'[61] Compared with his bleak existence in a hut at RAF Lyness on Hoy, with a straw-filled palliasse and pillow, Henry Brown was relieved to find that RAF Spitalgate was 'a permanent pre-war station'. Most of it comprised buildings 'solidly built of brick. The barrack blocks were two storeys high, each block having a central entrance hall with a dormitory on either side, upstairs and down, plus a shared ablutions room.'[62] Contrastingly, an erk who'd previously served on compact stations in urban environments considered that Elsham Wolds 'stretched out into the distance on all sides' into the Lincolnshire countryside, and initially this was overwhelming.[63]

Some airfields/stations had very good reputations within the Service. One NCO described how RAF Tangmere, of Battle of Britain fame, was like a:

> Shangri-la in the Air Force in those days. It was the most desirable station in the whole of the UK. Situated adjacent to Chichester, which is a nice little town, adjacent to the coast, for yachting and everything else which the gentlemen of the private flying club which was the RAF in those days ... very handy for London. And it just was a jolly good station for commissioned types or non-commissioned types. The SWO had always been carefully chosen.[64]

At RAF St Athan in South Wales, where comprehensive technical training was given, there were similarly lavish facilities, including an Olympic-sized gymnasium, presided over by a flight sergeant who was none other than pre-war heavyweight boxer Jack London.

Some stations had much better accommodation than others. Erks enjoyed brick-built billets, at RAF Binbrook, with 'civilised ablutions', and had space to store kit and possessions in a locker by their beds. Nearby there was an airmen's mess and a NAAFI, plus workshops, hangars and stores were conveniently located. An airman who served there claimed that 'the camp had a good atmosphere, a sense of "happy ship". Many friendships were formed, airmen worked well together, usually in pairs who shared the same box of tools. We all got on with the job we had been trained to do, it had become our way of life.'[65] In contrast, during 1942, Eric Marsden was posted to RAF Marston Moor, Yorkshire, where 1652 Heavy Conversion Unit was based. He found that there was:

> no centralisation at all. Billets were dispersed around the station in the form of Nissen huts and the ablution blocks and dining room and cookhouse separate from the billets. This place had been built during autumn and the approach of winter, there was mud everywhere although at the moment it was frozen solid. The billets were unwelcoming. Curiously enough they were still building huts with windows in and painting them black … in view of the fact we might get bombed.[66]

Given the dispersed layout of the station, it was a considerable walk from billets to flight offices, for instance. As on other large stations, this necessitated an issue of bicycles, first to senior ranks, before they became more widely available. A corollary of this was that bicycle theft became a significant issue.

There tended to be a significant divide between operational stations and training establishments. Eric Marsden bluntly explained, places such as RAF Uxbridge and RAF Cardington where recruits were handled, were, 'regarded with horror'. He discovered 'that stations which had a name like this, seemed to infect the people who were posted there. All the people in Orderly Rooms and so on were the most miserable gits you could ever come across, dyed in the wool "bull artists" and so it's not surprising that these places got these bad names.' Transit camps, such as West Kirby near Liverpool, where personnel were processed before going overseas or on arrival from an overseas posting, also had bad reputations. This was because the atmosphere and the living conditions were poor, and the NCOs from the permanent staffs that ran them 'were often on the fiddle'.[67]

Food was another important issue. Sooner or later, personnel became accustomed to the delights of the cookhouse, such as a breakfast consisting of 'the traditional forces' porridge, very thick and gooey, not very warm, and little or no milk, not even of the well-watered variety. Steamed fish of uncertain vintage or species, and bread and jam.'[68] At his isolated radio station at RAF Scampton, Jack Ambler found they had to draw rations from the camp cookhouse and do their own cooking. 'Our extensive menu was centred around, beans on toast, sausages and beans, sausages and chips, chips and beans – and if we could "scrounge" some flour and egg powder – the occasional pancake as a special treat. Drinking water had to be collected in buckets.'[69] This was because there was no water supply, other than a water butt, which provided water for washing, and the only 'pipes' allowed were deeply laid telephone cables.

For some airmen, another distinctive feature of airfield life at squadron level was the absence of women. Recalling his service with Bomber Command, Len Bower commented:

> The WAAF did exist, but at Binbrook we saw little of them. I have recollection of only a handful who were drivers of MT. Otherwise the girls and ladies of our lives were the friendly untouchables behind the counters of the NAAFI or the ever welcome NAAFI girl who drove her small van around the aircraft dispersals and to our hangar in all weathers to sell us, for coppers, hot tea and 'wads' (rock buns) as a welcome break for the ground crews.[70]

From the perspective of the average erk, or junior NCO, working within a squadron demonstrated these were comparatively small units. Even on an airfield, where there was more than one squadron operating, didn't necessarily guarantee that the individual knew anybody outside his immediate sphere of work. Explaining the situation he found himself in with Fighter Command, Eric Marsden observed:

> A squadron was a very small unit, a flight an even smaller unit and if you were on a big station like Tangmere where there were possibly 2,000–odd people on the station, you would know by name not necessarily all the people within your own flight. You would know, probably the pilots 8–15 of them and some of the pilots in the other flight in the squadron. You would know your NCOs. You would probably not know any or many of the names of the ground crew in 'A' Flight if you were in 'B' Flight as we were. And of the rest of the people on the station, you would know the name of the SWO, you might know the name of the SP [Service Police] in charge of the Guard Room, you would possibly know the name of the station commander, not necessarily. It's quite possible to get through without knowing these things. It was a very parochial kind of life and that would apply to any station at all.[71]

Although most non-flying types admired aircrews, there was often a distinct divide between those that flew and the rest. According to a bomb disposal officer, an airfield's primary function was to support flyers, 'and except for adjutants, control-room and intelligence types, lesser lights minded their own business since hero worship caused embarrassment, and the lack of wings on their tunics brought an inferiority complex into being which made them remain aloof' and ensured it was difficult to forge friendships with 'fighter or bomber men'.[72]

Most ground-based personnel were to some extent shaped by their specific working environment, be they an intelligence officer, a fitter or a clerk, for example. Stanley Wright commenced his war in 1939 as a plotter in the Operations Room at RAF North Weald, Essex, and was on duty when it was bombed during the Battle of Britain. He recounted that:

> An ops room is a peculiar looking place. You've a well with a large map in it, it's gridded rather like an OS grid, purely an outline one and sitting around it are in those days' airmen with ear phones on and they had plots from what was known as RDF (now radar) Radio Direction Finding stuff for the sea areas and from the Observer Corps from the land side of it. All of the plots were sent up to Stanmore [RAF Stanmore Park, Middlesex, part of 11 Group, a non-flying administration/HQ establishment], they were filtered, in other words they were sorted out so that two or three raids should have been one because several people were looking at them and they were sent back again to the different sector stations. Overlooking the map were a couple of daises, on the centre of the top dais sat the Duty Controller. On one side of him he had the Army with the search lights, and one or two odds and ends. To his right-hand side were the people who dealt directly with Group. You had people drawing maps of any action that happened. …
>
> You worked a three watch system in the early days. It later became four because it became a bit more hectic. The Ops Room itself was an ordinary brick building on the surface. It had an earth wall around it but no way of stopping anything very solid … underneath the daises were the radio operators who sat there logging everything that was said by the Controller or the aircraft, and of course defence network tele-printer rooms where people sat there collecting written orders on tele-printers. Two or three GPO engineers and that was the full strength of the thing.[73]

Another facet of airfield life was that recreation was important in maintaining morale, including sports and pastimes. While serving with the WAAF at RAF Waddington, Pip Beck found that their 'choral society expanded into a dramatic society', ably assisted by two airmen with 'professional stage' backgrounds.[74] To relieve boredom on Sullom Voe in the Shetlands, members of the RAF Regiment obtained permission to turn an abandoned church into a recreational centre for use off duty. This worked well, although some embarrassment was caused when the padre wanted to use it for services, as one serviceman had 'painted some excellent nudes on the walls – but quite tasteful'. Once these were covered with curtains, services proved popular with airmen, especially the opportunity to sing 'a bloody good hymn'.[75]

Cinemas, cafés and pubs provided useful relaxants when off duty. Many air force personnel posted to Lincolnshire, effectively 'Bomber County', enjoyed visiting the larger urban areas, such as Lincoln and Grimsby, and these provided a welcome change from camp life. Arguably, alcohol was an even more important form of relief, especially at isolated stations, such as RAF Lyness. After being posted there as a clerk, Henry Brown admitted: 'I had not been much of a drinker, but now, with nothing to do in the evenings but drink in the NAAFI, play table tennis or cards I had become used to consuming five or six pints of beer per night.'[76]

Overseas service

Of those men and women who served overseas during the course of their wartime service, this was sometimes as a result of an immediate posting. Having passed out at RAF Halton, Wing Commander Harry Blee briefly served at RAF Portreath, near his home in Cornwall, as an airframe fitter. He then volunteered for training as a flight engineer, because four-engine bombers had been introduced, and he attended a course at RAF St Athan. After embarkation leave following completion of the course, he was ordered to go to India. In a pattern familiar to Service personnel throughout the war, he 'said goodbye to Helen [his future wife] on Gloucester railway station after a short meeting, not knowing when, or if, we would see each other again'.[77]

Alternatively, others volunteered for an overseas posting. In Eric Marsden's case, this was because he was 'absolutely cheesed off with winter flying in Yorkshire [at 1652 HCU] and the amount of flying we were doing on the conversion unit', which ensured ground crew like him had little 'spare time and were worn thin'.[78] Subsequently, he attended a course to become a junior NCO at RAF Cosford, Shropshire, and then learnt how to operate mobile oxygen plants. From late 1942 until early 1944, he worked with a mobile oxygen unit, first supporting the Royal New Zealand Air Force in New Zealand, and then on attachment to the United States Navy on Vella Lavella, Solomon Islands. 'We were supposed to be supplying breathing oxygen [for aircraft] to all the islands forward of Guadalcanal, which meant a fair number of fighter squadrons.'[79]

Not all personnel went to such far-flung or exotic locations. Although not technically overseas, the Orkneys, as Henry Brown discovered, were classed as active service. Consequently, at RAF Lyness all airmen were issued rifles and, when necessary, ammunition from the armoury.[80] By mid-1944, increasing numbers of women were allowed to serve overseas, including in North-West Europe after D-Day. As she'd been brought up in France, Jeanne Truman was keen to serve there, and after liberation worked as an intelligence officer at SHAEF (Supreme Headquarters Allied Expeditionary Force). One of her duties included updating maps. 'I went for intelligence briefings every morning, and then changed the maps. Anyone could go in and see how the advances were. What I found very odd was that an awful lot of the places, especially on the Russian front, had the same names and I thought I do hope I've moved them into the right places and not the wrong ones!'[81]

In contrast, other overseas postings exposed personnel to the dangers of the front line. When Stanley Wright and his mobile radar unit landed with American troops in Normandy, it proved:

> dangerous because we'd done a bit of training with them dressed in khaki. We did our landing in air force blue and once you get air force blue salty and damp ... well the Germans shot at us because they knew who we were, the Americans shot at us because they knew that everything that looked grey-blue was German, and we had a very uncomfortable time there.[82]

Disease was another threat, particularly in the Far East. Having trained as a nursing orderly, Morton Charlton was posted to a medical unit in Burma before being invalided home, suffering from a 'complaint peculiar to the tropics, called "Sprue". This is a failure to digest food, and one is therefore unable to get any nourishment from it, so that eventually it is passed through the body and excreted in the same form in which it is ingested.'[83]

Clearly, transporting personnel to somewhere close to Britain, such as Normandy, was comparatively straightforward. However, to ferry large bodies of personnel further afield required troopships, as large aircraft that could whisk personnel or entire units en masse to anywhere around the globe weren't available in the 1940s. Many troopships were converted liners, including RMS *Windsor Castle*. She'd been rebuilt in 1937, and 'with new engines, new bows and two funnels' was one of 'the loveliest ships that the Union-Castle Line ever had'.[84] Invariably, these weren't fast enough to outpace U-boats, and so sailed in convoys in a zigzag pattern, usually with a naval escort. Typically, convoys set sail from Liverpool and/or the Clyde, and met up with their escort to negotiate the Atlantic, sailing the long way round to the Middle East, stopping off in West Africa and South Africa en route. Others sailed on to India via a similar route, or even as far as Australia and New Zealand. One erk aboard the *Duchess of Richmond*, in January 1941, recorded that they were part of 'a fast convoy escorted by corvettes, destroyers, a cruiser' and for a while, the battleship HMS *Ramilles* formed 'an impressive sight from the bridge of our ship leading the starboard of three columns'.[85]

Officers, some NCOs, and anyone with special duties, such as working on a gun crew, could expect to have reasonable accommodation – a cabin shared between four persons. However, for the vast majority of erks, conditions were cramped, claustrophobic and tinged with uncertainty, as for security reasons most didn't know exactly where they were headed. When he was posted abroad in March 1942, Peter Jago remembered it was rumoured they were bound for Trincomalee, Ceylon (Sri Lanka). Aboard the *Windsor Castle*, 'We were crammed together under the decks so tightly that we were even sleeping on the stairs leading up to the deck.'[86] A nursing orderly who sailed aboard the *Franconia* likened descending to the troop decks 'as near to hell as one could get, the humidity was almost unbearable and the stench of perspiring bodies was not very sweet either, for the only ventilation was funnelled down canvas tubes from the upper decks, and was minimal by the time it reached this far down.'[87] For many, seasickness was an issue, especially in stormy weather. Bertram Hughes found that during appalling weather, his voyage overseas was characterised by: 'Three days of moaning, cursing, wailing, swaying disillusioned seasick bodies. The delights of kipping in a hammock were enjoyed to the full – nobody slept a wink.'[88]

Conditions at sea were ameliorated somewhat as most airmen had to perform duties such as acting as a mess orderly or having to look out for U-boats. Card games, bingo, raffles and quizzes helped pass time, and sometimes an officer might provide personnel with an update about the war. Another popular activity was the traditional 'Crossing the Line' ceremony, when a ship crossed the equator, and its crew paraded in costumes, and 'much hilarity ensued'.[89] Stopovers in ports were another means of relieving the monotony of a long voyage. At Freetown, Sierra Leone, airmen often 'encountered the "bum-boatmen" who dived for coins and sold us fruit which we hauled up in baskets'.[90] While at Durban, South Africa, there was usually plenty of scope for sightseeing, and some local white/Afrikaans families would entertain servicemen. There was also the famous 'Lady in White', who'd greet troopships by belting out traditional patriotic songs.[91]

Meals provided another break from the boredom of troopship routine, but at best tended to consist of typically bland Service-type food. Personnel aboard the SS *Dominion Monarch* felt particularly aggrieved when they were served rotten kippers more than once, after passing West Africa. Eric Marsden, who as a junior NCO was in charge of a mess table during the voyage to New Zealand, explained the situation:

> We were served kippers one day … distinctly off … so we shovelled them all back into the mess tin and they were taken back to the galley. Big mistake – because we got them again. These had been served up as rations and we were supposed to eat them. So we sent them back again. What we didn't know was that the sergeant's mess were doing the same thing. A third time although we didn't realise it at first, they were served up to us again, this time in the form of what the cooks laughingly described called 'American Dry Hash'. And simply the kippers had been taken off

the bone and mashed up with a little bit of potato to produce a plasticine-like paste that smelt vile and tasted worse. So we did the same thing again only some … modelled them into graves, crosses and swastikas on their plates and solemnly took them back on their plates and put them on the counter of the galley.

In response, the head cook complained to the purser, who in turn accosted the OC Troops, and the airmen were disciplined for 'treating Service rations improperly'. They had to mount a punishment parade daily from 2.00 to 5.00 pm in the blazing hot sun at their abandon ship station.[92]

Boat drills formed another aspect to the routine endured by airmen aboard troopships. Morton Charlton commented how: 'Lifeboat stations were called every morning, and we had to line up at our appointed posts complete with our life-jackets which were our constant companions on board ship,' even forming 'an adequate pillow or cushion' when needed.[93] Sometimes there weren't enough lifeboats, forcing airmen aboard the *Dominion Monarch* to discuss the desperate idea of making a raft from their mess tables and benches, in the event of having to abandon ship. In March 1943, convoy KMF 11 was attacked, and the *Windsor Castle* hit by an aerial torpedo 110 miles north-west of Algiers. She took a few hours to sink, and for Peter Jago, it was his worst experience of the entire war. After spending time in the water he was so cold that he couldn't climb aboard the destroyer that rescued him, and had to be dragged up on deck by sailors, where he and other survivors were given piping-hot coffee. He vividly recalled trying to comfort another airman: 'I was trying to fold his hands round the coffee and warm him up a bit, and he just died in my arms. Shock I suppose.'[94]

Code and cypher officers were the first WAAF personnel to be deployed overseas, initially to America, and then elsewhere, including the Middle East. However, later in the war other trades had followed, and it became possible for women to volunteer and experience a variety of tours. For Dorothy Marsh, a farmer's daughter, this was exciting, as she experienced service with the ferry organisation in North America. After a successful interview at the Air Ministry, she was posted to Dorval, Montreal, and later, 'Elizabeth City, North Carolina, where the Catalina flying boats were being ferried out to Murmansk by Russian pilots'. Another posting followed 'in June 1944 to Goose Bay, Labrador. More planes going to Russia, this time Mosquitoes,' after which she returned to Dorval, and then back to the UK.[95]

Erks and other ground-based personnel could potentially serve in a variety of theatres during the Second World War. Morton Charlton provides an example. Having qualified as a nursing orderly, he served in Britain before a posting to Burma, from where he went on to serve in Nationalist China, before being invalided home in 1943. On recovery he joined a mobile field hospital in North-West

Europe during 1944–45, and by the time he was demobilised in 1946 had been posted to twelve different countries during his service, effectively experiencing three wars for the price of one.

As one erk explained, on active service, 'Your immediate surroundings dominate your thought process.' This could lead to 'a heightened awareness and a definite tension', amplified by 'conflicting rumours' about the war's situation.[96] During the North African campaign, airmen typically had to endure harsh, hot, dusty living conditions, made worse by sandstorms. They were divorced from civilisation and female company, and routinely faced with 'miles and miles of shimmering nothingness'. Yet some discovered that there was 'a strange pleasure in conditions of adversity'.[97] Most were aware that the loss of Tobruk would prove disastrous, and for a period, rumours abounded that it was threatened, leading to despondency. After the Second Battle of El Alamein during October–November 1942, attitudes changed, and as one airman with a fighter squadron commented: 'Life was more interesting and purposeful and there was considerable exhilaration in constantly moving forward.'[98]

Contrastingly, by January 1945, it appeared that the Italian campaign had ground down to a virtual standstill. Ground crews tended to glean information from publications such as *Eighth Army News*, a forces newspaper, and inferred that because their own sector was static, others must be as well. Despite this, they worked servicing aircraft, and in fighter squadrons, patrols continued even though little aerial opposition was met. As a fitter with 145 Squadron, Bertram Hughes experienced extensive service in Italy during 1943–45. For him it was characterised by periods of action, such as 'on readiness' at dawn, and 'stand down' at dusk, interspersed by 'endless inspections; the checks on everything that moved – and everything that didn't; the endless take-offs, the endless landings; the failed take-offs, the failed landings; the big accidents; the small accidents; the ever-lasting lifting, and pushing and carrying; the weariness; the frustration; the duff gen; and always the lurking fear that' pilots might fail to return.[99]

Compared with the above, the war in North-West Europe during 1944–45 appeared to have more purpose. In a message to the troops on D-Day, the Supreme Commander Allied Forces Europe, General Eisenhower, even dubbed the ensuing campaign to liberate Nazi-occupied Europe a 'Great Crusade'. Yet it was conducted against a resilient foe, and conditions could be tough for airmen. Stanley Wright and members of his mobile radar unit led an uncomfortable existence, reliant upon basic facilities, 'living like troglodytes', as they drove into northern Germany towards Denmark.[100]

Living and working conditions were a challenge for personnel serving in the Far East as well. As an instrument repairer with 322 Maintenance Unit in Cawnpore, India, Albert Bennett was intimately involved in servicing aircraft for the Burma campaign, mainly Hurricane fighters and Dakota transport aircraft.

'As one can imagine with the temperature 120 degrees plus, working in the nose of a Dakota was somewhat exhausting and if the aircraft had been carrying mules, often somewhat overpowering.'[101] Although they weren't directly involved in combat, many ground-based personnel came under fire, such as when airfields were attacked by the enemy. An armourer at Feni, Bengal, recorded the moment when he sheltered in a dummy gun pit during a raid by Japanese bombers. 'I lay there trembling, listening to the nearing explosions, and muttering, "Please, God don't let them hit me," over and over until I became ashamed and changed it to, "Please, don't let me be in such a funk."'[102] Another feature of the Far East was that owing to the isolation, harsh climatic conditions, threat of disease, and being ground down by their routine, airmen risked becoming 'puggled'. This was a phrase adapted from the Urdu, and applied especially towards the end of a tour, when a man might appear especially weary and confused.[103]

One of the most distressing and disturbing experiences endured by chair polishers from the RAF during the entire war, was when dealing with the concentration camp at Belsen, shortly after its liberation in May 1945. A nursing orderly who entered the camp with a collection of cigarettes and chocolate from his unit, recorded:

> the scenes were appalling, with emaciated bodies, little better than skeletons, lying all over the place, mostly huddled together. The fact that an eye moved was about the only visible signs of life, for it would have been difficult to say that they were still breathing. It was a most sickening sight, which no amount of pictures could graphically portray with any degree of accuracy. Apart from the degradation there was the awful stench which pervaded everywhere, and from which there was no escape. The smell lived on in the memory for a long time afterwards, and the scenes were never to be forgotten.[104]

Members of Stanley Wright's unit were deployed in an attempt 'to clear the place up'.

> The only thing that stopped me getting drunk or sleeping was Belsen. Driving a 3-ton Chevrolet truck towards it, you could smell it 2 miles away, over the smell of your engine. It smelt of burnt leather and burning bodies. We were all covered in DDT, given some spare shirts, and then told over there are some huts. If you go towards those huts, if you see any bodies put them in the back of your truck and put them beside the huts. We did in a big way – you'd walk along there and see a chap in his pyjama suit [concentration camp uniform] sort of tottering down the path towards you, dusty paths. You'd go and do something, unload some gear

or put some bodies beside the truck and they were put into great open graves that were dug by bulldozers. And you'd find them dead beside the road and put them in there. I have a nasty feeling that several of the camp staff went into the same graves.[105]

Numerous factors helped personnel to cope with conditions overseas. Discipline was important, and tended to contrast with that of the British Army. In an operational setting, as Wing Commander Harry Blee stated, 'The RAF version was essentially self-discipline – many airmen worked in small groups to perform their tasks, sometimes solo. Corporals and senior NCOs really made the system work and the good ones were very successful in getting the job done against the odds.'[106] As in Britain, erks weren't necessarily motivated by a desire for promotion, and many were happy to stay with their units. In North Africa, Bertram Hughes recounted how he and fellow ground crew, 'weren't ambitious, not in that direction, and we consoled ourselves with the thought that our remuneration was equivalent to that of a sergeant in Group Five, engaged on general duties.'[107]

Underpinning discipline was the issue of morale. In this context it can broadly be defined as factors that enabled airmen to better withstand the stresses and strains of active service, and do their jobs to the best of their ability. While teamwork, a military ethos and comradeship were essential, other aspects were equally significant. Access to tobacco and alcohol was important. Smoking was immensely popular in the 1940s, an era before widespread knowledge about its health hazards, and offered relief from the tedium of Service life. One of the most widely available cigarette brands available overseas was the 'V' for Victory, cheaply produced, and derided by many airmen as tasting like 'camel shit'. Beer was also welcomed, although it varied in quality. According to one airman, the local brew on Malta 'was about as strong as dandelion and burdock watered down', making the drinker increasingly downcast the more he consumed.[108]

Mail brought relief from the routine overseas, although news from home could be good, bad or indifferent, and 'Dear John' letters usually caused misery. Food was equally as important. Lawrence Wheatley spent part of his war as an armourer in the Middle East, and recalled: 'We lived on bully and biscuits, very fatty, tinned bacon, and tinned tomatoes or beans or occasionally eggs for breakfast; and Machonochie's [a tinned beef stew with vegetables] or bully beef stew in the evening.'[109]

Recreation was another vital feature in helping personnel to cope overseas. Albert Bennett found that regulations in India stated that after six months in the sweltering heat of Cawnpore, 'you were sent away to the hills and a cooler climate for three weeks' leave'. In his case this was to 'a hill camp called Chakrata', although he was rushed away after only a few days to join a Spitfire squadron.[110] Lawrence Wheatley remembered that during the North African campaign, reading was valued, especially any Penguin paperbacks that he and his fellow irks could obtain. In his squadron, several games were played in off-duty moments, including chess, and card games proved popular, notably brag and pontoon. Junior NCOs even had a mah-jong set that had been bought in Singapore.

When practicable, sports provided another useful release from Service life abroad. In Colombo, Ceylon (Sri Lanka), for example, there was ample scope for airmen to play football, hockey and rugby. A corollary of such activities was that they could stave off boredom, and keep Service personnel occupied and free from trouble. This included reducing the danger posed by venereal disease, a particular challenge in front-line areas, where it could be difficult to regulate prostitution. As an official RAF manual advised, to counter the threat of VD, 'Healthy sports should be organised in the men's spare time or when circumstances permit, and concert parties etc., arranged to occupy the evening.'[111]

Chapter 7

Accidents, Crashes, Shot Down and Taken Prisoner

Flying with the wartime RAF was potentially a dangerous business, whether on operations, during training, ferrying aircraft or in any other capacity. Apart from the obvious risk of being shot down when in action, pilots and aircrews could be faced with a host of mechanical and other challenges that put both their aircraft and lives in jeopardy. Consequently, accidents and crashes were very much a part of wartime life and could have a profound impact on both flying types and ground-based personnel.

There were numerous causes of accidents and crashes. One issue that had striking resonance from a flying perspective were the awkward handling characteristics of particular types of aircraft, both when airborne and on the ground. The Spitfire could prove awkward to handle on grassy airstrips in Britain and forward airfields overseas, both of which tended to become muddy in poor weather. As one pilot explained, such conditions were hated, because 'wind from the propeller would whip up mud and throw it into the radiator, blocking it and causing the engine to overheat', plus the design of the Spitfire ensured that on the ground its 'very heavy engine ... stuck out so far in front that it could cause the aircraft to tip over onto its nose and smash the propeller'.[1]

Some accidents led to fatalities, whereas others were less serious. Equally, many wartime pilots and aircrew had what might be termed close shaves during their service. At 16 OTU, a twin-engine Wellington bomber fitted with dual controls for instructional purposes had its port engine cut out at barely 20 feet. The instructor immediately took over, but was unable to retract the undercarriage as this could only be done via the port motor. 'Take-off flap was still on and the aircraft was nose up and starting to climb, whilst still on a low airspeed – a fatal combination.' Yet the instructor managed to wrestle control of the aircraft, relying on the starboard motor at full power, and safely landed the aircraft, only too well aware of how close they'd all come to being killed. He thoroughly deserved the green endorsement that appeared in his log book.[2]

Accidents of varying magnitudes also occurred on the ground. Airfields by their very nature were potentially dangerous work environments, with numerous aircraft taking off and landing and taxiing on a routine basis, plus large quantities of bombs and petrol stored in the vicinity. Ground crew working on aircraft could potentially suffer mishaps as well, such as accidentally putting a foot through the fabric skin covering the geodetic structure of a Wellington bomber.

Unsurprisingly, aircrew were usually glad to make it safely back to base after a sortie, particularly when nearing the end of a tour. A skipper of a Lancaster from 101 Squadron vividly recalled returning from a raid on Munich on 9/10 March 1943, their last operation. When he and his crew looked back they realised that they might have been for the 'chop' several times. 'We did breathe a sigh of relief when we thought what might have been.'[3] However, if they survived a crash or bailing out over hostile territory, pilots and aircrew stood a good chance of going into the bag if they didn't evade the enemy. Whether as a POW in Europe or the Far East, most endured a miserable existence in captivity, although there were opportunities to mount escapes or antagonise their captors, which could boost the morale of those behind the wire.

Accidents and crashes

There were many causes of flying accidents, including mechanical failure, pilot error, and poor weather. Sometimes it wasn't possible to identify an exact reason. On 25 April 1944, Liberator EW148, bound for India, ploughed into buildings in downtown Montreal, shortly after take-off from Dorval. It was piloted by an experienced former Polish Airlines pilot in his late forties, who'd escaped from Europe to join the RAF. The weather was indifferent, the cloud base at around 300 feet, light rain and visibility of 3 miles, which should have been acceptable for flying. Inexplicably, the pilot kept low, below the cloud, before crashing, killing himself and the four other crew members, plus ten civilians. Despite scores of witnesses, 'no real clue emerged' as to why the aircraft crashed. According to a senior officer: 'There were reports of damage on take-off, malfunction of controls, illness of Burzinski [the pilot], but neither by any radio message nor by any item of evidence could we pin anything down.'[4]

As indicated, design characteristics of particular aircraft types could play a role in accidents or make them awkward to handle. A number of Liberators found their way into RAF service via Lend-Lease arrangements. Although it appeared a brute of an aircraft, it proved sturdy and comparatively reliable. As the flight engineer leader for 'A' Flight 358 Squadron, Wing Commander Harry Blee developed an affinity for this American-manufactured four-engine bomber. His squadron deployed the Liberator from bases in India, undertook one bombing operation in support of ground troops attacking Mandalay, and became heavily involved on 'special duties' dropping supplies and agents to secret groups working behind the lines in Japanese-occupied South-East Asia.

There were Pratt and Whitney Twin Wasp Engines on the Liberator: two banks, with 17.5 litre capacity in its engine. Your boost was set to go up to 28 inches and revs to 27.50. Of course both of these depended on the settings for a particular aircraft. The revs for take-off, was 27.50 and that really was an issue related to the propeller blade. ... Although it didn't matter overmuch the vibration could be reduced once you're in the air really. It didn't matter on the ground the wheels absorb the rough and the banging. But once you're airborne the easier it was to synchronise the propellers and you can do it by looking along the blades ... smoother ride and less noise, just a gentle pulsing. ... Liberators seemed comfortable in a hot atmosphere and worked well. ... I can't remember that I had any failure issues with engines etc. So I had a clear run. ... It got me home.[5]

In contrast, other aircraft achieved unenviable reputations. The Handley Page Hampden served with both Bomber and Coastal Command during the early half of the war. Given its strange appearance with a distinctive pencil-like fuselage, RAF personnel often dubbed it the Flying Coffin, particularly as the chop rate on operations was invariably high. An extremely costly raid against German warships in the Heligoland area occurred on 29 September 1939, when eighteen of the twenty-four aircrew that embarked on it were killed, including the commanding officer of 144 Squadron.[6] A member of the ground crew at RAF Scampton vividly remembered seeing damaged Hampdens over his airfield, returning from this operation.

One day we saw eleven aircraft go over, heading out over Lincoln and heading east. And the buzz went round that they were from further along the road at Hemswell [a nearby RAF station] and they were doing a daylight bombing raid on Heligoland or in that area. And we thought 'oh my word, daylight!' A couple or three hours later five came back and it was certainly the most horrid sight I'd seen up to that time. They were tattered, they were struggling, three engines were miss-firing, they were wobbling all over the sky, and they'd obviously been shot up pretty rotten, and they were the remains of the squadron of that raid. ... It brought home to all of us on the deck that things were not quite as bright as the journalists made out in terms of RAF aircraft, that our Hampden with their single Vickers guns and so on were not up to the opposition. The station commander at Hemswell stood and wept we were told because several of them bellied in and were unable to make normal landings. There were crashes all over the field and they were pretty bloody inside, a fair number of dead and wounded and so on.[7]

As a torpedo bomber, the Blackburn Botha proved fundamentally unsound. Of all the wartime roles performed by the RAF, delivering torpedoes against targets at sea was one of the most difficult, and resulted in high losses to aircrew. According to one navigator with Coastal Command, who encountered the Botha during training, it was 'a twin-engined, high winged, four to a crew plane which was unstable and under-powered and not suitable for aggressive operations'.[8] At least one crew room was decorated with a verse that summarised how poorly this aircraft performed:

> My abject all sublime,
> Is to make a Botha climb,
> On one engine at a time …
>
> Later someone added in pencil, 'Done it! – for two seconds.'[9]

The Bristol Beaufort proved better suited as a torpedo bomber, but wasn't without its foibles. It 'was of all-metal construction, twin engine, with a high wing-loading, that is very weighty for the area of wing and therefore its stalling speed was very high and necessitated a steep angle of approach when landing. Mostly it could not maintain height on a single engine and if ditched in the sea, sank very quickly.'[10]

Given that accidents/crashes were an inevitable part of flying, personnel had to confront this reality. One former RAF officer explained:

> What people in the business do is carry out emergency drills, various practices that are necessary to make sure if certain things happen there is a plan and it's a workable one and its well-tried. Having said that, they work on a system that if it happens at all, it will be to somebody else not me. … Although necessary to prepare for emergency eventualities, no case to brood on it, it's a fact of life, so you make whatever arrangements you can to deal with it and get on with life. That was the flying business in wartime.[11]

Operational experience of an aircrew from 101 Squadron provides an example. During late 1942, the squadron started to re-equip with Lancaster bombers, and supported the bombing offensive against Germany as well as minelaying sorties and operations against Italy. It started using the 'Airborne Cigar' (ABC) operationally, a radio countermeasures apparatus that jammed German R/T transmissions, and required a specially equipped Lancaster, replete with a German-speaking operator who accompanied the crew. From January 1944 to April 1945, the squadron flew 2,477 sorties, including those with the Airborne Cigar, and dropped 16,000 tons of bombs on enemy targets.[12]

A Lancaster from 101 Squadron suffered problems during a raid against the Krupp armaments works at Essen, in the Ruhr. Once over Europe, the port outer engine began to overheat and had to be feathered; then over the target, the starboard outer engine received a hit. This provided most of the electrical power for the aircraft, so the bomb release system failed, forcing the crew to release their bombs manually – never an easy task – and they were unsuccessful. On only two engines and with a full bomb load, they managed to limp homewards, expecting to make a pancake landing, and were directed to the emergency airfield at Carnaby, near Bridlington. 'To the scene of a greatly excited crowd of ground crew people,' the fortunate crew 'climbed out, and kissed the earth, one and all'. Although mightily relieved to have survived their ordeal, they soon discovered that their sortie didn't count towards their tour's total, as it was classed as 'aborted' because they'd failed to deliver their bombs over the target.[13]

Weather was a significant factor in many flying accidents and crashes, both in Britain and overseas. On 25 August 1943, C.A. Faulks, a wireless operator/air gunner, was part of an aircrew despatched on an air sea rescue mission. No survivors were found, and on return to base his aircraft encountered an electrical storm, ensuring that they were off course. They were instructed to head due east, and in accordance with procedure, Faulks logged the wireless signal, and told the pilot to change course.

> We were about 80 miles west of Wick [North-East Scotland], whereas we would normally be about half that distance. The course they had given us was a correct one, and all was well. But what the ground station had failed to warn us about, was that Ben Loyal, a 2,500 foot mountain was in our flight path, and we were flying at our normal operating height, below that level. Suddenly there was a blinding red flash in my head then nothing![14]

He was the only survivor of the crash, having fortuitously been thrown clear of the aircraft on impact, although with both legs badly broken. For the next year and five months, he was treated in various military hospitals before eventually returning to duty and being posted to RAF Leuchars.

Equally, weather was an issue for aircrews in the Far East, including those flying large multi-engine aircraft on lengthy sorties. On 7 May 1944, two aircraft from 356 Heavy Bomber Squadron 'assisted in searching the Bay of Bengal for a missing Liberator of 355 Squadron. Crash located near KHARGPUR.'[15] Although not specified in the Operations Record Book, weather might have been a contributing factor in the crash. Liberator crews from 358 (Special Duties) Squadron found that weather:

> was the major problem, people shooting at us was not really the issue you could always keep away from it. There weren't many outfits in the jungle

with anti-aircraft weapons but if you flew near Bangkok or Hanoi, the main towns they did have anti-aircraft weapons but then why go there? Air supply was into uninhabited jungle, special operations support local groups etc. out of town. During the monsoon you could be flying from south to north over the Arabian Sea, Calcutta at the top, and it was just a wall as far as you could go. So it was a case of making an assessment of where to go into it. The problem was really very strong up and down drafts, and this probably explained aircraft that didn't come back. If you were low down then a serious down draft made it likely that you'd hit the water. The mantra we followed was to be at least 5–6,000 feet, which gives you some room to manoeuvre. But different skippers chose different ways to deal with it.

Unless you've been in a tropical area during monsoon season, you can't quite appreciate how overarching it is. It is floor to ceiling, left to right everywhere you looked, no easy way through. And furious rain storms as well, not that they in themselves were a problem. The turbulence was the issue inside these large formations.

Plenty of crews, including mine, had some very rough rides. And if you hit it really hard you had to knock out the auto-pilot [known as 'George'] or else it would go mad trying to keep straight, and fly manually then once it stabilised a bit bring 'George' back in.

The crews coming from Europe had nearly always done a tour in Europe [with Bomber Command]. And during winter months in Europe the weather can be a major factor as well. ... In many ways flying to Berlin, the weather could be just as bad. So it wouldn't have been new, but probably more violent.[16]

In the Mediterranean and Middle East, sandy conditions were a challenge, and accounted for the crash of a Martin Maryland, a light bomber/reconnaissance aircraft. After examination of the wreckage, the pilot recalled, 'it was found that the left wheel's brake had partially seized, thereby accounting for my inability to hold the aircraft straight on take-off. We always had a lot of trouble with sand getting into the moving parts of aircraft.'[17] Human error was another significant issue. A tragic situation was witnessed by Des Curtis, a navigator with Coastal Command, who served on Beaufighters and the fearsome Mosquito Tsetse. He'd been part of an ASR sortie, where together with other aircraft he'd directed Canadian warships to the site of 140 German seamen who required rescuing.

We came back five aircraft [Beaufighters]. The CO said: 'Let's just do a gentle fly pass in formation. Tighten up.' So we were five aircraft in formation doing a low-level run across the airfield. We were tucked in, number two aircraft on the starboard side, and another aircraft was on our starboard side and making the outside wingman. We came over the airfield and the leader did not say: 'Break away, break away, go' which was the standard instruction. He made no remark at all [and lived to deeply regret what occurred next]. And he suddenly started, the leader suddenly started turning sharply to starboard. My pilot realised that something was going wrong and pulled the stick back, opened the throttles and we climbed until we had run out of power virtually, and then turned back to see what was happening, and I looked round to see one aircraft in two pieces, spiralling down to the sea off the coast of RAF Portreath [Cornwall] and another aircraft with a wing and a half. One half of the wing had been sheared off.[18]

Regardless of their cause, flying accidents entailed a human cost, not only in terms of losing aircrew, but also owing to the emotional impact on other personnel. As an R/T operator with the WAAF based at RAF Waddington, Pip Beck was routinely in contact with aircrews, especially as they returned from operations. Once, a low-flying Wellington crashed nearby, 'and a great rush of flame spurted from the broken aircraft'. There were no survivors, and the inexperienced pilot might have 'panicked a bit and turned on his duff side and stalled'. Beck was extremely shaken. 'It had all happened in moments, and in that short space five young men had died in the smoking pyre of their aircraft; mine had been the last voice they had heard – would ever hear.'[19] Sadly, this was far from uncommon, and during the war plenty of aircrews were lost over home soil as well as over the Reich.

Knowing that an aircraft was in trouble was distressing. As a wireless operator, Jack Ambler was stationed in a hut on the edge of an airfield, from where he experienced receiving faint and disturbing messages from aircraft on operations. These were difficult to cope with because he was ordered by Signal HQ not to acknowledge them and keep silent. On one occasion he was:

Sitting at the radio set and just quietly listening, as instructed, when I suddenly heard an extremely faint signal from one of our planes, slow but methodically clear I heard the message: 'Hit on Fire.' And I immediately conveyed this over the direct line to Airfield Control. It was from the leading aircraft who had been hit by enemy fire. This time I again learned that I had been monitored by signals HQ – but they had not heard the message come over the air, and were astounded. I had this time kept silent as told to do, sadly realising I could not even acknowledge this distressing message, and so the HQ people heard nothing.[20]

No doubt some personnel found it easier than others to cope with losses. During his service in India, Wing Commander Blee witnessed a horrific incident resulting in the death of a close comrade, but explained how he managed to deal with it psychologically.

> I actually saw a friend of mine blown up. Ken Wells. I was the Flight Engineer Leader for 'A' Flight 358 Squadron and he was the Flight Engineer Leader for 'B' Flight. He was doing an air test with the crew of a Liberator and they were doing a wide circuit. ... And we never did know why it blew up but the suspicion was that fuel got onto hot metal somewhere in the system, which theoretically could happen of course and probably did.
>
> You sort of shut your mind to it really. I mean it's a fact, it happened. I saw it and I am 95 and still remember it ... having said that, I haven't spent the intervening years worrying about it. These sort of things they happen and if your number's up it is, so that's the way I sort of look at these things.[21]

Pip Beck was deeply moved by her experience of the Augsburg Raid. On 17 April 1942, six Lancasters from 44 (Rhodesia) Squadron based at RAF Waddington, and another six from 97 (Straits Settlements) Squadron, based at Woodhall Spar, undertook a daring low-level strike against the MAN diesel engine factory at Augsburg, Southern Bavaria. This entailed a difficult, lengthy flight over enemy territory, much at extremely low level. Eight crews reached the target and bombed it, but overall losses were so great that such raids weren't repeated. For his leadership during the operation, Squadron Leader (later Wing Commander) John D. Nettleton was awarded the Victoria Cross.[22] Of 44 Squadron's aircraft, his was the only one to return, and after the raid, there were 'thirty-five empty bunks, thirty five-five empty places at table, shared between the Officer's and the Sergeant's Messes. Many of us wondered whether it was worth it.'[23]

Unsurprisingly, the prevalence of accidents and crashes, and the risk of being shot down, raised the spectre of Lack of Moral Fibre. While serving as a sergeant with a mobile radar unit after D-Day, Stanley Wright became aware of another NCO who'd previously been branded LMF.

> We had a code and cipher sergeant over in Normandy, who had LMF stamped across his papers. Now he'd been an air-gunner in Blenheims from Manston [RAF Manston, Kent] and went off one morning with twelve of them, and went off later that morning with the six that were left. Later that afternoon he was one of three that were going on the next trip and he said: 'No, I am going to live.' And he was LMF. Frankly I reckon he'd earnt his pay by going on two trips.[24]

According to Stanley Wright, such a sympathetic viewpoint was pretty universal amongst airmen towards those classed as LMF, especially after these individuals had endured significant action.

Inevitably, numerous less serious accidents occurred, although aircraft and equipment might have been damaged. Early in the war, Eric Marsden witnessed one at RAF Tangmere, Sussex, and recorded the uncharitable reaction of the ground crew.

> The Station Commander had a beautiful Hawker Hind/Hart, this beautiful silver bi-plane polished up to the knocker. And he would occasionally have it wheeled out and take a flight in it. And we all admired it because the Hart series are pretty aeroplanes. I remember he'd brought it down onto the end of the east-west runway, the 25 runway, and it was sitting at the western end, ready for take-off, and a Hurricane came in to land, and landed smack on top of it. And no one was injured, which was the remarkable thing. ...
>
> All rotten types like the ground crew just stood about laughing of course, and didn't go anywhere near it in case we got involved in the work of clearing it up.[25]

Many flyers endured close shaves during their war service, when under different circumstances there might have been more tragic consequences. Pilot Officer J.R.A. Hodgson flew with Bomber Command and spent a period seconded to Coastal Command at RAF St Eval, Cornwall, to gain operational experience. During August 1942, he was returning from an anti-submarine patrol when his twin-engine Whitley bomber suffered engine failure.

> I had come down low, 500 feet or so, as the clouds were right down. The other motor wouldn't hold her so out went the SOS and back went the boys to the ditching stations. I held her for another five minutes and then stuck her down on the sea. We got the dingy out OK and the aircraft sank in seven minutes – not bad for a Whitley.[26]

They endured several hours adrift in their dingy, were pestered by a basking shark, which attempted to eat their fluorescein tablet, but eventually they were spotted. The ASR system went into operation, and a motor launch picked them up and transported them to the Scillies.

As a fighter pilot with 1 Squadron, flying Hurricanes, Paul Richey recounted how, over France, he heard a loud 'bang' and felt a jolt run through his aircraft.

> I throttled right back again, then cautiously opened the throttle, watching my rev counter. It whirled right round the clock to about 3,000, so

I hastily snatched back the throttle and switched off. The entire prop had disintegrated. All this feverish activity took just a few seconds.[27]

Fortunately, he was able to glide back to his airfield from around 20,000 feet and safely touch down on the grass without further problems, although his hands were trembling with tension.

Another fighter pilot, Tony Tooth, had various scrapes flying Spitfires in North Africa. At Maison Blanche (Dar El Beïda), Algeria, 'There was only one runway, and that with a hump in the middle, and no Air Traffic Control, so everyone just took off or landed in the most convenient direction, causing many near misses but so far as I know no collisions.' He experienced a near miss, having followed his flight commander in to land one evening.

luckily I did a bad landing and immediately left the runway onto the grass, as I did so a US B-26 Marauder bomber came past me doing at least 125 mph, to my 75! He had seen me in front of him but was determined to get down first try. There is only one word for his action, murderous. ... I should say that the Spitfire was not a nice plane to fly at night as the engine produced spectacular amounts of flame exactly in the direction the pilot would be looking when landing. As I taxied back in the dark after that little incident I didn't see a new bomb crater and went straight into it![28]

On another occasion, his flight was fitted with a 90-gallon, long-range fuel tank, which affected performance on take-off.

Unknown to me a bomb disposal team was digging up an unexploded bomb from the runway just over the hump and so out of sight from us at the end of the runway, consequently as I went over the hump there they were just in front of me! By hauling back hard on the stick I managed to get airborne and so did not go straight into the team or their crater, but the wheels did just clip the earth thrown up sufficiently hard to smash the undercarriage. I, however, could not see what damage had been done, so I decided to do a belly landing ASAP. As it would be extremely dangerous to land on top of 90 gallons of high octane-petrol, I had to get rid of that tank so I flew over the sea and released it, hopefully into the water. I then flew back to the airfield and pulled off a perfectly good landing on the grass beside the runway. Luckily the fire-crew had seen my plight and were waiting in exactly the right place, so they were able to haul me straight out and put me in the ambulance to be taken for a check-up. It transpired that I was 'high' on a mixture of petrol fumes and ethylene glycol from the radiator. The collapsing undercarriage had punctured the radiator and the fuel tank so the cockpit had been filling with very noxious fumes. Then to cap it all the tank had not released and so I had landed on top of it. Why on earth it did not explode or catch fire, no one could fathom – Very definitely my lucky day![29]

Personnel working on the ground also faced potential hazards. A wartime instrument repairer with Bomber Command commented: 'On the ground one had to be very alert and watchful, keeping eyes and ears open for things spinning, slipping, turning, catching fire and falling,' and 'the need for vigilance' was impressed upon them by their NCOs. Moreover, 'fire vigilance was constant, especially in the vicinity of petrol, oil, bombs and ammunition; and you had to keep an eye on taxiing aircraft, swinging tail planes, and slip-streams.'[30]

Handling bombs was often fraught with danger, and there were several cases of armourers being blown up during the war, and others, including WAAF tractor drivers towing bomb trains to aircraft. At RAF Skellingthorpe, Lincolnshire, a raid was cancelled and the aircraft recalled. Although ordered to jettison their bombs, 'some returned with long-delay fused bombs still aboard'. While the armourers attempted to deal with one aircraft, a bomb exploded, killing them and blowing out the glass windows of Flying Control, fortunately with no further casualties. 'Anxiety was great in case the explosion set off a chain reaction in the other still bombed-up aircraft,' but luckily, that didn't transpire.[31]

Other forms of ordnance could be problematic. Lawrence Wheatley served as an armourer overseas, including at an airfield near Colombo, Ceylon (Sri Lanka). Here two new armourers were tasked with removing flares from a Fairey Albacore of the Fleet Air Arm, an aircraft intended to replace the antiquated Swordfish.

Unfortunately, they forgot to remove the fusing device from the carrier and as the flare dropped to the ground the safety fork was jerked out activating the delay mechanism that allowed the flare to fall clear of the aircraft when in flight. Instead of pushing the flare away from the aircraft and removing themselves, the armourer at the nose end of the flare remained kneeling and clutching the flare apparently mesmerised. The small explosive charge which ejected the flare from the case and ignited it blew the fusing pistol into the poor chap's forehead fracturing his skull. He died very shortly afterwards in the station sick bay.[32]

Various other accidents befell ground-based personnel, which although not necessarily serious, were still painful and awkward for those concerned. Armourers employed bomb trolleys, which comprised a 'T-girder' onto which were bolted supports to carry bombs, and a wheel assembly at either end. At the front was a tow bar for fitting to a tractor. In the Middle East, an affable older armourer from Scotland put his index finger through the holes to ensure they married up, when unfortunately, the two erks holding the girder dropped it, severing the end of his finger. He was hurriedly treated by the MO, but left with a 'finger ... like the end of a sack of flour. ... For some days afterwards airmen would approach another with a cheery, "Here, cop hold", drop the end of his finger into the other's palm.'[33]

Shot down: bail out or crash-land?

One of the most terrifying prospects facing wartime flyers was that of being shot down in a burning bomber over enemy territory. Assuming they weren't killed or badly injured after being hit, initially their chances of survival rested on whether the skipper could keep their damaged aircraft airborne and fly homewards. If not, crews would have to brace themselves for a crash-landing or bail out by parachute, neither of which necessarily proved straightforward in the heat of action.

Wing Commander Ken Rees recalled the agonising moments when BK309 'N for Nuts', the Wellington bomber he was piloting, came under anti-aircraft fire during an attempt to lay mines along the Karmsund, Norway, a channel between the island of Karmoy and the mainland, south of Haugesund, which offered protection to enemy shipping heading for sheltered waters inland of Stavanger. The anti-aircraft defences in the area had recently been reinforced. Initially, he wasn't surprised, as he'd often encountered light flak, but then it became heavier:

> red balls of tracer fire, rising lazily towards us from the ground, accelerating viciously as they whizzed close by. Our sky was quickly filling with flak ... hitting us like dozens of sharp stones, and with a loud bang the oil tank in the fuselage exploded, taking the two pigeons [carrier pigeons] out completely, our first casualties. We were now well alight, and some of the flak hit the cockpit, great balls of fire.

With the intercom and lights down, instruments unresponsive, fire taking hold, and crewmen injured, *N for Nuts* was in a perilous state. 'Suddenly, a massive thump, and the starboard engine was dead; it felt as if the propeller had been shot off.' By skilful airmanship, he managed to bring the stricken aircraft down to crash-land into the waters of Lake Langavatn.[34]

On 29/30 May 1942, four Wellingtons were lost out of a mixed force of seventy-seven bombers that attacked the Gnome et Rhône aircraft engine factory at Gennevilliers, near Le Bourget, France. In a foretaste of later Pathfinder tactics, the raid incorporated twelve 'Wimpeys' bombing from low level (2,000 feet) to illuminate the target for heavier four-engine aircraft bombing from 10,000 feet. Carlton Younger, a navigator with 460 Squadron, was among those shot down that night. Approaching the target, 'a fiery web of tracer of various colours and a cone of searchlights made for a beautiful sight but the low-level attack now seemed like a suicide mission.' During its bombing run, Younger's aircraft was hit amidships, and 'a red streak shot in front of us, travelled along the starboard wing and set it ablaze.' The aircraft was clearly doomed, although the skipper stayed with her so that surviving crew members could bail out. As it went into a steep dive, he ordered Younger to jump. 'I thought it was futile but had nothing to lose, so I jumped. … I felt hot flames over my head then the jerk as my parachute opened, at the same moment as I heard the crash. I brushed a tree and hit the ground chin first.'[35]

Percy Carruthers, a decorated NCO pilot, recounted how it felt when his Martin Baltimore was hit while leading a bombing run in North Africa.

> The intensity of the battering did not abate. A sickening rending blast somewhere below my feet shattered the aircraft, admitting a force so violent that my eyelids were fluttered uncontrollably and the flesh on my cheeks and lips were rippling with the force. The control column, hinged at the floor between my legs, thrashed at me as though crazed.[36]

Although he didn't realise it, he'd received several wounds, and soon after lost his port engine. Given the hopelessness of the situation, he ordered the crew to bail out, before following, only to land amongst German troops who promptly captured him.

Alternatively, bombers might be attacked by fighters or night fighters. In early December 1942, Halifax *'P for Popsie'* was one of over 270 aircraft sent to bomb Mannheim, an operation that achieved little success as in cloudy conditions most aircraft had to bomb by dead reckoning.[37] During the raid, *P for Popsie* was savaged by a German night fighter over Alsace-Lorraine, leading the pilot to put the aircraft into a steep dive to try to douse the flames before ordering crew members to bail out. The wireless operator, Henry Robertson from Northumberland, recorded the experience: 'The silence in the aircraft was suddenly and rudely shattered by a loud sustained burst of heavy cannon or machine-gun fire. The bomber shuddered violently' and soon became 'bathed in bright orange light coming from the blazing port engines'.[38]

While they didn't appreciate it at that moment, they'd fallen prey to a new Luftwaffe night-fighter tactic of employing upward-firing guns (*Schräge Musik*). The night-fighter pilot was directed by ground control onto a specific bomber, and approached his target from the rear and below, proving hard to detect. He'd then fly directly underneath the bomber's belly and unseen by either of its gunners, open fire with the upward-firing guns specifically aiming for the engines.

Personnel who bailed out and survived invariably became members of the Caterpillar Club: 'a unique band of men and women whose lives have been saved by the aid of an Irving parachute'.[39] When Tony Johnson, a wireless operator/air gunner in a Wellington, earned his membership of the Caterpillar Club, he was struck by the contrast of his peaceful descent compared with the mayhem of the stricken bomber he'd just vacated.

> I started to tumble as soon as I hit the slip stream, and I pulled the ripcord as soon as I had judged that I was clear of the tail-plane. The canopy blossomed into a lifesaving mushroom which instantly checked my rapid descent. Gyrating considerably slower earthwards, I was amazed by the uncanny silence compared to the bedlam I had experienced during the previous ten minutes [when his aircraft had been hit by an 88mm anti-aircraft shell]. It was so quiet I could hear the gentle rustle of the parachute shroud lines as the chute drifted on the breeze.[40]

Others recalled that they were dominated by uncertainty, tinged with fear as they hurled themselves free of their burning aircraft. As he parachuted down, 'somewhere over Europe', Henry Robertson was initially struck by the realisation that he'd miss bacon and eggs in his sergeants' mess that night, then thought: 'What would my people at home think if they could see me now?' Subsequently, the cold reality of his predicament stuck him: 'Where was the night fighter? Was he still mooching about looking for me, to finish the business with another burst of fire? Would he accidentally fly into me or the parachute in the darkness?' Not likely as he reckoned it was probably following the blazing Halifax to confirm its 'kill'. He began to wonder where he was, and pondered: 'What kind of reception, if any, awaited me when I landed?' Although he couldn't see anything in the darkness, he 'kept as loose-limbed as possible to ensure an accident-free landing'.[41]

An alternative to crash-landing on land or bailing out was to ditch in water. William (Jim) Hunter joined the RAFVR in 1939, qualified as an observer (navigator) and served on Beauforts with Coastal Command. In July 1941, he was shot down while attacking the German battle cruiser *Scharnhorst*. The port engine was hit and belched 'smoke in large quantities', and with the starboard engine struggling to cope, the surviving crew members braced themselves for landing on the sea, which proved to be text book-like in its precision.

> Everything became very quiet. By God it was quiet after the previous din. Digger [the pilot] was then making his way out through the hatch above his cockpit and I soon followed. The last ridiculous thing I remembered doing before I left was to lift the Syko machine over the side of the depleted nose and into the sea! [The Syko machine was for encoding/decrypting messages, generally between a flying aircraft

and a ground station]. Within seconds of our entering the sea Ted [the gunner] appeared from the turret, having apparently suffered no real harm. The pity was that Pip [wireless operator] didn't make it. We had to leave him in the aircraft which with her back broken took no time in sinking, and without trace. The three of us trod water, inflated our Mae Wests and waited for something to happen.[42]

Consequently, they became members of the Goldfish Club, that select band of aviators who'd made a successful forced landing into water. They were subsequently picked up by the crew of the *Scharnhorst*, and although they didn't understand everything said to them, the gist was clear: 'For you the war is over.'[43]

Fighter pilots could be faced with the decision of whether to bail out or make a crash-landing, either during combat or owing to problems such as engine failure. Having engaged enemy fighters during Operation Husky, the Allied invasion of Sicily in July 1943, Tony Tooth's engine 'blew up' and large quantities of smoke belched from his Spitfire's exhaust.

I didn't fancy climbing up leaving a spectacular trail of smoke in enemy territory so decided to stay with it. It turned out that my luck held out, as we went thru the mountains we got slower and slower and lower and lower till suddenly we were over a large cultivated field. I could see that there was a large irrigation ditch crossing the field so I knew I had to try to stop before I went into that. The only answer was to push the plane down onto the ground as quickly as possible and hope that we would stop in time.[44]

Another Spitfire pilot, American William Ash, who served with the RAF, was involved in a sweep over the Continent in March 1942 when hit from behind during an engagement with enemy fighters. He turned to face his attackers and attempted to present a smaller profile. However, by flying straight at them his aircraft received several further hits. 'I knew that there are few worse ways to go than being trapped in a cockpit on fire,' and this left him only two choices: choose somewhere to crash-land, or bail out.[45] Fearing that parachuting would provide German troops the opportunity to watch him descend before capturing him on the ground, or that the fighters might shoot him, he decided to crash-land. Desperate to avoid a French church, he reached the ground and his Spitfire dug a wing tip into the earth.

Almost instantly my plane began a cartwheel, careering over the ground. Flashes of grass and sky alternated as pieces of the plane started to disintegrate. One wing was practically ripped off and a shuddering crunch close behind me told me my fuselage had probably gone too. I finally came to a stop, not too far from the church, which – like myself – was miraculously intact.[46]

Evading capture

If they survived a crash-landing or bailing out, pilots and aircrew risked becoming a prisoner of war. Yet the Air Ministry was initially slow to realise the potential of evasion by downed aircrew who were uninjured and able to get free of an aircraft. Interrogation of returning aircrew who'd successfully escaped from enemy territory revealed that many were captured within a few hours after landing by parachute or climbing out uninjured from their crashed aircraft, simply because they'd made little or no effort to leave the area and hide before German search parties arrived. Given this, it became increasingly important as the war progressed that all operational RAF personnel were encouraged to become more evasion conscious. Typically, senior officers instructed flyers that it was their duty to evade capture if shot down or escape if they were captured. When Tony Tooth crash-landed over Sicily, then enemy territory, he recalled:

I stayed down in the ditch [where he'd crashed] and kept going for an hour or so, heading south, and then laid up and hid as I thought I was safe from pursuit. In point of fact I think that most Germans that day would have had much more pressing business than chasing stray airmen![47]

Once dark, he set off again and walked towards the sea, eventually making it to one of the American invasion beaches, from where he was returned to his squadron.

Early in the war, intelligence officers started to be briefed on escape and evasion techniques and this information was relayed by them to operational squadrons. Clearly this was a step in the right direction. By 1944, specialist training in this field frequently relied on personnel with invaluable first-hand experience. Ahead of D-Day, Squadron Leader Denis Peto-Shepherd was posted to No. 3 Group Escape School at Methwold, Norfolk, before commencing an operational tour with 90 Squadron, Bomber Command. He recalled that trainees were addressed by a number of airmen who'd proved successful as evaders, and attention was given 'to toughening physical exercise, aimed largely at fitting us for the life of long-distance movement in the open that this would involve'.[48]

The loss rate in Bomber Command was running at about 4 per cent per operation by late 1943. Consequently, it was good for the morale of aircrew and squadrons to know that if personnel survived being shot down and evaded capture there was a chance they'd make it home. Instruction on evasion stressed that movements were best conducted at night, and that evaders should lie up during daylight hours and avoid built-up areas where there were liable to be enemy troops. Yet lectures could be enlivened by amusing anecdotes that hammered home particular points. One that did the rounds in the 1940s, and highlighted the need to promptly vacate a crash site as well as the value of seeking help from locals, was probably apocryphal. It concerned an NCO pilot shot down near to a French convent. Before the Germans closed in he was hurriedly hidden by the nuns, and disguised in a habit of their order. Soon he found himself in the company of an especially beautiful nun, who resisted his careful advances, stating in a deep masculine voice: 'Don't be a bloody fool, I've been here since Dunkirk.'[49]

The British authorities recognised that in France priests were likely to be particularly helpful, albeit they had to be approached with caution. Alternatively, places such as isolated farmsteads could be approached. Evasion training advised that it was sensible to keep watch on such properties first, to ascertain whether they were safe. As Henry Robertson discovered, when he and another crewmember from *P for Popsie* successfully evaded capture in occupied France from December 1942 to March 1943, the absence of German troops visiting a property often ensured that it was approachable. Moreover, he soon realised that much depended on their ability to obtain help from locals sympathetic to the Allied cause, 'aided by oodles of luck'.[50] During his period as an evader, he was at one time disguised as a Breton forestry worker so as to account for any language difficulties, because Bretons spoke virtually impenetrable French. Another time, he hid in a hayloft, with the Germans agonisingly close. Eventually, he made it from near Bar-le-Duc in Alsace-Lorraine, where he was shot down, to Spain via Paris, Western France and Vichy France. He reflected that he was immensely grateful for the assistance and hospitality shown to him by families in the Ruffec area, which 'proved a vital factor to the success of our subsequent journeying in France, the Pyrenees and Spain'.[51] Like many evaders temporarily stopping over in Paris so as to use the rail network, he found that Parisian prostitutes were only too keen to do anything to hit back at the Germans, including sheltering Allied airmen in brothels.

Airmen expected to become a POW if captured, provided the enemy could be certain of their identity; otherwise they might be viewed as a spy. This was straightforward so long as the RAF evader could 'produce his service identity discs'.[52] Contrastingly, the many courageous individuals who assisted them risked being sent to a concentration camp at best, or summarily shot, if caught by the Germans. Although the reappearance in Britain of personnel who'd previously been thought to have been lost in action was a tremendous boost to morale, it posed problems for security. Returnee evaders were liable to be deluged with questions by their comrades, which could compromise the safety of those who'd helped them on the Continent. Successful evaders were therefore drilled on the importance of remaining tight-lipped.[53]

If help from locals wasn't forthcoming, evaders on the Continent were encouraged to attempt to walk towards unoccupied France, repeating pleas for assistance when appropriate. This was potentially an extremely daunting task, but it was hoped that by doing this they'd eventually be put in contact with the local Resistance and/or some form of escape organisation. Even so, evading capture could potentially be an isolating, unnerving experience, and the successful evader required the mental fortitude to persevere. For Henry Robertson, thoughts of the beautiful countryside in his native Northumberland, and that he might live to see it again, acted as a mental stimulus during his lengthy evasion experience.

Escape lines became more developed and effective as the war progressed, but constantly ran the risk of being infiltrated by enemy agents or, in some cases, betrayed by those working for them. One of the most well known in Western Europe was the PAO Line (better known as the Pat Line), overseen by MI9 – that part of the British Directorate of Military Intelligence at the War Office tasked with fostering an escape and evasion culture in the Armed Forces and supporting European resistance networks, particularly by urging them to help airmen evading capture. From October 1941, the Pat Line was run in the field by a Belgian Army medical officer, Albert-Marie Guérisse (who'd escaped to Britain in a commandeered vessel and was given the assumed name of Lieutenant Commander Patrick O'Leary (Royal Navy)), and it aided around 600 persons per year to evade capture, including Henry Robertson. Using a variety of safe houses across the Continent, evaders were provided with civilian cover and eventually guided, usually by smugglers, across the Pyrenees and into neutral Spain. This was a significant challenge in itself, especially owing to the threat of poor weather and tough walking. From Spain, many British personnel travelled homewards via Gibraltar.[54]

Another notable enterprise was the Comet Line, founded by Belgian nurse Andrée de Jongh, better known as Dédée, or the 'Little Cyclone' – a nickname her father gave her on account of her prodigious energy as a child. In 1941, she and friends began to hide British servicemen evading capture, initially troops left behind at Dunkirk. Subsequently, with help from her family and MI9, she established an escape line that specialised primarily in guiding Allied airmen fleeing from occupied Europe, again to eventual safety across the Pyrenees. From July to October 1942, the Comet Line brought out fifty-four people, mainly aircrew, and this was an impressive effort before winter set in. It was deemed so successful that Hermann Göring, as head of the Luftwaffe, personally ordered its destruction.[55] Alternatively, some evaders, again mainly airmen, were picked up by high-speed vessels off Brittany and spirited away to safety at Falmouth, via what became known as the 'Shelburne Route'.[56]

However, approaching locals for help didn't always produce the desired result. When the crew of *N for Nuts* crash-landed in Norway, they had to make the agonising decision to leave a badly injured crew member behind, before putting as much distance as possible between themselves and the crash site. Still suffering from shock, they approached a few properties for help, before eventually finding a house occupied by two brothers. Here they were able to dry out their uniforms, while one of the crew received basic attention for burns, although their efforts to obtain a map went unheeded. Suddenly, the door burst open and they were confronted by half a dozen Germans pointing pistols and sub-machine guns at them, compelling them to surrender. As Wing Commander Ken Rees commented, 'You don't fool around with all that ammunition directed at you.'[57]

Others barely had the chance to seek help from locals or make any attempt at evasion. When Trevor Utton, an 18-year-old air gunner in the mid-upper position on a Lancaster, was shot down over Bonsecours, France, in May 1944, he bailed out and landed in the grounds of a large house. After looking around he spotted a lean-to shed, so took off and folded his parachute, and hurriedly hid with it a corner of the shed. 'After about two or three minutes the tallest German I ever saw with a rifle and bayonet came in and said *"Raus"* [Out] which I did.'[58] Unfortunately, he'd landed in the grounds of the Château Baugnies, which was adjacent to the École du Centre Filles, which billeted the local German garrison.

In contrast, some RAF evaders became involved in helping the French Resistance or other partisan type groups during their time behind enemy lines. Denys Teare, the bomb aimer in Lancaster ED571 *'S for Sugar'* from 103 Squadron, bailed out over occupied France on 5 September 1943, after a raid on Mannheim. During his evasion experience he became involved in assisting the Resistance in receiving a supply of weapons via an airdrop. The drop zone was to be marked by three red lights, shining upwards and spaced at regular intervals.

> I myself was to stand 100 metres from the end of the red line, and as the aircraft circled, I was to flash a letter S with a white light. We were warned to keep a sharp look-out not only for patrolling Nazis but for the heavy metal canisters as they came floating down in the darkness; a hit from one of those could easily prove fatal.[59]

Airmen could rely on numerous devices to help them evade capture. Yet, landing in occupied territory could be a disorientating experience. The much decorated Squadron Leader Tom Cooke was shot down over France while engaged on 'special duties' supporting SOE, having already completed over fifty operations with Bomber Command. He found:

> The main problem initially was to find out exactly where I was. I had some maps and the sky was cloudy, so there was no way one could look at the stars and get a direction. None of the road sign posts had been taken

down in that part of France but this didn't help unless you've pinpointed the area you were in.[60]

Consequently, all flying personnel became equipped with officially produced escape kits, such as the small box employed by Henry Robertson, which contained a compass, pills for purifying water, a water bottle, silk map of France and Belgium, antiseptic and sunburn cream, French and Belgian currency.[61] A knife was important as well, particularly so that an airman could cut himself free of an obstacle, such as a tree, should his parachute become entangled in it. Denys Teare always carried a sheath knife on operations, and when he bailed out employed it on landing, 'to cut off the tops of my sheepskin flying boots [so as to make them more like civilian shoes] and remove my brevet [his bomb-aimer's badge] and sergeant's stripes'.[62]

Some of the challenges facing Teare were ameliorated by the standard issue of flying boots, which were essentially shoes with leather leggings that were attached around the calves over thick socks. If the airman landed in occupied territory, the leggings could swiftly be removed, making it appear as if he was wearing normal civilian shoes.

Officially produced emergency packs, comprising food in concentrated form, plus matches, a needle and cotton, a razor and shaving soap, were all useful to the evader. It was generally reckoned that most French peasants were clean-shaven, so these last items had resonance beyond personal hygiene. A fishing line was provided in some escape kits, which could at the very least help evaders pass the time if in hiding near water. Alternatively, if not employed for its intended purpose, the line could serve other uses, such as acting as replacement braces on trousers when these broke. Aircrew were also advised to take passport-sized photographs with them, so these could be used in forged identity documents.[63]

While serving as the station commander at RAF Linton-on-Ouse, Group Captain (later Air Vice-Marshal) John Whitley undertook several bombing sorties. After avidly listening to several escape and evasion lectures, he attempted to go one better than officialdom and developed his own escape kit. Firstly, he removed maker's labels from a lounge suit jacket, put a tie in its pocket, and rolled these up with a peaked cap in a haversack. 'He sewed a strap on the haversack and thereafter kept the haversack with his parachute canopy pack so both could be clipped to his harness in a second.' On operations he wore the trousers for the suit (with labels removed) underneath his uniform trousers, 'and under his uniform shirt wore a blue check shirt with collar attached'. In his pockets he carried 'a Rolls razor, tube of brushless shaving cream, toothbrush; tube of tooth-paste, nail file and tiny compass'.[64]

Much thought went into the development of escape/evasion devices, under the inspirational leadership of Christopher Clayton Hutton, known as 'Clutty', whose job it was to design them for the armed services, as part of MI9. Notably, maps demonstrated great ingenuity. Using pectin to coagulate the ink, it became possible to print handkerchief-sized maps of Germany that were readily concealable. Later versions had Germany printed on one side and France on the other. As Denys Teare recalled, 'I had found two handkerchiefs in my waterproof escape packet, one printed with the map of Germany on one side and Northern France on the reverse side, the other one with maps of Italy and Southern France.'[65] It even proved possible to produce maps using an extremely fine but durable paper, which could be scrunched into a ball and then smoothed out with hardly a crease. Various compasses were designed for aircrew, without which these maps would have been of limited value. One compass was manufactured so that it could be hidden inside a button on RAF uniform, and another was so small it could readily be concealed within an item such as a tobacco pipe or cap badge.[66]

For RAF flying personnel in the Far East, a piece of lightweight clothing suitable for tropical conditions was developed, dubbed the 'Beadon suit'. This incorporated several items for use by any would-be evader, such as maps, a compass, a hacksaw, a machete, anti-malaria tablets and an escape kit, all kept in securely buttoned pockets.[67] However, anyone of European descent faced two sizeable problems in attempting to evade capture in the Far East, which made conditions significantly more challenging than in Europe. 'One was the sheer size of Asia – the colossal distances, covered on foot, across formidably severe terrain. The other was that it was impossible for a white or black-skinned escaper to make himself look like the population round him.'[68]

Despite this, the situation facing British airmen did improve as the course of the war against Japan turned more in their favour. In early September 1944, Warrant Officer A.C. Farrell, a Hurricane pilot operating over Burma, was forced to crash-land near Japanese positions. He managed, with a degree of luck as well as skill, to evade capture and 'survived for five days on nuts, raisins and vitamin tablets, and then met some locals who befriended him till E Group could collect him'.[69] This was a rescue and intelligence organisation that had been established independently in the Far East during 1941, and performed similar tasks to MI9 in Europe. Another vital factor that helped pilots such as Farrell was the prompt reporting by other pilots of where and when other aircraft were seen to crash, as these could be followed up, hopefully with good results from an RAF perspective.

Life in captivity

Around 10,500 personnel from Bomber Command alone became a *Kriegsgefangener*, or POW, usually shortened to the more manageable *'kriegie'* by the British. They and other RAF *kriegies* faced a life of uncertainty. Wireless operator 'Jack'

Foster was captured in France during May/June 1940, having been posted there as part of a small RAF contingent tasked with co-operating with spotter planes supporting army units from the British Expeditionary Force. After over a year in captivity, he recorded that it felt as if:

> The end of the war seemed years away. Jerry was racing through Russia, and as a POW you have no idea how long you will be behind barbed wire. This is one of the hardest things to overcome, a criminal is given a sentence, and knows he will be free at the end of it.[70]

During the summer of 1940, his group of prisoners faced a long, hot and dusty march into captivity, often 'being herded ... like animals'.[71] Initially, he was taken to a *Dulag Luft*, or *Durchgangslager* (transit camp), at Frankfurt-on-Main for interrogation. Like all RAF personnel, he was drilled to only provide name, rank and Service number, if captured. For flying types, this was even more important, as the enemy was understandably keen to extract information about units, aircraft, specialist equipment and so on. Typically, prisoners were held in a cell 'about 8ft long by 6ft wide and 8ft high. The only communication with the guards was by pulling a piece of wood set in the door, which when pulled, stuck out of the door into the corridor.'[72]

When Percy Carruthers was held at the Dulag Luft after being transported from North Africa, he was subjected to typically tough treatment. The temperature in his cell was freezing. He'd complain and the heating would be turned up so much, he could 'hardly breathe'. Subsequently, he was advised that he only had himself 'to blame for the discomfort of the "unpredictable" heating system', and that he should 'complete the "Red Cross" (bogus) form and answer some simple questions'. However, if he remained uncooperative, he was assured that his stay in the cell would be prolonged and uncomfortable, plus the safety of his 'family in England could not be guaranteed when the Germans marched into the British Isles'.[73] As Tony Johnson and other members of Bomber Command who became POWs and passed through German cities discovered, they were routinely branded by irate locals as *'Terrorfliegers'* (terror flyers) or *'Luftgangsters'*.[74]

For evaders who were caught, the situation could be worse. William Ash was hauled out of the Paris flat where he'd been hiding and taken to Gestapo HQ. His interrogator refused to believe he was a pilot, as he'd been captured in Paris wearing civilian clothes, unless he provided the names of everyone who'd assisted him since he crash-landed. Soon he received a thorough beating from the guards, which started when:

> One ... hauled me to my feet and grabbed my arms behind my back. The other hit me a vicious punch in the face. I turned my head and the

next blow crashed into my stomach. I tried to clench my muscles but a third crashing blow to my solar plexus left me gasping for breath as he returned to hitting me around the face.[75]

Badly bruised and bloody, he was threatened with being shot as a spy unless he co-operated and proved his identity. However, a blazing row ensued between his Gestapo interrogator and a Luftwaffe officer who'd arrived and proceeded to take him into custody. By comparison, the Luftwaffe proved more humane, not least because they knew that hundreds of their own pilots and aircrew were held as prisoners by the Allies, so that acts of brutality wouldn't be to their interests.

In the Far East, the Kempei-Tai (Japanese secret/military police), like the Gestapo, were universally dreaded. As a member of 205 Squadron operating flying boats, Charles McCormac was captured when Singapore fell to the Japanese. He was interrogated thoroughly and occasionally beaten with fists, although he tried to give nothing away. Subsequently, he was taken before Teruchi, a Kempei-Tai officer later sentenced to death as a war criminal. After administering further beatings and shouting several questions, Teruchi 'pulled his Samuari sword out of its bamboo scabbard' and jabbed the blade at McCormac, who:

> tensed and waiting, managed to jerk his head aside in time to save his eye. The point speared through the fold of skin at the corner of his eye, grated on the bone and tore through and out ... Teruchi jabbed again and once more McCormac ducked and the point sliced across his cheek by the corner of his mouth, but did not go through into the mouth.[76]

Having been interrogated and processed, which included the issue of a metal identity disc, *kriegies* were transported to some form of permanent camp, often by rail. For many this involved being packed into cattle trucks for an uncomfortable journey. As one former Wellington pilot recalled, there was: 'only just enough room to sit down or stand up in your own little space. ... No windows just a barred ventilator about two feet by ten inches,' located near the roof so 'not much chance of seeing out, unless someone lifted you up'.[77] Pretty soon most prisoners became aware of the attitude of their guards. Not all were thugs or sadists, but according to Tony Johnson, many Germans 'thoroughly enjoyed baiting us, in the hope that we would overstep the mark and provide the excuse to maim or kill'.[78] Notably, late in the war, some RAF prisoners were moved westwards to escape the advancing Russians. Conditions on these marches were appalling, and one especially horrendous episode occurred at Stalag Luft IV (Gross Tychow), when a group of prisoners were subjected to the infamous 'run up the hill'. During this, they 'were made to run at the double to the camp while being set upon by dogs and by guards' rifle butts and fixed bayonets', and at least 228 men were injured.[79]

In the Far East, guards were noted for their cruelty, including one at Hakodate POW Camp in north Japan, 'a proper bastard' who routinely would 'kick into the legs of all the sick who had leg ulcers from beri-beri, causing them terrible pain and bleeding'.[80] Alan Carter, an airman first class and wireless operator with 605 (County of Warwick) Squadron, was one of about 4,500 persons unlucky enough to be captured by the Japanese in Java after the fall of Singapore and Sumatra. He witnessed the above treatment, and explained one way in which Far East POWs coped with it was to give all guards nicknames. In this they found some humour in their dire situation, and had much in common with *kriegies*, who adopted the same practice. The above guard was dubbed 'Billy Bennett', after a pre-war stage act who was billed as 'almost a gentleman', and because 'he was anything but a gentleman', the name stuck.[81]

Like *kriegies*, FEPOWs had to be transported to permanent camps, or from one camp to another. The way in which this was achieved between countries and islands within the Japanese Empire was via the notorious 'hell ships', merchant vessels whose foetid holds were packed with neglected prisoners and cargo. It is estimated that 10,800 of the 50,000 prisoners transported by sea like this died during their journey.[82] Alan Carter was one of those who endured voyages aboard such vessels from Java to Japan, via Singapore, Indo-China (Vietnam) and Formosa (Taiwan). Recalling conditions aboard the *Tofuku Maru*, he noted, 'each man's ration was a loosely packed cup of rice and a cup of [watery] soup', possibly with potato peelings floating in it or daikon, a type of radish.[83] As they approached Japan:

> We prisoners ... would be glad to vacate the ship as our death toll had grown considerably since leaving Singapore and every day brought further deaths from dysentery ... in a way this work [he and a few other prisoners acted as stokers] was our salvation because it occupied our minds and bodies as well as providing us with the means of obtaining extra food – a life saver in the conditions we were living in.[84]

POW camps varied in size and location, but there were similarities, even between those in different operational theatres. Hakodate Camp comprised 'a collection of long wooden huts surrounded by an eight foot high fence with double gates' replete with guardhouse, guards' living quarters, store room, bathhouses, cookhouses, administrative buildings and so on.[85] Percy Carruthers was held in three different camps in Europe, and observed that 'all were built on sandy soil to discourage tunnelling', while accommodation was also in wooden huts, and these were on stilts, again to deter tunnelling. All the camps were split into compounds, within two barbed wire fences, and a single strand of 'warning wire', beyond which any unauthorised person could be shot. There were roofed watchtowers, complete with searchlights and machine guns. Entry to these camps was via the 'Vorlager ... a separate compound containing the German administration offices and accommodation quarters'.[86]

Unlike the Japanese, who didn't recognise the Geneva Convention, the Germans did (at least in theory) abide by its terms. However, NCOs and other ranks were usually put to work by the Nazis. Trevor Utton found that working as an NCO orderly in an officer's camp, carrying out domestic chores, helped 'fill your time', and conditions were 'better ... than the privates in the army had'.[87] Jack Foster was initially put to work picking out cobblestones from a ditch beside a road. He and his fellow prisoners 'messed about, picking up one stone and then stopping for a chat', so a German workman was put 'in the ditch and set the pace, so we would then drop every other one', and 'got the sack'.[88] This was typical of a great many POWs, who if possible tried not to work too hard, or even tried to sabotage the projects they were given. In the Far East, Alan Carter and his comrades were forced on demanding labouring jobs, although these sometimes had perks. While working as 'stevedores' at Hakodate docks, the opportunity arose for prisoners to help themselves from a box of frozen oysters, something they did eagerly in order to supplement their meagre diet.

Contrastingly, officers held captive in Europe were not expected to go on work parties. As a black RAF officer, originally from British Guiana (Guyana), Cy Grant was a rarity. Yet, his experiences as a navigator with 103 Squadron had much in common with other airmen. His Lancaster was shot down over Holland in 1943, when the unfortunate crew were on only their third operation. After evading capture, he was later handed over to German troops, and in keeping with Nazi ideology, dubbed 'A Member of the RAF of Indeterminate Race'. Initially held at Belaria POW camp for officers, he likened the experience to receiving a university education. There was:

> an opportunity to reflect upon my life, about who I was, what I was doing there and what had brought me into that situation. ... I was in the company of men who were officers, well-educated and above average intelligence. We were able to organise ourselves into a highly efficient community.[89]

Activities included an escape committee, music groups such as a jazz band, plus theatre/drama groups and a library, supported by the Red Cross. The food was poor, and at first there was little news from home or on how the war was progressing. Carlton Younger recounted that at his camp, a thirty-two-piece orchestra, made up from *kriegies*, proved popular, along with the camp's theatre in one of the wooden huts. This offered:

> full-time jobs for many, for dress designers and 'seamstresses', and all the other makers and menders. The feminine roles ... were now convincingly

played by a small group who were dressed and made up with much cunning. ... Music, debating, literature, the theatre – they were new and exciting worlds to many.[90]

Another officer POW remembered at his camp, education began to take off, and was enjoyable, if nothing else. '[T]he subjects varied a great deal even if most amounted to little more than talks. But they were popular and, with the arrival of the RAF, their scope was widened considerably.' This was because the RAF drew on those with a technical background, plus many at officer level were well educated, and overall comprised a wide variety of life experiences from across the Commonwealth and beyond. Consequently, it was an experience 'to listen to some backwoodsman of an Australian talking on "riding the range" and making such digressions as only these people could was a riot in itself'. Such experiences enabled one to 'leave the realms of the POW camp' for a while, although serious lectures on topics such as astronavigation, mathematics, law, and languages also occurred.[91]

Sporting activities also helped *kriegies* pass time and acted as a diversion from their plight. At Stalag Luft III (Sagan), one prisoner recalled: 'We played a lot of sport; this was mainly soft-ball or "golf" in the summer, and football. We also had a sports day and crazy days when, for bets, folk would push a ball around the "circuit" with their noses!'[92] Not only did these activities fill time, they also boosted morale, provided relief from the routine and conditions of captivity, and even had educational benefits. Likewise, *kriegies* of all ranks concocted pastimes for similar purposes. One example of this was witnessed by Jack Foster, who described how a craze was established in his camp one summer:

which entailed catching a large fly [plenty of which could be found in the latrines], tying cotton to its legs, then making a drogue from cigarette paper and tying it to the cotton. We would then climb up to the top bunk and let it go ... then ... see who could get one to fly the furthest.[93]

However, the above shouldn't imply that POW life was akin to a holiday camp. It certainly wasn't. Apart from boredom, most experienced an emotional cocktail of fear, frustration and uncertainty. Some became suicidal, or 'wire-happy', and encouraged the Germans to shoot them by climbing the wire. For aircrew, captivity was a painful experience, as these men were typically highly motivated individuals and missed the challenge of operational flying. Some made up for this by 'Goon baiting', or intimidating guards, mounting escapes, and generally making life as awkward as possible for their captors. Simultaneously, there were those who considered themselves fortunate to have survived being shot down and felt they'd already contributed to the war effort enough by flying on operations, and were resigned to their fate as a POW.[94]

Food was a major issue for all POWs, especially, 'the lack of it, and its quality was nothing to rave about'.[95] Often, prisoners in Europe and the Far East were denied Red Cross parcels, which made matters worse, and had serious implications for their health. As Jack Foster found, *kriegies* were so weak that if they sat up in bed too quickly they became dizzy, and owing to their poor diet, lacked strength to properly combat illnesses or infections. According to Cy Grant, typical rations consisted of: 'one-fifth of a loaf bread, an ounce of margarine, six potatoes, and a bowl of soup per diem ... made from worm-infested peas and horsemeat, but we scooped out the worms and wolfed it down'. Consequently, many mentally 'planned gourmet feasts' as a coping strategy.[96]

In the Far East, the food was similarly appalling, compounded by the harsh climate and threat of tropical diseases, plus conditions such as dysentery. At Hakodate, prisoners were routinely fed rice, which 'contained weevils and maggots too numerous to be removed before cooking', and out of desperation they'd eat 'bones from any fish ... stolen and cooked', plus horse bones used by the cookhouse as stock for soup, 'boiled for so long that they were soft and easy to chew'.[97]

Unsurprisingly, POWs, wherever they were held, frequently attempted to improve the conditions of their captivity. This could involve making secret radios (there were plenty of RAF prisoners with the appropriate skills) used to garner news on the war, which boosted morale. Alternatively, less technical pursuits included making home-made brew from dried fruit in Red Cross parcels, or holding delousing sessions by running a lighted taper along the seams of uniforms, making lice pop. Jim Burtt-Smith, a working-class lad from London, volunteered for the RAF, became a bomber pilot with 115 Squadron, and was shot down and captured. He remembered how prisoners at Stalag VIIIb (Lamsdorf) sought to improve life by using their ingenuity to build home-made 'immersion heaters', with items scrounged from around the camp, including round cigarette tins.

> You would turn the tin upside down and nail a piece of wood across the bottom leaving the head of the nail protruding. Then lay the tin, supported by the wood across your billy can, so that the tin was suspended upside down in the water you wanted to heat up. Get two pieces of wire and attach one bared end to the nail and the other to the small folding handle of the billycan. Then connect to the electricity supply for the hut's lights. The water would boil almost immediately.[98]

Escape efforts

Escaping in the Far East was an extremely difficult proposition. Nevertheless, attempts were made, including one from a camp near Bibai, to where Alan Carter had been moved by mid-1945. A warrant officer and an American prisoner appeared to have successfully escaped, only to be paraded at roll call (*tenko*) after a few days, with ropes 'fastened to their arms which were pulled up behind their backs and connected to a noose around the neck'.[99] If they dropped their arms the noose tightened, choking them, and they'd both received severe beatings. They acted as a warning to the other prisoners, against the folly of escaping, before being handed to the Kempei-Tai. As all FEPOWS had been coerced into signing a document waiving their right to escape or face death, it was assumed that they'd be executed.

In contrast, escaping from a permanent POW camp in Italy or Nazi-occupied Europe was more practicable. Many camps had an escape committee that vetted proposed escape plans, although they didn't necessarily have the authority to ensure all prisoners helped with escapes. However, many did, and this included tunnelling, providing forged documents, and manufacturing suitable civilian clothing. In this regard, POWs found that their blankets smoothed with a sharp knife provided a good basis for making escape clothing. As many camps were akin to university behind the wire, this ensured that those engaged in activities such as the theatre could transfer their skills towards escaping or helping escapists.

Parcels containing escape equipment were sent to all camps by MI9 under the auspices of fictitious welfare organisations, such as the 'Welsh Provident Society' or 'Prisoners' Leisure Hours Fund', complete with authentic postmarks, and wrapped employing newspaper from the supposed locality of the sender. These provided invaluable support to escapists by supplying items such as maps hidden in Monopoly boards, or hacksaws concealed within the handles of cricket bats and the like. To counterbalance these 'special' parcels, thousands of ordinary parcels were despatched from Britain containing items such as coffee and tobacco, which could be used to bribe guards.[100]

Although achieving a 'home run' was difficult, the official RAF policy was that it was the duty of every airman to escape once captured, or continually attempt to do so, because this would distract the enemy and tie down a number of his troops in search parties. Many wholeheartedly embraced this philosophy, including Wing Commander Douglas Bader, who despite missing his legs, gained considerable notoriety among the Germans for the lengths he went to 'Goon bait' guards. After mounting a number of failed escape attempts, he was eventually incarcerated in the supposedly 'escape-proof' Oflag IVC at Colditz.[101]

Yet attitudes towards escape differed among *kriegies*. Some felt that the activities of escapists were in essence those of a selfish minority, because life in a POW camp was grim at the best of times, and their actions made it all the more intolerable for the rest. RAF Sergeant Richard Passmore reckoned that the whole business of escaping was effectively a 'form of escapism' in itself, hindered by the difficulty of making a 'home run'. Keep in mind that by May 1945, he'd been imprisoned at Stalag Lufts I, III and VI, and during his captivity he'd done his fair share of assisting escapers, including the terrifying experience of helping to excavate a tunnel that collapsed, plus he'd already risked his life for his country by flying operationally. Another issue that caused him and other POWs considerable resentment was that they perceived back at home were men 'both in and out of uniform, who were doing quite nicely out of the war'.[102]

The best time to escape was soon after capture, before an individual had been processed as a POW or during transit to a camp. This was not necessarily practicable for men who'd suffered the ordeal of being shot down and were still recovering from it. Consequently, escaping from a permanent camp offered an alternative. There were three main ways of doing this: 'over (the wire), through (the gate), or under (the wire)'.[103] 'Over the wire' was extremely risky, and liable to lead to an escapee being shot. However, 'through the gate' would often require some form of subterfuge to be successful. Alternatively, 'under the wire' essentially entailed tunnelling, a potentially dangerous and awkward activity reliant on several prisoners.

RAF Sergeant George Grimson demonstrated great ingenuity and fortitude as an escapist, and favoured the first two methods, assisted by an ability to speak passable German. At Stalag Luft III (Sagan) he disguised himself as an 'engineering ferret', one of the German workmen who repaired telephone lines and lighting, propped his ladder up against the perimeter fence, having first cleared this with a guard, then dropped some tools on the wrong side of the fence. He swore loudly in German, before asking the guard if he could climb over and retrieve them. This enabled him to enter the German sector of the camp, whereupon he hid before exiting through the gates using forged papers. Once it was safe, he took off his work clothes to reveal a smart civilian suit underneath, and continued his escape. Although recaptured, in early 1944 he escaped again, this time from Stalag Luft VI (Heydekrug), by bluffing his way out of the gate in a German uniform obtained from the camp interpreter, who was sympathetic towards the Allied cause. Outside the wire, he bravely remained under cover for a period, and attempted to organise his own escape line via the Baltic ports to help other escapees reach Sweden. It seems probable that he was eventually caught and shot by the Gestapo.[104]

Kriegies could use work parties as opportunities for escaping once outside a camp. Some RAF officers attempted to escape by swapping identities with other ranks engaged on labouring tasks, then looking for an opportune moment to slip away. Instead of using a work party, bluffing their way out of a camp's gate, or getting over the wire, tunnelling presented another option. Famously, this was achieved during the 'Great Escape', the massed breakout from Stalag Luft III in March 1944 that resulted in fifty escapees being caught and executed. It's no coincidence that many of the RAF personnel involved in this mammoth enterprise had considerable previous escape experience to draw upon.[105]

Typically, tunnelling required determination, skill, planning and an element of luck to be successful and remain undetected. The Germans often employed microphones buried in the ground to detect signs of tunnelling. One way for the noise of the excavators to be shielded was for several prisoners to walk around and stamp their feet, as if to keep warm, in the hope of 'deafening some unfortunate guard given the tedious job of listening to the soil for eight hours at a stretch'.[106] Another was for tunnels to be dug deeply, below microphone level. This was fine in theory, but depending on the local geology, there was always a danger that a tunnel might collapse or become flooded. It could also be extremely unnerving for the men involved with the digging, under claustrophobic conditions, to know that a considerable weight of earth rested over their heads, the deeper and longer a tunnel became.

Concealing the spoil from excavations was a related challenge faced by all tunnel diggers. At Oflag XXIB (Schubin), a major tunnel was dug and spoil hidden by adding it to the latrines, which unfortunately 'flooded with winter rains or a blockage', so that diggers were covered in 'a vile liquid'.[107] This made it harder to clean up and conceal their activities, as well as being unpleasant for their room-mates. Unsurprisingly, materials scavenged from around a camp, such as bed boards and packaging from Red Cross parcels, were invaluable in shoring up tunnels. Providing an air supply to men in a tunnel was another key issue. The tunnel at Schubin was 300 feet long and dug to a depth of 20 feet to avoid underground obstacles. It had a 'fully supported roof' and on 3 March 1943, forty men used it to get under the wire and into the relative cover of a potato clamp. It employed home-made bellows fashioned from an old army kitbag to provide air for the diggers, 'and was lit by fat lamps'. These large bellows were attached to an air pipeline made of Klim milk tins saved from Canadian Red Cross packages. As these tins were slightly smaller at one end than the other, they could be readily slotted into each other to form the necessary tubing.[108]

As Willian Ash, one of those who took part in this daring breakout, cautioned, their troubles really only just began once they emerged from the tunnel and sought to evade capture. He was on the run for a week before being slung into a civilian jail. Yet the 'escape was a great success in terms of getting the German army out looking for us' owing to the large numbers of POWs involved. According to him, they may have been 'hunted' by as many as '300,000 regular troops, police, militia, civilians and Hitler Youth'.[109] This made it exceptionally difficult to achieve a 'home run' but graphically demonstrated how such activities could enable POWs to contribute towards the war effort.

Chapter 8

Demobilisation and Coming Home

Victory over the Axis powers during the summer of 1945 brought conflicting emotions for RAF personnel. A decorated veteran of 420 operational sorties described how initially, there was a sense of 'bewilderment', coupled with 'gladness and regret'. After the 'jollifications' that had characterised VE-Day, his airfield experienced an 'unaccustomed silence' and there was a palpable sense of 'the snapping of nervous tension' that felt 'dreadful, as painful as a surgical operation'.[1] Another fighter pilot recounted how during the war he'd encountered 'the magnificent "esprit de corps" that the Royal Air Force rejoiced in', and this was different from the civilian life facing him on demobilisation, which forced him to take a room in a boarding house, 'to give myself time to sort myself out'. For him, a particularly notable feature had been 'the amazing accessibility and friendliness of the most famous and successful pilots', who with few exceptions were 'as friendly and pleasant as could be. My lowly rank meant nothing.'[2]

Yet it wasn't just flyers who missed wartime RAF life. As the date for her discharge approached, WAAF officer Muriel Pushman conceded that she 'was sad, not just at the thought of leaving my friends but also at leaving behind this part of my life'. Soon she had to tidy her room, 'morosely emptying draws, and making two neat little piles on my bed – WAAF issue to be returned to Stores in one, and my own private bits and pieces in the other'.[3] Others were shaken by the devastation that the war had caused. This included one WAAF who was taken on an official RAF sightseeing trip flying over Germany shortly after the war. She was horrified by the devastation that had been rendered to cities such as Hamburg, where 'there wasn't a roof to be seen!'[4]

Equally, there were those 'sick to the death of living out of a kitbag', and who refused any inducement to sign up for another four years, the terms of enlistment offered with the post-war RAF.[5] Leslie Baker, who'd been ground crew and a Commando, reflected, 'I am very proud to have played my small part in an Allied victory. I have learned the value of true comradeship and I hope that such a major war will never happen again.' However, this was tinged with regret on a personal level because, as he put it, 'my career was absolutely shattered by this war and I had to struggle to make my way to the best of my ability.'[6]

One officer commented how, during the war, conditions had 'been getting more and more informal', and that it was becoming increasingly difficult 'to keep the troops occupied'.[7] Notably, during January 1946, at least 50,000 airmen committed what was technically an act of mutiny in the Far East, when they collectively refused to perform work for a short period or attend parades wearing their best blue uniforms. What had started as a small, peaceful protest at RAF Drigh Road (Karachi) rapidly spread as far as Singapore. A major factor contributing towards the airmen's dissatisfaction was the slow rate of demobilisation and poor conditions, although some mutineers may have had genuine left-wing or even communist sympathies. Courts martial occurred, although afterwards a sense remained among senior military officers that many airmen effectively 'got away with it'.[8]

Various dispersal points for the transition from RAF to civilian life were established, including those at Wembley in London, and Cardington in Bedfordshire. Former Spitfire pilot Tony Tooth recounted how, in July 1946, 'I got a gratuity of £186, roughly £4,000 today, and an outfit of civilian clothes which I disposed of immediately as it was so horrible!'[9] One rumour that did the rounds was that if personnel slipped the tailor a five pound note, they'd be given the best demob clothing. On 17 August 1945, Henry Brown was officially released early from the RAF on medical grounds, and received his Form 1394. He proceeded to a demobilisation centre at RAF Padgate, Lancashire – ironically, the same station where he'd enlisted in 1941 – and underwent a process familiar to countless wartime airmen. His draft was met by a 'fiery drill corporal' who briefly showed them around and cautioned that they'd have to be ready for a final parade at eight o'clock the following morning. Subsequently, they were marched to a large hangar, 'laid out like a giant Marks & Spencer store' with an array of civilian clothing on display. To him, the choice and quality seemed good:

> I chose a brown pin-striped suit which I wore for years ... brown shoes and socks, brown striped shirt and tie and a natty brown trilby hat ... nothing blue. I had enough of that colour for now. We changed and handed in our service kit, not without a little nostalgia. Then we collected our railway warrants from the Guard Room, signed out for the last time [as a civilian]. ... A new life had started.[10]

Three categories of release existed for both men and women: Class A was based on a person's age and length of service; Class B (National Reconstruction) incorporated those released 'at the request of the Ministry of Labour and National Service, in order to perform work of national reconstruction'. However, these individuals could be recalled for duty 'if at any time prior to the date on which the Emergency is declared ended ... [they] ceased to perform the work for which' they'd been released. Finally, Class C incorporated those released on extreme compassionate grounds, in advance of other personnel.[11] Demobilised personnel hoped the RAF would provide a good reference that could help them find civilian employment or successfully return to their former jobs. Wireless operator Jack Ambler received 'a reference in my Certificate of Service Book, intended to help me reclaim my job in civilian life', which read: 'LAC Ambler is a most reliable and keen worker, very efficient and can be depended upon.'[12]

Many Service men and women were entitled for the award of the 1939–45 Defence Medal, for services in Great Britain and overseas from 3 September 1939 to 8 May 1945, and/or the War Medal, 1939–45, with its distinctive red, white and blue ribbon. To qualify for this, an individual had to be a full-time member of the British and Commonwealth Armed Forces, and have completed a minimum of twenty-eight days' service in either an operational or non-operational capacity. Additionally, those who'd served overseas were potentially eligible for a range of campaign stars, and the 1939–45 Star if they'd served operationally during 3 September 1939 to 15 August 1945. After operational flying with Coastal Command, followed by service with Transport Command, Flight Lieutenant E.F. Carlisle-Brown was demobilised in April 1946, after six and half years' service. He received the following British medals: the 1939–45 Star; Aircrew Europe Star (France and Germany Clasp); Africa Star (North African 1942–43 Clasp); the 1939–45 Defence Medal; General Service Medal and Air Efficiency Medal (AE).[13]

As individuals had to apply to the Air Ministry for the various Second World War campaign medals, not all felt obliged to do so, especially as they attempted to put their war years behind them. An issue that caused even greater resentment was that, despite their efforts, members of Bomber Command weren't granted a specific campaign medal. As one veteran stated in 2003, 'the absence of the Bomber Command medal somehow passes the buck of recrimination [for the bombing offensive] to them – the RAF aircrews' and 'it leaves a somewhat bitter taste in the mouths of many' flyers and the ground crew who supported them.[14] However, many members of Bomber Command, as well as other aircrew, were eligible for the Aircrew Europe Star, awarded for operational flying from British bases over Europe (including Britain), for a period of two months from the outbreak of war on 3 September 1939 to 4 June 1944. In recent years, a Bomber Command Memorial has been unveiled in London, and the International Bomber Command Centre established in Lincoln. Although, sadly, such recognition has come too late for a great many veterans, these will hopefully ensure that future generations are made aware of the sacrifices made by the crews of Bomber Command.

Many personnel remained liable to be recalled to duty until their commission was relinquished or terms of enlistment ceased to apply, not something that was necessarily welcomed. Having joined the RAFVR in the late 1930s, and been called up for war service, Stanley Wright eventually served as an NCO and radar operator in North-West Europe, 1944–45. After demobilisation, he embarked on a career as a teacher in London, at a school for children with sight problems, when:

> I suddenly got a notice saying 'G' Reserve: 'You are recalled to the air force. Go to Browning Street and have a medical and then you'll get your papers etc.' I wasn't a bit happy. God damn it, I'd done six years of the blasted air force. I didn't want to get called up for another fortnight, and it didn't strike me as being fair that someone who'd been chucked out as early as I had on old age and general decay [he'd always suffered from poor sight] should be whipped back in again so quickly.[15]

During the immediate post-war period, the RAF was also tasked with having to run down what had been a vast organisation in wartime. By May 1945, it had grown to a strength of over 55,000 aircraft and 1,079,835 Dominion and Allied officers and men. The WAAF had made a significant contribution to the war, with women serving in at least eighty ground-based trades. The future Women's Royal Air Force (WRAF), as the WAAF was rebranded, would have to be much smaller, although women were still expected to perform vital functions such as air traffic control. Simultaneously, the RAF had to contend with the onset of the Cold War, including the Berlin Airlift of 1948, and countering Communist guerrillas during the Malayan Emergency.

With the advent of atomic weapons delivered by air, and arrival of jet aircraft, the nature of aerial warfare appeared to be changing too. A much decorated fighter pilot observed how the arrival of jet propulsion was, 'the greatest step forward since man had learnt to fly', and that with aircraft such as the British Meteor jet, 'a prospect opened of inspiring possibility and absorbing interest'.[16] Under Air Staff Plan E of 1947, it was envisaged that the RAF would rely on a front-line strength of 1,500 aircraft, incorporating 51 fighter squadrons, 41 bomber squadrons, 13 squadrons of maritime aircraft, 42 squadrons of transport aircraft, plus 12 reserve squadrons. This proved unfeasible in the austere post-war economic climate, and within a year, aircraft numbers had been reduced to about half those suggested in 1947. Post-war reliance was also being placed on National Servicemen (conscripts), although not to the same extent as the army, and this had particular implications for the training cycle, as the RAF required technically competent individuals, but National Servicemen were only with the Service for a relatively short period (two years by the time of the Korean War).[17]

However, demobilisation took time, and for many individuals victory in 1945 didn't bring an abrupt end to their RAF service. In July, Flight Lieutenant Anthony Goulty transferred to 7 Intelligence Assault Unit (7 IAU), which was to partake in Operation Zipper, the proposed liberation of Malaya.

the plan was for us to storm ashore just behind the first wave of landing craft, and round up Japanese orders of battle etc. before they got too burnt in the incinerators the fleeing Japs were sure to put them in. We had a compliment of 27, drawn from all three Services, under the command of Colonel De Quesne, who was a Rhodesian.[18]

Owing to the dropping of the atomic bombs on Hiroshima and Nagasaki, and subsequent Japanese surrender, the operation never occurred. Instead:

troops were urgently needed in many countries to take over from the occupying Japanese. There we were, all kitted out, keyed up and ready to go somewhere! So 7 IAU was flown the very next day 'over the hump' to Donmuang Airfield in Bangkok, I myself being in the second Dakota to land, about ten minutes after the first one. As soon as our aircraft came to a stop, Gurkha troops who had flown with us, jumped down and surrounded the aircraft, with rifles pointing in all directions – while we, rather unmilitary intelligence officers, followed gingerly with our hands hovering over our revolvers. We needn't have worried. Japanese officers came up, bowing and scraping, full of deference. Our aircraft was closely followed by another, bearing personnel of one of the rehabilitation units, which the Army most commendably had trained in readiness to look after the pitiful wrecks of prisoners of war who had somehow clung to life through all the incredible hell of horrors capture by the Japanese had meant for them.[19]

Those on regular engagements continued to serve with the post-war RAF, ensuring it had a cadre of highly experienced personnel to draw upon, although not all could expect to continue to fly operationally, given the reductions being made. Having received a permanent commission in 1945, Harry Blee embarked on a post-war air force career, eventually retiring in 1975 as a wing commander. He recalled that after experiencing the thrill of operational flying with 358 Squadron, he was compelled to move to the Administration Branch.

Since the war was over, the RAF was obviously going to be greatly reduced in size. ... They established at Blackpool an Aircrew Reallocation Centre. And all surplus aircrew were sent there and parked in various hotels and interviewed and asked individually as to what their future was to be. In my case as I was originally an apprentice and then a full-time voluntary airman, not a National Serviceman, I was entitled to continue to serve, but of course this had all been superseded by the commission.

And so the issue then was to say: 'is he going to be a permanent officer?' And the long and the short of it, was the answer: 'Yes.' And so I was allocated a permanent commission which signed me on to age 55. And of course at that stage they didn't want aircrew bods and were busy wrecking all the Lancasters and the rest, so in my case I decided on the Admin Branch and was posted to Glasgow Recruiting Office – my first experience of a ground job.

Most of my time was spent interviewing National Servicemen at Robertson Street, Glasgow, bear in mind they weren't volunteers, and many strongly resisted the idea of joining up at all. My favourite question was: 'Why have you chosen the RAF?' All these bods would say it beats crawling around in the Army in the mud. Most of them were not wanted because we had a list of the trades we were looking for and if they weren't on there we didn't want them but they were entitled to an interview.[20]

Like many airmen, Jack Ambler was relieved to have survived the war. 'I thank God for – I was spared – and came out of it all unharmed. My father had lost three brothers in World War One. Two killed in action at the Battle of the Somme in France, and one died of Pneumonia in the trenches, so I had been lucky.'[21]

In contrast, others were adversely affected by their wartime experiences, even if it took time for the symptoms to show. As ground crew, Dick Ashley spent part of his war with an RAF salvage team, including supporting American B-17 Flying Fortress units. Routinely this entailed the grisly task of dealing with the burnt-out wrecks of crashed bombers, including recovering the charred bodies of American airmen, many of whom he'd known socially. Despite this, he became hardened to the work, before years later, in old age, suffering nightmares that he attributed to his wartime experiences.[22] Albert Bennett was deeply moved by the period he spent in Singapore, shortly after VJ-Day, when his unit faced the task of helping to evacuate former FEPOWS. 'This was an experience I shall never forget and memories of the release of these men and their appalling condition will always remain with me.'[23]

During 1945, the RAF became heavily involved in efforts to repatriate recently liberated POWs, both in Europe and the Far East. Jim Hunter, a former *Kriegie*, vividly recounted flying out from an airfield near Lüneburg Heath, in an overcrowded Lancaster from 460 Squadron Royal Australian Air Force, packed with former POWs. From the nose he 'had a wonderful view as the sun shone down on England's green and pleasant land. The fields had never been greener or more welcoming than now.' On landing they were greeted by members of Princess Mary's Royal Air Force Nursing Service and Queen Alexandra's Royal Army

Nursing Corps, who served food and generally made a 'fuss' of them, before they were taken to RAF Cosford, and processed prior to being reunited with family members.[24]

Not all former POWs had such a welcome. Having endured life as a *Kriegie*, and the chaotic scenes that typified the fall of Nazi Germany, Carlton Younger was repatriated via boat. 'We landed at Tilbury and entrained for Fenchurch Street station in London. ... I was alone, with no money. Not for me the hugs and kisses from WAAFs and Red Cross girls, the food and drinks, the exciting welcome home that all my friends had been given when they landed. ... I was scruffy, unshaven, wearing an Australian battledress top and RAF grey trousers, both the worse for wear,' plus a tie and an ill-fitting field service cap.[25]

However, there were many for whom RAF service had been a highly positive experience. With Coastal Command, Des Curtis experienced the exhilaration of flying Beaufighters and Mosquitoes on operations, and was still only 22 years old when his career as a navigator ended. This was followed by a period in RAF Public Relations and Administration, prior to leaving the Service, all of which helped enormously in his future business career.

> I had been taught the skill of self-reliance, the skill of thinking quickly on my feet. Not being afraid too much of what other people might regard as a bit frightening, because death had been too close, too often. It didn't make one careless, but it made one realise that only death was the most frightening thing. So one had a degree of self-reliance that I would not at all, I couldn't hope to have acquired had I lived a bank clerk's life in Barclays Bank in London for example.[26]

Many, regardless of rank, and in which branch of the RAF they'd served, were keen to embark on civilian careers. For some, marriage and starting families were another priority in the new post-war world. In this regard, Sir William Beveridge's report of 1942, promulgating the creation of a welfare state, had a significant impact on many men and women in the armed forces, including those serving with the RAF. Many may have viewed the report's content as an ideal worth fighting for, 'a new Jerusalem', something that made their sacrifices worthwhile. Although fewer than half of servicemen actually voted, 60 per cent of those that did chose Labour, and this has often been considered to have contributed towards the Labour landslide victory during the July 1945 General Election.[27]

As indicated, unless they remained in the post-war Service, many men and women were eager to put their air force days behind them on demobilisation. Yet the transition to civilian life could be problematic, and something of a culture shock after years of experiencing a regimented life in the RAF, plus the intensity of war service. Former NCO Eric Marsden discovered that 'you had to adjust to the RAF "not being mother" and that you were on your own, had to get your own food, pay and work organised etc.' In his case, embarking on a teaching job in Chesterfield 'helped dispel the sense of disorientation from demob'.[27]

Many were not necessarily interested in talking too much about their experiences after 1945. Clearly those who'd suffered traumatic episodes, such as becoming a POW, had good reason for this. Jack Foster, for example, spent five of his six years in the RAF behind the wire, with all the deprivation that entailed, plus towards the end of the war he was injured when Allied aircraft mistakenly strafed a group of POWs.[29] On the fiftieth anniversary of VJ-Day in August 1995, former wartime RAF intelligence officer Anthony Goulty was moved by the sight of the commemorations in London to open up about his war.

He explained his reasons for keeping quiet for so long about the details of his service, something that had been exacerbated by the secret nature of his work.

> I was so drilled in keeping absolutely silent about it, that this had become instinctive. There was no official date of release from one's obligation to keep mum, under the Official Secrets Act – so that, even today, fifty years later, I have great difficulty in convincing myself that I can now reveal that from the time I was barred by a medical board from flying (which was a big blow at the time), I was trained for, and then engaged in cryptography in reading Japanese radio signals. ...
>
> The second reason is simpler. Just relief to have done with the war [a feeling shared by many veterans]. The delight of married life at home ... very soon having a family to bring up, and having to concentrate on earning a living.
>
> The third reason for bottling it all up was probably the simplest of all. Probably nobody would have been interested! Our work was important, but it was nothing to shoot a line about, compared with those who had been in the thick of battles.[30]

Much of the above would have chimed with other RAF war veterans, especially those who didn't experience combat flying. There was (and still is) a tendency among surviving veterans to mentally compartmentalise their war experience in an effort to cope with their lives since the war. Consequently, many have tended to be reticent about discussing their war service, or at least been selective about what they highlight, regardless of their rank and specific duties. This had particular resonance for those who'd served in the Far East, because that campaign was widely perceived as 'the forgotten war', not least owing to its geographical remoteness from Britain, and because of the withdrawal from Empire that commenced soon after the Second World War.

Glossary

AA	anti-aircraft
AAF	Auxiliary Air Force
AASF	Advanced Air Striking Force
ABC	Airborne Cigar (radio countermeasures apparatus)
AC1	aircraftman first class
AC2	aircraftman second class
ACH/GD	aircraft hand/general duties
ADGB	Air Defence of Great Britain
AFM	Air Force Medal
AG	air gunner
AI	airborne interceptor
ALO	air liaison officer
AOC	Air Officer Commanding
ASDIC	An early form of sonar – the British term ASDIC derived from the Anti-Submarine Detection Investigation Committee established to develop the methods used in the First World War.
ASI	air speed indicator
ASR	Air Sea Rescue
ASV	Air-to-Surface Vessel
ATA	Air Transport Auxiliary
ATFERO	Atlantic Ferrying Organization
ATS	Auxiliary Territorial Service
AVM	air vice-marshal
BEF	British Expeditionary Force
BEM	British Empire Medal
BFTS	British Flying Training Schools
BOAC	British Overseas Airways Corporation
CFI	chief flying instructor
CPF	Coastal Patrol Flight
DDT	dichloro-diphenyl-trichloroethane
DF	direction finding
DFC	Distinguished Flying Cross

DFM	Distinguished Flying Medal
DI	daily inspection
DWI	Directional Wireless Installation
E/A	enemy aircraft
EFTS	Elementary Flying Training School
FAA	Fighter Area Attacks
FCP	Forward Control Post
FEPOW	Far East prisoners of war
FIDO	Fog Investigation and Dispersal Operation
GCI	Ground Control of Interceptions
GR	general reconnaissance
H2S	airborne, ground-scanning radar system
HCU	Heavy Conversion Unit
h.p.	horsepower
HSL	high-speed launch
IAU	Intelligence Assault Unit
IO	intelligence officer
ITW	Initial Training Wing
IWM	Imperial War Museum
IWM/DS	Imperial War Museum/Department of Sound
KG	Kampfgeschwader (German bomber unit)
LACW	leading aircraftwoman
LDV	Local Defence Volunteers (initially, then became Home Guard)
LFS	Lancaster Finishing School
LMF	lack of moral fibre
MAD	magnetic anomaly detector
Mae West	slang for life jacket
mg	machine gun
MID	Mention in Despatches
MO	medical officer
MT	motor transport
MTE & D	Medical Training Establishment and Depot
MU	maintenance unit
NAAFI	Navy, Army and Air Force Institute
NCO	non-commissioned officer
OPSUM	operational summary
OTC	Officer Training Corps
OTU	Operational Training Unit
PFF	Pathfinder Force
PLE	prudent limit of endurance
POW	prisoner of war

PRU	photographic reconnaissance unit
PTI	physical training instructor
RAFVR	Royal Air Force Volunteer Reserve
RCAF	Royal Canadian Air Force
RCM	radio countermeasures
RDF	radio direction finding
RP	rocket projectile
RSM	regimental sergeant major
R/T	radio telephony
SEAC	South East Asia Command
SFTS	Service Flying Training School
SHAEF	Supreme Headquarters Allied Expeditionary Force
SL	searchlight
SOE	Special Operations Executive
SP	Service Police
SPT	sparking plug tester
SWO	station warrant officer
SWWEC	Second World War Experience Centre
TA	Territorial Army
TAF	Tactical Air Force
TI	target indicator
TNA	The National Archives
USAAF	United States Army Air Force
USN	United States Navy
U/T	under training
VCP	Visual Control Post
VLR	Very Long Range
WAAF	Women's Auxiliary Air Force
WOP	wireless operator
WRAF	Women's Royal Air Force
WRNS	Women's Royal Naval Service

Notes

Introduction

1. Imperial War Museum/Department of Sound (IWM/DS) 19585, Reel 1, Rupert Cooling.
2. Guy Gibson, *Enemy Coast Ahead* (Wilmslow, Cheshire: Goodall, 1995), p. 22.
3. Richard Hough, *One Boy's War* (Barnsley: Pen & Sword, 2007), p. 83.
4. Statistics from: Katherine Bentley Beauman, *Partners in Blue: The Story of Women's Service with the Royal Air Force* (London: Hutchinson, 1971), p. 162 & Patrick Bishop, *Air Force Blue: The RAF in World War Two – Spearhead of Victory* (London: William Collins, 2017), p. 66.
5. Ken Rees with Karen Arrandale, *Lie in the Dark and Listen: The Remarkable Exploits of a WWII Bomber Pilot and Great Escaper* (London: Grub Street, 2006), p. 12.

Chapter 1: Recruitment and Training

1. Denis Peto-Shepherd, *The Devil Take the Hindmost* (Bishop Auckland, Co Durham: Pentland, 1996), p. 79.
2. Pip Beck, *A WAAF in Bomber Command* (London: Goodall, 1989), p. 13.
3. See for example, Chaz Bowyer, *The Royal Air Force 1939–1945* (Barnsley: Pen & Sword, 1996), pp. 22–7.
4. Lawrence Wheatley, *An Erksome War* (Braunton, Devon: Merlin, 1991), p. 11.
5. 5,000 figure is from: Denis Richards, *Royal Air Force 1939–1945: Volume I: The Fight Against the Odds* (London: HMSO, 1953), p. 17.
6. Ibid, pp. 16–17.
7. Richard Hillary, *The Last Enemy* (London: Penguin, 2018), p. 30.
8. IWM/DS 13265, Reel 1, Eric Marsden.
9. IWM/DS 19585, Reel 1, Rupert Cooling.
10. Patrick Bishop, *Air Force Blue: The RAF in World War Two – Spearhead of Victory* (London: William Collins, 2017), p. 72.
11. IWM/DS 12135, Reel 1, Kazimierz Budzik.
12. Morton Charlton, *Mandalay and Beyond: Tales from a Medical Airman's Diary* (Braunton, Devon: Merlin Books, 1996), pp. 2–3.
13. Vincent A. Ashworth, *'Artie' Bomber Command Legend: The Remarkable Story of Wing Commander Artie Ashworth DSO, DFC and Bar, AFC and Bar, MID* (NZ: Fighting High, 2014), p. 21.
14. See Helen Doe, *Fighter Pilot* (Stroud, Gloucestershire: Amberley, 2016), esp. pp. 25–8.
15. Jack Currie, *Wings Over Georgia* (London: Goodall, 1989), p. 12.
16. Hillary, *The Last Enemy*, p. 15.
17. Tony Spooner, *Clean Sweep: The Life of Air Marshal Sir Ivor Broom* (London: Goodall, 1994), p. 16.

18. W.E. 'Bill' Goodman, *Of Stirlings and Stalags: an air-gunner's tale* (London: Publish Nation, 2013), p. 34.

19. Albert & Ian Smith, *Mosquito Pathfinder: A Navigator's 90 WWII Bomber Operations* (London: Goodall, 2003), p. 11.

20. Rees with Arrandale, *Lie in the Dark and Listen*, p. 16.

21. F.R. Chappell, *Wellington Wings: An RAF Intelligence Officer in the Western Desert* (London: William Kimber, 1980), p. 20.

22. Henry Brown, *Per Astro Ad Asbestos* (New Waltham nr Grimsby: Ashridge, 1999), p. 8.

23. Spooner, *Clean Sweep*, p. 17.

24. Charlton, *Mandalay and Beyond*, p. 4.

25. IWM/DS 30386, Reel 1, Ronald Frederick Pate.

26. Peto-Shepherd, *The Devil Take the Hindmost*, p. 92.

27. Ibid, p. 94.

28. Second World War Experience Centre (SWWEC), Acc. No. 2000.676, Albert William Bennett, 'Memories of the RAF & SE Asia Command', p. 1.

29. Ron Smith DFM, *Rear Gunner Pathfinders* (London: Goodall, 1987), p. 9.

30. Cyril Clifford in Roger A. Freeman, *Chocks Away! Through the Eyes of Airmen* (London: Orion, 2004), p. 13.

31. SWWEC, Acc. No. LEEWW 2006.510, C.A. Faulks, an excerpt from the T/S memoirs of 'Guy' Faulks entitled: 'A Life Luckier Than Most', July 2006, p. 2.

32. Christobel Mattingley, *Battle Order 204: A Bomber Pilot's Story* (Crows Nest NSW, Australia: Allen & Unwin, 2007), p. 24.

33. Martin Mason in Freeman, *Chocks Away!*, pp. 9–10.

34. Richard Hough, *One Boy's War* (Barnsley: Pen & Sword, 2007), p. 7.

35. For more details on RAF wartime slang see: Chaz Bowyer, *The Royal Air Force 1939–1945*, pp. 115–17; Chappell, *Wellington Wings*, pp. 269–72; Peto-Shepherd, *The Devil Take the Hindmost*, p. 96; Hough, *One Boy's War*, pp. 9–10.

36. Beck, *A WAAF in Bomber Command*, p. 15.

37. Peto-Shepherd, *The Devil Take the Hindmost*, p. 100.

38. SWWEC, Acc. No. LEEWW 2006.597, Reminiscences of James Anthony Tooth (PO later Fl/Lt and Spitfire Pilot with 130, 152 & 287 Squadrons), p. 2.

39. Figure from: Richards, *Royal Air Force 1939–1945: Volume I*, p. 17.

40. Gibson, *Enemy Coast Ahead*, p. 40.

41. Statistics from: Bowyer, *The Royal Air Force 1939–1945*, p. 84.

42. Muriel Gane Pushman, *We All Wore Blue* (London: Futura, 1990), p. 9.

43. Joan Rice, *Sand in my Shoes: Coming of Age in the Second World War: A WAAF's Diary* (London: Harper Perennial, 2007), pp. 3–4.

44. Laura McGeown quoted in Beryl E. Escott, *Our Wartime Days: The WAAF in World War II* (Stroud, Gloucestershire: Alan Sutton, 1995), p. 5.

45. IWM/DS 9106, Reels 2 & 3, Gwendoline Saunders.

46. Irene Storer in Freeman, *Chocks Away!*, p. 11.

47. Irene Park quoted in Escott, *Our Wartime Days: The WAAF in World War II*, pp. 12–13.

48. IWM/DS 9106, Reel 2, Gwendoline Saunders.

49. Ibid, Reel 3.

50. Bowyer, *The Royal Air Force 1939–1945*, p. 80.

51. Rice, *Sand in my Shoes*, p. 8.

52. Pamela Anderson quoted in Escott, *Our Wartime Days: The WAAF in World War II*, p. 6.

53. Sylvia Pickering, *More Tales of a Bomber Command WAFF* (Bognor Regis: Woodfield, 2003), p. 59.

54. For a good overview of the ATA see: Mike Ryan, 'Hurricanes and Handbags: Women RAF Ferry Pilots during the Second World War' in Celia Lee & Paul Edward Strong (Eds), *Women in War from Home Front to Front Line* (Barnsley: Pen & Sword, 2012), pp. 117–24.

55. Virginia Nicholson, *Millions Like Us: Women's Lives during the Second World War* (London: Penguin, 2012), pp. 64–7.

56. Beauman, *Partners in Blue*, pp. 98–9.

57. Beck, *A WAAF in Bomber Command*, pp. 18–19.

58. Richards, *Royal Air Force 1939–1945: Volume I*, p. 180.

59. For more detail on Cpl Pearson GC award see: Beauman, *Partners in Blue*, pp. 87–8.

60. Sam Pritchard in Bishop, *Air Force Blue*, p. 92.

61. Rees with Arrandale, *Lie in the Dark and Listen*, p. 16.

62. IWM/DS 12524, Reel 1, Cyril Bob Brown.

63. Peto-Shepherd, *The Devil Take the Hindmost*, p. 96.

64. Bruce Lewis, *Aircrew: The Story of the Men Who Flew the Bombers* (London: Cassell, 2000), p. 22.

65. J.R.A. Hodgson letter home in David Hodgson, *Letters from a Bomber Pilot* (London: Methuen, 1985), pp. 27–8.

66. Michael Allen, *Pursuit Through Darkened Skies: An Ace Night-Fighter Crew in World War II* (Shrewsbury: Airlife, 1999), p. 37.

67. Hough, *One Boy's War*, p. 9.

68. Currie, *Wings Over Georgia*, p. 24.

69. W.G.G. Duncan Smith, *Spitfire into Battle* (Oxford: ISIS, 2003), p. 8.

70. Bowyer, *The Royal Air Force 1939–1945*, p. 22.

71. See 'RAF Aircrew Training in the USA 1941–1945' in Currie, *Wings Over Georgia*, pp.7–8.

72. SWWEC, Acc. No. LEEWW 2006.597, Reminiscences of James Anthony Tooth, pp. 3–4.

73. Ibid.

74. See for example, David Mondey, *British Aircraft of World War II* (London: Chancellor, 1995), pp. 72–3.

75. Roald Dahl, *Going Solo* (London: Puffin, 2016), p. 84.

76. Spooner, *Clean Sweep*, p. 19.

77. Based on info in: Rees with Arrandale, *Lie in the Dark and Listen*, pp. 21–2.

78. Currie, *Wings Over Georgia*, p. 33.

79. Geoffrey Wellum, *First Light* (London: Penguin, 2003), pp. 12–13.

80. Mondey, *British Aircraft of World War II*, pp. 168–9.

81. J.R.A. Hodgson, letter to his brother in Hodgson, *Letters from a Bomber Pilot*, p. 30.

82. Lewis, *Aircrew*, p. 23.

83. Duncan Smith, *Spitfire into Battle*, p. 4.

84. SWWEC, Acc. No. LEEWW 2006.597, Reminiscences of James Anthony Tooth, p. 5.

85. Hough, *One Boy's War*, p. 24.

86. Currie, *Wings Over Georgia*, pp. 62–3.

87. SWWEC, Acc. No. LEEWW 2006.597, Reminiscences of James Anthony Tooth, p. 17.

88. Duncan Smith, *Spitfire into Battle,* p. 11.

89. Dahl, *Going Solo*, p. 87.

90. Hillary, *The Last Enemy*, p. 32.

91. SWWEC, Acc. No. LEEWW 2006.597, Reminiscences of James Anthony Tooth, p. 4.

92. Wellum, *First Light*, p. 32.

93. IWM/DS 30386, Reel 2, Ronald Frederick Pate.

94. AM Broom in Spooner, *Clean Sweep*, pp. 21–2.

95. IWM/DS 19585, Reel 1, Rupert Cooling.

96. Hough, *One Boy's War*, pp. 66–9.

97. Rees with Arrandale, *Lie in the Dark and Listen*, p. 28.

98. IWM/DS 19585, Reel 1, Rupert Cooling.

99. Duncan Smith, *Spitfire into Battle*, pp. 27–31.

100. J.R.A. Hodgson, in Hodgson, *Letters from a Bomber Pilot*, p. 43.

101. Spooner, *Clean Sweep*, p. 25.

102. Albert & Ian Smith, *Mosquito Pathfinder*, pp. 37–8.

103. Goodman, *Of Stirlings and Stalags: an air-gunner's tale*, p. 71.

104. Don Charlwood, *No Moon Tonight* (London: Goodhall, 1990), p. 31.

Chapter 2: The Experience of Bombing Operations

1. Denis Peto-Shepherd, *The Devil Take The Hindmost* (Durham: Pentland, 1996), p. 64.

2. See for example, Richard Overy, *Why The Allies Won* (London: Pimlico, 1995), p. 105, and John Terrain, *The Right of the Line* (Ware, Hertfordshire: Wordsworth Editions, 1997), p. 251.

3. Terrain, *The Right of the Line*, p. 261.

4. Richard Overy, *The Air War 1939–1945* (London: Papermac, 1987), p. 106.

5. John Ellis, *Brute Force: Allied Strategy and Tactics in the Second World War* (London: Andre Deutsch, 1990), p. 180.

6. Malcolm Smith, 'The Allied Air Offensive' in John Gooch (ed), *Decisive Campaigns of the Second World War* (London: Frank Cass, 1990), p. 68.

7. Overy, *Why The Allies Won*, p. 111.

8. See for example, Paul Brickhill, *The Dam Busters* (London: Pan, 1955), and John Sweetman, *The Dam Busters Raid* (London: Cassell, 2003).

9. Author's interview: Wing Commander Harry Blee, 12 August 2019.

10. F.R. Chappell, *Wellington Wings: An RAF Intelligence Officer in the Western Desert* (London: William Kimber, 1980), pp. 76.

11. Ibid, p. 194.

12. Ken Rees with Karen Arrandale, *Lie in the Dark and Listen: The Remarkable Exploits of a WWII Bomber Pilot and Great Escaper* (London: Grub Street, 2006), p. 37.

13. David Mattingley quoted in Christobel Mattingley, *Battle Order 204: A Bomber Pilot's Story* (Crows Nest, NSW, Australia: Allen & Unwin, 2007), p. 129.

14. American types operated by the RAF in limited numbers included the: Lockheed Ventura; Douglas A 20 Boston; B-17 Flying Fortress; B-24 Liberator; and B-25 Mitchell.

15. See for example, Ralph Barker, *Strike Hard, Strike Sure* (London: Pan, 1965), pp. 25, 40.

16. Details about aircraft in this section are based on: Johnathan Falconer, *RAF Bomber Command 1939 to 1945 Operations Manual* (Yeovil, Somerset: Haynes, 2018), pp.68–81, and David Mondey, *The Hamlyn Concise Guide to British Aircraft of World War II* (London: Chancellor, 1994).

17. Mike Henry DFC, *Air Gunner* (Wilmslow, Cheshire: Goodhall, 1997), p. 27.

18. Denis Richards, *Royal Air Force 1939–1945 Volume I The Fight At Odds* (London: HMSO, 1953), pp. 113–14.

19. Max Hastings, *Bomber Command* (London: Pan, 1999), p. 65.

20. Tony Spooner DSO, DFC, *Clean Sweep: The Life of AM Sir Ivor Broom KCB, CBE, DSO, DFC and two bars, AFC* (Manchester: Goodall, 1994), p. 36.

21. Henry, *Air Gunner*, pp. 80, 108.

22. AVM D.C.T. Bennett CB, CBE, DSO, *Pathfinder* (London: Goodall, 1988), p. 141.

23. Jack Currie, *Mosquito Victory* (London: Goodall, 1983), p. 121.

24. Albert & Ian Smith, *Mosquito Pathfinder: A Navigator's 90 WWII Bomber Operations* (Manchester: Goodall, 2003), p. 135.

25. Spooner, *Clean Sweep*, p. 156.

26. IWM/DS, 30386, Ronald Frederick Pate, Reels 3 & 5.

27. Hastings, *Bomber Command*, pp. 82–3.

28. Guy Gibson, *Enemy Coast Ahead* (Wilmslow, Cheshire: Goodall, 1995), p. 56.

29. Hastings, *Bomber Command*, p. 83.

30. Bennett, *Pathfinder*, p. 104.

31. Leonard Cheshire, *Bomber Pilot* (St Albans, Herts: Mayflower, 1975), p. 119.

32. J.R.A. Hodgson letter to a friend in David Hodgson, *Letters from a Bomber Pilot* (London: Methuen, 1985), p. 56.

33. IWM/DS 19585, Rupert Cooling, Reels 2 & 3.

34. W.E. 'Bill' Goodman, *Of Stirlings and Stalags: An Air-Gunner's Tale* (London: Publish Nation, 2013), p. 72.

35. Gibson, *Enemy Coast Ahead*, p. 163.

36. Don Charlwood, *No Moon Tonight* (London: Goodall, 1990), p. 68.

37. Jack Currie, *Lancaster Target* (Manchester: Goodall, 2008), pp. 27–8.

38. Jack Currie, *Mosquito Victory* (London: Goodall, 2008), p.17.

39. Charlwood, *No Moon Tonight*, p. 57.

40. Alan Mellor quoted in Edward Smithies, *Aces, Erks and Backroom Boys: Aircrew, ground staff and warplane builders remember the Second World War* (London: Cassell, 2002), p. 207.

41. Walter Thompson DFC, *Lancaster to Berlin* (Manchester: Goodall, 1997), p. 135.

42. Leslie Mann, *And Some Fell on Stony Ground: A Day in the Life of an RAF Bomber Pilot: A Fictional Memoir* (London: Icon, 2015), pp. 101–102.

43. IWM/DS 30386, Ronald Frederick Pate, Reel 4.

44. Pip Beck, *A WAAF in Bomber Command* (London: Goodall, 1989), pp. 34–5.

45. Hastings, *Bomber Command*, pp. 199–200.

46. R.C. Rivaz, DFC, *Tail Gunner* (London: Arrow, undated), p. 36.

47. IWM/DS 19585, Rupert Cooling, Reel 3.

48. For an overview of Sqn Ldr Peto-Sheperd's war service see: James Goulty, *Second World War Lives: A Guide for Family Historians* (Barsley: Pen & Sword, 2012), Ch. 6, pp. 64–78.

49. Peto-Shepherd, *The Devil Take The Hindmost*, pp. 252–4.

50. Goodman, *Of Stirlings and Stalags*, p. 76.

51. IWM/DS 30386, Ronald Frederick Pate, Reel 4.

52. Rivaz, *Tail Gunner*, pp. 33, 86, 90–1.

53. Goodman, *Of Stirlings and Stalags*, p. 66.

54. Anonymous RAF navigator quoted in Bruce Lewis, *Aircrew: The Story of the Men Who Flew the Bombers* (London: Cassell, 2000), pp. 6–7.

55. IWM/DS 19585, Rupert Cooling, Reel 2.

56. FO James Hudson DFC, RAFVR, *There and Back Again: A Navigator's Story* (Lincoln: Tucann, 2001), pp. 145–6.

57. Lewis, *Aircrew*, p. xv.

58. Hastings, *Bomber Command*, p. 75.

59. PO Dick Starkey quoted in Kevin Wilson, *Men of Air: The Doomed Youth of Bomber Command* (London: Cassell, 2011), p. 12.

60. SWWEC, Acc. No. 2000.456 (Box 1 of 5), Denis Noel Peto-Shepherd Papers, Unpublished Memoir, p. 498.
61. Gibson, *Enemy Coast Ahead*, p. 71.
62. Hastings, *Bomber Command*, p. 159.
63. Chappell, *Wellington Wings*, pp. 27–8.
64. SWWEC, Acc. No. 2000.456, Peto-Shepherd Papers, Unpublished Memoir, pp. 500–501.
65. David Mattingley quoted in Mattingley, *Battle Order 204*, p. 149.
66. Ron Smith DFM, *Rear Gunner Pathfinders* (London: Goodall, 1989), pp. 20–1.
67. Martin Middlebrook & Chris Everitt, *The Bomber Command War Diaries: An Operational Reference Book 1939–1945* (Barnsley: Pen & Sword, 2014), p. 41.
68. IWM/DS 19585, Rupert Cooling, Reel 2.
69. See for example Falconer, *RAF Bomber Command 1939 to 1945 Operations Manual*, pp. 116–18.
70. Thompson, *Lancaster to Berlin*, p. 126.
71. See for example, Middlebrook & Everitt, *The Bomber Command War Diaries*, p. 548; SWWEC, Acc. No. 2000.456, Peto-Shepherd Papers, Unpublished Memoir, pp. 516–19.
72. Smith, *Rear Gunner Pathfinders*, p. 46.
73. Thompson, *Lancaster to Berlin*, pp. 149–52.
74. Middlebrook & Everitt, *The Bomber Command War Diaries*, p. 570.
75. SWWEC, Acc. No. 2000.456, Peto-Shepherd Papers, Unpublished Memoir, pp. 552–4.
76. Ibid, pp. 554–6.
77. Reg Fayers (76 Sqn) quoted in Roger A. Freeman, *Chocks Away!*, p. 96.
78. Ibid, p. 95.
79. SWWEC, Acc. No. 2000.456, Peto-Shepherd Papers, Unpublished Memoir, p. 558.
80. For more details see, Falconer, *RAF Bomber Command 1939 to 1945 Operations Manual*, pp. 122–3.
81. Smith, *Rear Gunner Pathfinders*, p. 47.
82. SWWEC, Acc. No. 2000.456, Peto-Shepherd Papers, Unpublished Memoir, p. 515.
83. Chappell, *Wellington Wings*, p. 260.
84. Currie, *Lancaster Target*, p. 101.
85. For a good overview on the workings of the Kammhuber Line, see: Falconer, *RAF Bomber Command 1939 to 1945 Operations Manual*, Ch. 9 'Defending the Reich', pp. 126–35.
86. Bennett, *Pathfinder*, p. 140.
87. Smith, *Rear Gunner Pathfinders*, p. 51.
88. See for example, Vincent A. Ashworth, *'Artie' Bomber Command Legend: The Remarkable Story of Wing Commander Artie Ashworth DSO, DFC and Bar, AFC and Bar, MID* (NZ: Fighting High, 2014), pp. 129–30.
89. Ibid, pp. 130–1.
90. IWM/DS 30386, Ronald Frederick Pate, Reels 2 & 3.
91. Hastings, *Bomber Command*, p. 68.
92. Details based on: Form 1757 Royal Air Force: Observer's and Gunner's Flying Log Book: 902557 F/Sgt R.J. Wainwright (I am deeply grateful to Mr Charlie Wainwright for loaning me his father's log book).
93. IWM/DS 19585, Rupert Cooling, Reel 3.
94. Figures from: Falconer, *RAF Bomber Command 1939 to 1945 Operations Manual*, p. 6.
95. Charlwood, *No Moon Tonight*, p. 177.
96. Thompson, *Lancaster to Berlin*, pp. 102–103.
97. SWWEC, Acc. No. 2000.456, Peto-Shepherd Papers, Unpublished Memoir, p. 520.

98. IWM/DS 19585, Rupert Cooling, Reel 3.
99. Smith, *Rear Gunner Pathfinders*, p. 86.
100. Albert & Ian Smith, *Mosquito Pathfinder*, pp. 70–1.
101. Currie, *Lancaster Target*, p. 136.
102. Lewis, *Aircrew*, p. 70.
103. SWWEC, Acc. No. 2000.456, Peto-Shepherd Papers, Unpublished Memoir, p. 559.
104. Albert & Ian Smith, *Mosquito Pathfinder*, p. 45.
105. Charlwood, *No Moon Tonight*, p. 49.
106. Currie, *Lancaster Target*, p. 136.
107. Goodman, *Of Stirlings and Stalags*, p. 116.
108. For an excellent discussion regarding courage see: Hastings, *Bomber Command*, pp. 213–16.
109. For a useful overview on LMF see: Falconer, *RAF Bomber Command 1939 to 1945 Operations Manual*, pp. 62–5.
110. Currie, *Lancaster Target*, p. 34.
111. Charlwood, *No Moon Tonight*, p. 163.
112. Smith, *Rear Gunner Pathfinders*, p. 38.
113. Charlwood, *No Moon Tonight*, p. 50.
114. Hastings, *Bomber Command*, p. 204.
115. Currie, *Lancaster Target*, p. 138.
116. Smith, *Rear Gunner Pathfinders*, p. 111.
117. Cheshire, *Bomber Pilot*, pp. 29–30.
118. SWWEC, Acc. No. 2000.456, Peto-Shepherd Papers, Unpublished Memoir, p. 567.
119. Charlwood, *No Moon Tonight*, pp. 146, 148.
120. SWWEC, Acc. No. 2000.456, Peto-Shepherd Papers, Unpublished Memoir, p. 539.
121. For an excellent analysis of bombing during the Second World War see: Overy, *Why the Allies Won*, Ch. 4 'The Means to Victory: Bombers and Bombing', pp. 101–33.
122. Ibid.
123. IWM/DS 19585, Rupert Cooling, Reel 4.
124. IWM/DS 30386, Ronald Frederick Pate, Reel 6.

Chapter 3: Flying with Fighter Squadrons

1. James Goodson, *Tumult in the Clouds* (London: Penguin, 2018), p. 51.
2. AVM J.E. 'Johnnie' Johnson, *Full Circle: The Story of Air Fighting 1914–1953* (London: Pan, 1969), p. 139.
3. Stephen Bungay, *The Most Dangerous Enemy: A History of the Battle of Britain* (London: Arum, 2000), pp. 259–60.
4. Gordon Olive, DFC, *Spitfire Ace: My Life as a Battle of Britain Fighter Pilot* (Stroud, Gloucestershire: Amberley, 2016), p. 80.
5. Paul Richey, *Fighter Pilot* (Stroud, Gloucestershire: History Press, 2016), p. 78.
6. Figures in the introduction are from: Chaz Bowyer, *The Royal Air Force 1939–1945* (Barnsley: Pen & Sword, 1996), pp. 37–43.
7. For details of James Goodson's wartime career see: Goodson, *Tumult in the Clouds*.
8. IWM/DS 12524, Reel 2, Air Commodore Cyril, Bob Brown.
9. Ibid.
10. Comments by the station commander at RAF Warmwell quoted in Alan Brown, *Flying for Freedom: The Allied Air Forces in the RAF 1939–45* (Stroud, Gloucestershire: History Press, 2011), p. 16.

11. Sqn Ldr H. Fenton quoted in Helen Doe, *Fighter Pilot* (Stroud, Gloucestershire: Amberley, 2016), p. 93.
12. Olive, *Spitfire Ace*, p. 145.
13. IWM/DS 12982, Reel 2, Sqn Ldr Boleslaw, Henryk Drobinski.
14. IWM/DS 12135, Reel 1, Kazimierz Budzik.
15. Goodson, *Tumult in the Clouds*, p. 61.
16. Chiefs of Staff reports quoted in Brown, *Flying for Freedom*, p. 188.
17. Brown, *Flying for Freedom*, p. 20.
18. Hector Bolitho, *The Finest of the Few: The Story of Battle of Britain Fighter Pilot John Simpson* (Stroud, Gloucestershire: Amberley, 2010), p. 87.
19. Peter Hearne (65 Squadron) quoted in Roger A. Freeman, *Chocks Away!*, pp. 121–2.
20. Bolitho, *The Finest of the Few*, p. 18.
21. Freeman, *Chocks Away!*, p. 123.
22. Johnson, *Full Circle*, p. 111.
23. Details on aircraft in this section are from: David Mondey, *The Hamlyn Concise Guide to British Aircraft of World War II* (London: Chancellor, 1994).
24. Roald Dahl, *Going Solo* (London: Penguin, 2016), p. 94.
25. Olive, *Spitfire Ace*, pp. 84–5.
26. Ibid, p. 79.
27. Goodson, *Tumult in the Clouds*, p. 50.
28. IWM/DS 12524, Reel 1, Air Cdre Cyril, Bob Brown.
29. http://war-experience.org/lives/air-commodore-john-ellacombe-dfc/ accessed 14/3/19.
30. SWWEC, Acc. No. LEEWW 2006.597, Reminiscences of James Anthony Tooth (PO later Fl/Lt and Spitfire Pilot with 130, 152 & 287 Squadrons), p. 6.
31. Richard Hillary, *The Last Enemy* (London: Penguin, 2018), p. 85.
32. IWM/DS 12982, Reel 4, Sqn Ldr Boleslaw, Henryk Drobinski.
33. Geoffrey Wellum, *First Light* (London: Penguin, 2018), p. 104.
34. W.G.G. Duncan Smith, *Spitfire into Battle* (Oxford: Isis, 2003), p. 123.
35. IWM/DS 12135, Reel 1, Kazimierz Budzik.
36. Duncan Smith, *Spitfire into Battle*, pp. 29–30.
37. Antoni Murkowski quoted in Freeman, *Chocks Away!*, pp. 110–11.
38. Olive, *Spitfire Ace*, pp. 158–9.
39. SWWEC, Acc. No. LEEWW 2006.597, Reminiscences of James Anthony Tooth, p. 7.
40. Ibid, p. 9.
41. Duncan Smith, *Spitfire into Battle*, p. 87.
42. IWM/DS 21291, Reel 3, Wg Cdr James Gilbert Sanders.
43. Tony Spooner, *Night Fighter Ace* (Stroud, Gloucestershire: Sutton, 1997), p. 74.
44. http://war-experience.org/lives/air-commodore-john-ellacombe-dfc/ accessed 14/3/19.
45. Edward Lanchbery, 'Typhoon Troubles' in Gavin Lyall, *The War in the Air* (London: Book Club Associates, 1973), p. 204.
46. George Aldridge quoted in Freeman, *Chocks Away!*, p. 112.
47. Edward Lanchbery, 'Typhoon Troubles' in Lyall, *The War in the Air*, p. 204.
48. Gp Capt Desmond Scott quoted in Anthony Robinson, 'Tally Ho! 609 Squadron RAF: Normandy 1944' in *The Elite Vol. 2 Issue 18* (London: Orbis, 1985), p. 351.
49. SWWEC, Acc. No. LEEWW 2006.597, Reminiscences of James Anthony Tooth, p. 19.
50. IWM/DS 12982, Reel 5, Sqdn Ldr Boleslaw, Henryk Drobinski.
51. Doe, *Fighter Pilot*, pp. 71–2.
52. Wellum, *First Light*, p. 165.

53. Bolitho, *The Finest of the Few*, pp. 86–7.
54. IWM/DS 12135, Reel 2, Kazimierz Budzik.
55. Olive, *Spitfire Ace*, p. 144.
56. Ibid, p. 119.
57. Richey, *Fighter Pilot*, p. 19.
58. Laddie Lucas, *Flying Colours: The Epic Story of Douglas Bader* (London: Granada, 1983), pp. 120, 152.
59. 'Malan's Ten Commandments: Ten of my rules for air fighting' reproduced in Lyall, *The War in the Air*, pp. 45–6.
60. See for example, Bungay, *The Most Dangerous Enemy*, p. 152.
61. Johnson, *Full Circle*, p. 117.
62. See for example, Patrick Bishop, *Fighter Boys: Saving Britain 1940* (London: Harper Perennial, 2004), esp. pp. 46–7.
63. See for example, Bungay, *The Most Dangerous Enemy*, pp. 250–2; Leo McKinstry, *Hurricane Victor of the Battle of Britain* (London: John Murray, 2010), pp. 134–5.
64. IWM/DS 12982, Reel 2, Sqn Ldr Boleslaw, Henryk Drobinski.
65. IWM/DS 21291, Reel 2, Wg Cdr James Gilbert Sanders.
66. Ibid.
67. Dahl, *Going Solo*, pp. 137–8.
68. Hillary, *The Last Enemy*, p. 63.
69. IWM/DS 12524, Reel 2, Air Cdre Cyril, Bob Brown.
70. Richey, *Fighter Pilot*, Appendix III Formation Flying, pp. 202–209.
71. IWM/DS 12524, Reel 1, Air Cdre Cyril, Bob Brown.
72. Bungay, *The Most Dangerous Enemy*, p. 260.
73. Olive, *Spitfire Ace*, p. 83.
74. Nick Thomas, *RAF Top Gun: The Story of Battle of Britain Ace & World Air Speed Record Holder Air Cdre E.M. 'Teddy' Donaldson CB, CBE, DSO, AFC*, LoM (USA)* (Barnsley: Pen & Sword, 2008), p. 55.
75. Richey, *Fighter Pilot*, pp. 95–6.
76. IWM/DS 12524, Reel 2, Air Cdre Cyril, Bob Brown.
77. Richards, *Royal Air Force 1939–1945 Volume 1*, p. 193. (For further detail on this bitter controversy see: John Terraine, *The Right of the Line* (Ware, Herts: Wordsworth Editions, 1997), esp. pp. 194–205, 216–17.)
78. Johnson, *Full Circle*, p. 185.
79. IWM/DS 21291, Reel 2, Wg Cdr James Gilbert Sanders.
80. Olive, *Spitfire Ace*, p. 189.
81. John Simpson in Bolitho, *The Finest of the Few*, p. 55.
82. IWM/DS 21291, Reel 2, Wg Cdr James Gilbert Sanders.
83. Olive, *Spitfire Ace*, p. 94.
84. SWWEC, Acc. No. LEEWW 2006.597, Reminiscences of James Anthony Tooth, p. 9.
85. Ibid, pp. 14–15.
86. IWM/DS 12982, Reel 4, Sqn Ldr Boleslaw, Henryk Drobinski.
87. IWM/DS 12524, Reel 1, Air Cdre Cyril, Bob Brown.
88. John Simpson in Bolitho, *The Finest of the Few*, p. 59.
89. IWM/DS 12135, Reel 2, Kazimierz Budzik.
90. IWM/DS 21291, Reel 1, Wg Cdr James Gilbert Sanders.
91. IWM/DS 12135, Reel 2, Kazimierz Budzik.
92. IWM/DS 12982, Reel 3, Squadron Leader Boleslaw, Henryk Drobinski.

93. IWM/DS 12524, Reel 2, Air Cdre Cyril, Bob Brown.

94. Ibid, Reel 3.

95. Duncan Smith, *Spitfire into Battle*, p. 323.

96. Dennis Richards, *Royal Air Force 1939–1945 Volume 1: The Fight at Odds* (London: HMSO, 1953), p. 384.

97. Goodson, *Tumult in the Clouds*, p. 64.

98. IWM/DS 12982, Reel 3, Sqn Ldr Boleslaw, Henryk Drobinski.

99. Duncan Smith, *Spitfire into Battle*, pp. 144–5.

100. IWM/DS 12135, Reel 3, Kazimierz Budzik.

101. Edward Lanchbery, 'Tip and Run' in Lyall, *The War in the Air*, pp. 346–7.

102. 'Tony' Murkowski 316 (Polish) Squadron quoted in Freeman, *Chocks Away!*, p. 120.

103. IWM/DS 12982, Reel 4, Sqn Ldr Boleslaw, Henryk Drobinski.

104. Spooner, *Night Fighter Ace*, p. 18.

105. Michael Allen, *Pursuit through the Darkened Skies: An Ace Night-Fighter Crew in World War II* (Shrewsbury: Airlife, 1999), p. 10.

106. IWM/DS 21291, Reel 2, Wg Cdr James Gilbert Sanders.

107. Extract from a Combat Report by Sqn Ldr John Cunningham DSO, DFC in Lyall, *The War in the Air*, p. 86.

108. IWM/DS 12135, Reel 2, Kazimierz Budzik.

109. Ibid.

110. Allen, *Pursuit through the Darkened Skies*, p. 12.

111. IWM/DS 21291, Reel 3, Wg Cdr James Gilbert Sanders.

112. See for example, Allen, *Pursuit through the Darkened Skies*, esp. pp. 56–9, 61, 74–5.

113. IWM/DS 12524, Reel 3, Air Cdre Cyril, Bob Brown.

114. Ibid.

115. Ibid.

116. Allen, *Pursuit through the Darkened Skies*, p. 297.

117. Combat Report 11/5/44 reproduced in Ibid, p. 206.

118. Ian Gooderson, *Air Power at the Battlefront: Allied Close Air support in Europe 1943–45* (London: Frank Cass, 1998), esp. pp. 62–5.

119. SWWEC, Acc. No. LEEWW 2006.597, Reminiscences of James Anthony Tooth, p. 11.

120. Doe, *Fighter Pilot*, p. 158.

121. IWM/DS 12135, Reel 3, Kazimierz Budzik.

122. Richard Hough, *One Boy's War* (Barnsley: Pen & Sword, 2007), p. 136.

123. Ibid, p. 92.

124. Ibid, p. 117.

125. Belgian pilot Raymond Lallement quoted in Robinson, 'Tally Ho! 609 Squadron RAF: Normandy 1944', p. 355.

126. Doe, *Fighter Pilot*, pp. 166–7.

127. See: Gooderson, *Air Power at the Battlefront*, esp. pp. 87–9, 92–4, 171–3, 219, 239.

128. Hough, *One Boy's War*, p. 112.

129. Ibid, pp. 147, 149.

Chapter 4: At War with Kipper Fleet: Coastal Command

1. 'Kipper Fleet' was RAF wartime slang for Coastal Command.

2. See for example, Chaz Bowyer, *The Royal Air Force 1939–1945* (Barnsley: Pen & Sword, 1996), pp. 47–52.

3. Frank Tilsley, *The Boys of Coastal Command* (London: Cassell, 1944), p. 7.

4. ORB 220 Squadron, entry for 3/9/39 reproduced in Ron Selley & Kerrin Cocks, *I Won't be home next Summer: Flight Lieutenant R.N. Selley, DFC (1917–1941)* (Pinetown, SA, 30° South Publishers, 2014), p. 93.

5. See for example, Chaz Bowyer, *Coastal Command at War* (London: Ian Allan, 1979), pp. 56–7; *Coastal Command* (London: HMSO, 1942), p. 37.

6. Ted Rayner, *Coastal Command Pilot 1939–1945: Wartime Experiences with 220 & 269 Squadrons* (Bognor Regis: Woodfield, 2001), p. 94.

7. Anonymous RAF officer quoted in *Coastal Command*, p. 63.

8. Winston S. Churchill, *The Second World War Vol. III: The Grand Alliance* (London: Folio Society, 2002), p. 91.

9. 'Hudsons' Millionth Mile by A Squadron Commander of Coastal Command' in *Winged Words: Our Airmen Speak For Themselves* (London: William Heinemann, 1941), pp. 63–6.

10. Tom Minta quoted in Roger A. Freeman, *Chocks Away!*, p. 125.

11. Anonymous squadron commander in 'Sqn Ldr Tom Dudley-Gordon', *Coastal Command at War* (London: Jarrolds, undated), p. 192.

12. 'Christmas Day in Coastal Command' by A Squadron Leader, RAFVR in *Winged Words*, p. 1.

13. *Coastal Command*, p.27.

14. Leslie Baveystock, DSO, DFC and Bar, DFM, *Wavetops At My Wingtips* (Shrewsbury: Airlife, 2001), p. 152.

15. James Sanders, *Of Wind and Water: A Kiwi Pilot in Coastal Command* (Shrewsbury: Airlife, 1989), p. 131.

16. Unless otherwise stated, details on aircraft in this chapter are based on: David Mondey, *British Aircraft of World War II* (London: Chancellor, 1995).

17. Baveystock, *Wavetops At My Wingtips*, pp. 148–9.

18. See for example, Winston S. Churchill, *The Second World War Vol. I: The Gathering Storm* (London: Folio Society, 2002), pp. 334–5; Stephen Roskill, *The Navy at War 1939–1945* (Ware, Herts: Wordsworth Editions, 1998), pp. 35–6.

19. 'Christmas Day in Coastal Command' by A Squadron Leader, RAFVR in *Winged Words*, p. 3.

20. Rayner, *Coastal Command Pilot 1939–1945*, p. 50.

21. *Coastal Command*, p. 36.

22. Rayner, *Coastal Command Pilot 1939–1945*, p. 68.

23. Ibid, p. 192.

24. *Coastal Command*, p. 80.

25. Ibid.

26. Ibid, p. 97.

27. John Terraine, *The Right of the Line: The Royal Air Force in the European War 1939–1945* (Ware, Herts: Wordsworth Editions, 1998), p. 229.

28. Roy Larkins quoted in *Chocks Away!*, p. 128.

29. *Coastal Command*, p. 36.

30. Baveystock, *Wavetops At My Wingtips*, pp. 151–2.

31. Terraine, *The Right of the Line*, pp. 235–8; John Terrain, Ch. 3 'Setting the Scene' in *Seek and Sink Bracknell Paper No. 2 A Symposium on the Battle of the Atlantic 21 October 1991* (RAF Historical Society, 1992), p.10.

32. See for example, Terraine, *The Right of the Line*, p. 238; Ronald Lewin, *Ultra Goes to War: The Secret Story* (London: Book Club Associates, 1978), pp. 216–20; Edward Thomas, Ch. 6 'Intelligence' in *Seek and Sink*, pp. 38–47.

33. Churchill, *The Second World War Vol. III*, p. 100.

34. Baveystock, *Wavetops At My Wingtips*, p. 152.
35. Lewin, *Ultra Goes to War*, p. 216.
36. See for example, Terrain, *The Right of the Line*, pp. 226–7; Lt Cdr W.J.R. Gardner, Ch. 5 'The Course of Battle' in *Seek and Sink*, p. 22.
37. Churchill, *The Second World War Vol. III*, p. 100.
38. Bowyer, *Coastal Command at War*, pp. 22, 26.
39. Roy Larkins quoted in *Chocks Away!*, p. 128.
40. Denis Richards & Hilary Saunders, *Royal Air Force 1939–1945: Volume I The Fight Avails* (London: HMSO, 1954), p. 345.
41. Norman L.R. Franks, *Search Find And Kill: Coastal Command's U-boat Successes* (Bourn End, Bucks: Aston, 1990), pp. 124–5; H.T. Lenton & J.J. Colledge, *Warships of World War II* (London: Ian Allan, 1980), pp. 164–5.
42. AC 'Taffy' Powell, *Ferryman: from Ferry Command to Silver City* (Shrewsbury: Airlife, 1982), p. 15.
43. Rayner, *Coastal Command Pilot 1939–1945*, pp. 108–109.
44. Denis Richards, *Royal Air Force 1939–1945: Volume I The Fight at Odds* (London: HMSO, 1954), p. 344.
45. Hilary G. Saunders, *Royal Air Force 1939–1945: Volume III The Fight is Won* (London: HMSO, 1954), p. 58.
46. Franks, *Search Find and Kill*, p. 10.
47. *Coastal Command*, p. 101.
48. See for example, *Ibid*, p. 98.
49. 'Sinking a U-boat' By A Squadron Leader of the Royal Australian Airforce in *Winged Words*, pp. 102–103.
50. Terraine, *The Right of the Line*, p. 233.
51. Tony Spooner, DSO, DFC, *Coastal Ace: The Biography of Squadron Leader Terence Malcolm Bulloch, DSO and Bar, DFC and Bar* (London: William Kimber, 1986), p. 138.
52. Ibid, p. 135.
53. Richards & Saunders, *Royal Air Force 1939–1945: Volume II*, p. 105.
54. Spooner, *Coastal Ace*, p. 123.
55. Dr Alfred Price Ch. 7 'Development of Equipment and Techniques' in *Seek and Sink*, p. 50.
56. See for example, Saunders, *Royal Air Force 1939–1945: Volume III*, pp. 55–6; R.V. Jones, *Most Secret War: British Scientific Intelligence 1939–1945* (London: Coronet, 1979), p. 409.
57. Spooner, *Coastal Ace*, p. 125.
58. Tony Spooner, DSO, DFC, *In Full Flight* (Canterbury: Wingham, 1991), p. 153.
59. Baveystock, *Wavetops at My Wingtips*, p. 218.
60. See Baveystock, *Wavetops at My Wingtips*, pp. 227–31, 243–50; Franks, *Search Find and Kill*, pp. 108–109, 120–1.
61. Richards & Saunders, *Royal Air Force 1939–1945: Volume II*, pp. 101–104.
62. Spooner, *In Full Flight*, pp. 243, 245.
63. See for example, J.P. Mallmann Showell, *U-Boats Under The Swastika* (London: Ian Allan, 1973), pp. 107–108.
64. Sgt E. Cheek quoted in Norman Franks, *Conflict over The Bay* (London: William Kimber, 1996), p. 175.
65. Saunders, *Royal Air Force 1939–1945: Volume III*, p. 58; Thomas, Ch. 6 'Intelligence' in *Seek and Sink*, p. 46.
66. Squadron Leader T. Bulloch (224 Squadron) quoted in Franks, *Conflict over The Bay*, p. 145.
67. Ibid, pp. 142–5.

68. Anonymous RAF officer quoted in *Coastal Command*, p. 133.

69. Richards & Saunders, *Royal Air Force 1939–1945: Volume II*, p. 95.

70. Terraine, *The Right of the Line*, p. 422.

71. Richards, *Royal Air Force 1939–1945: Volume* I, pp. 353–4.

72. R.E. Gillman DFC, DFM, *The Ship Hunters* (London: A Star Book, 1979), p. 151.

73. Ibid, pp. 38, 45.

74. 'Torpedoing a German Tanker' by Anon Wing Commander in *Winged Words*, p. 204.

75. Gillman, *The Ship Hunters*, pp. 49–50.

76. Ronnie Selley quoted in Selley & Cocks, *I Won't be home next Summer*, pp. 125–6.

77. *Coastal Command*, p. 129.

78. Sanders, *Of Wind and Water*, p. 38.

79. *Coastal Command*, p. 130.

80. Rayner, *Coastal Command Pilot 1939–1945*, p. 125.

81. *Coastal Command*, p. 132.

82. Patrick Gibbs DSO, DFC and Bar, *Not Peace But a Sword* (London: Grub Street, 1993), pp. 90–1.

83. Ibid, pp. 106–107.

84. Ibid, p. 107.

85. Sanders, *Of Wind and Water*, p. 115.

86. Ibid, p. 117.

87. Ibid.

88. Patrick Gibbs DSO, DFC and Bar, *Torpedo Leader on Malta* (London: Grub Street, 2002), p. 62.

89. Ibid, pp. 231–2.

90. *Coastal Command*, pp. 137–8.

91. IWM/DS 12135, Reel 1, Kazimierz Budzik.

92. Gibbs, *Torpedo Leader*, p. 47.

93. Ibid, p. 52.

94. Bowyer, *Coastal Command at War*, p. 83.

95. Spooner, *In Full Flight*, p. 167.

96. Bowyer, *Coastal Command at War*, p. 83.

97. Norman Carr (pilot 143 Squadron) quoted in Chaz Bowyer, *Beaufighter* (London: William Kimber, 1987), p. 76.

98. Anonymous Beaufighter pilot quoted in Bowyer, Beaufighter, p. 90.

99. For further details see for example, Philip Birtles, *Mosquito: A Pictorial History of the DH98* (London: Jane's Publishing, 1980), pp. 105–15.

100. SWWEC, Acc no. CUR002–3, Tape 687: Transcript of Interview with Des Curtis by Dr Peter Liddle, July 2001.

101. Richards, *Royal Air Force 1939–1945: Volume I The Fight at Odds*, pp. 362–3.

102. *Coastal Command*, p. 141.

103. Terraine, *The Right of the Line*, p. 422; Richards; Saunders, *Royal Air Force 1939–1945: Volume II The Fight Avails*, p. 99.

104. For further details see for example, Jonathon Falconer, *RAF Bomber Command 1939–1945 Operations Manual* (Yeovil: Haynes, 2018), p. 94.

105. 'Minelaying by Air' by A Canadian Pilot Officer in *Winged Words*, p. 115.

106. Ibid, p. 116.

107. Ibid, p. 115.

108. Ibid, p. 116.

109. W.J. 'Jim' Hunter, *From Coastal Command to Captivity: The Memoir of a Second World War Airman* (Barnsley: Leo Cooper, 2003), p. 29.
110. Nick Berryman, *In the Nick of Time: The Experiences of an RAF Air Sea Rescue Pilot with 276 Sqn* (Bognor Regis: Woodfield, 2000), p. 161.
111. See for example, Graham Pitchfork, *Shot Down and in the Drink: RAF and Commonwealth aircrews saved from the sea 1939–1945* (Kew, The National Archives (TNA), 2005), pp. 264–5.
112. Pop Ewins quoted in *Chocks Away!*, p. 134.
113. Pitchfork, *Shot Down and in the Drink*, p. 3
114. Richards & Saunders, *Royal Air Force 1939–1945: Volume II*, p. 88.
115. SWWEC, Acc. No. FIE003–1, H.J. Field, handwritten 8-page 'Memoir' outlining his war service, p. 4.
116. SWWEC, Acc. No. FIE003–2, H.J. Field, handwritten 4-page 'Memoir' regarding ASR, p. 2.
117. Mike Henry, *Air Gunner* (Manchester: Goodhall, 1997), pp. 141–2.
118. Pitchfork, *Shot Down and in the Drink*, p. 46.
119. SWWEC, Acc. No. FIE003–2, H.J. Field, handwritten 4-page 'Memoir' regarding ASR, p. 2.
120. Berryman, *In the Nick of Time*, p. 139.
121. LAC Ken Border quoted in Tom Docherty, *Dinghy Drop: 279 Squadron RAF 1941–46* (Barnsley, Pen & Sword, 2007), p. 137.
122. Berryman, *In the Nick of Time*, p. 138.
123. F/Lt Frank Rashleigh (279 Sqn) letter to his mother 22 November 1941, quoted in Docherty, *Dinghy Drop*, p. 2.
124. Berryman, *In the Nick of Time*, p. 125.
125. Ibid, p. 131.
126. Anon, *Air Sea Rescue*, (London: HMSO, 1942), p. 16.
127. Ibid, p. 30; Pitchfork, *Shot Down and in the Drink*, pp. 32–7.
128. Anon, *Air Sea Rescue*, p. 17.
129. Jack Foss quoted by Hector Bolitho in Gavin Lyall 'In the Drink' in *The War in the Air* (London: Book Club Associates, 1968), p. 288.
130. Pilot Officer Tadeusz Turek quoted in Norman Franks, *Another Kind of Courage: Stories of the UK-based Walrus Air-Sea Rescue Squadrons* (Sparkford, nr. Yeovil: Patrick Stephens, 1994), p. 142.
131. Docherty, *Dinghy Drop*, pp. 74–5.
132. W.G.G. Duncan Smith, *Spitfire into Battle* (Oxford: Isis, 2003), pp. 234–41.
133. For further details see: Pitchfork, *Shot Down and in the Drink*, pp. 24–7.
134. Anon, *Air Sea Rescue*, p. 9.
135. See for example, Pitchfork, *Shot Down and in the Drink*, p. 28; Anon, *Air Sea Rescue*, p. 14; Docherty, *Dinghy Drop*, pp. 6, 220.
136. Pitchfork, *Shot Down and in the Drink*, pp. 31–2.
137. Ibid, pp. 59–61; Docherty, *Dinghy Drop*, pp. 30, 32.
138. Docherty, *Dinghy Drop*, pp. 75–6; TNA, AIR 27/1609, Operations Record Book 279 Squadron September 1943, entries for 4/9/43.

Chapter 5: Service with Ferry/Transport Command

1. AC 'Taffy' Powell, *Ferryman: From Ferry Command to Silver City* (Shrewsbury: Airlife, 1982), pp. 74–5.
2. Don McVicar, *Ferry Command* (Shrewsbury: Airlife, 1981), p. 13.

3. Anon, *Atlantic Bridge: The Official Account of RAF Transport Command's Ocean Ferry* (London: HMSO, 1945), p. 21.
4. Ibid, p. 38.
5. McVicar, *Ferry Command*, p. 75.
6. D.C.T. Bennett, *Pathfinder: A War Autobiography* (London: Goodall, 1988), p 87.
7. Anon, *Atlantic Bridge*, p. 24.
8. Powell, *Ferryman: From Ferry Command to Silver City*, pp. 51–5.
9. Ibid, pp. 23–4.
10. McVicar, *Ferry Command*, p. 13.
11. Tony Spooner, *Coastal Ace: The Biography of Squadron Leader Terrence Bulloch DSO and Bar, DFC and Bar* (London: William Kimber, 1986), p. 115.
12. Bennett, *Pathfinder*, p. 91.
13. Powell, *Ferryman: From Ferry Command to Silver City*, p. 43.
14. Anon, *Atlantic Bridge*, p. 34.
15. Bennett, *Pathfinder*, p. 90.
16. Anon, *Atlantic Bridge*, pp. 42–3.
17. Spooner, *Coastal Ace*, p. 120.
18. McVicar, *Ferry Command*, pp. 73–4.
19. Bennett, *Pathfinder*, p. 100.
20. Ibid, p. 98.
21. McVicar, *Ferry Command*, p. 81.
22. Ibid, p. 69.
23. McVicar, *Ferry Command*, pp. 21–2.
24. Bennett, *Pathfinder*, p. 83.
25. McVicar, *Ferry Command*, pp. 24, 158.
26. Ibid, p. 67.
27. Ibid, p. 87.
28. Ibid, p. 68.
29. Ibid, p. 67.
30. Ibid, p. 33.
31. Ibid, p. 136.
32. Spooner, *Coastal Ace*, pp. 104–106, 111.
33. Anon, *Atlantic Bridge*, pp. 53–4.
34. Powell, *Ferryman: From Ferry Command to Silver City*, pp. 67–8.
35. McVicar, *Ferry Command*, p. 87.
36. Spooner, *Coastal Ace*, p. 116.
37. Anon, *Atlantic Bridge*, p. 64.
38. Ibid, p. 70.
39. Patrick Bishop, *Air Force Blue: The RAF in World War Two: Spearhead of Victory* (London: William Collins, 2017), pp. 233–5.
40. See for example, Powell, *Ferryman: From Ferry Command to Silver City*, pp. 88–9.
41. Author's interview/discussion: Wg Cdr Harry Blee, 12 August 2019.
42. Anon, *Atlantic Bridge*, p. 37.
43. Keith Wilson, *RAF Transport Command* (Stroud, Gloucestrshire: Amberley, 2017), p. 5.
44. SWWEC, CAR005–1, E.F. Carlisle-Brown 8-page memoir entitled: 'World War II – 1939–46: Some Personal Memories of my Service', p. 7.
45. LACW Edna Birbeck quoted in Arthur Pearcy, *Dakota at War* (London: Ian Allan, 1982), p. 76.

46. SWWEC, Acc no. 2001–1363, Tape 1165: Transcript of interview with Mr James Quinn by Dr Peter Liddle, November 2001, p. 8.
47. See for example, Wilson, *RAF Transport Command*, pp. 8–9; Roderick Bailey, *Forgotten Voices Victoria Cross* (London: Ebury Press, 2010), p. 272.
48. See for example, Group Captain George F.K. Donaldson RAF (retd), 'No. 177 Wing – Operation Thursday' in Pearcy, *Dakota at War*, pp. 54–62.
49. SWWEC, Acc No. LEEW 2007.233, Flt/Lt (152812) Brian Oswald Sibree (RAF Ret'd) 24-page memoir entitled: 'Wartime Memories', p. 7.
50. IWM/DS 19585, Reel 4, Rupert Cooling.
51. See for example, Group Captain George F.K. Donaldson RAF (retd), 'No. 177 Wing – Operation Thursday' in Pearcy, *Dakota at War*, pp. 54–62.
52. Gibbs, *Torpedo Leader on Malta*, p. 153.
53. I am deeply grateful to Mr Charlie Wainwright for supplying a copy of his father's (Flt/Sgt R. Wainwright's) AFM citation.
54. Likewise, I am most grateful to Mr Charlie Wainwright for allowing me to consult: Form 1757 Royal Air Force: Observer's and Gunner's Flying Log Book: 902557 F/Sgt R.J. Wainwright.

Chapter 6: Ground Crews and Other Non-Flying Personnel

1. Ted Mawdsley, *An Erk's Eye View of World War II: A Former Airman's Experiences with 103 Squadron at RAF Elsham Wolds, Lincolnshire 1942–43* (Bognor Regis: Woodfield, 2003), p. 67.
2. Bertram Hughes, *An Erk Goes To War* (Ringwood, Hampshire: Navigator, 1996), p. 17.
3. IWM/DS 13265, Reel 1, Eric Marsden; Chaz Bowyer, *The Royal Air Force 1939–1945* (Barnsley: Pen & Sword, 1996), pp. 15–21.
4. SWWEC, Acc. No. BAK001–02, Leslie F. Baker 'Untitled Memoir', pp. 2–8.
5. Harry Old quoted in Edward Smithies, *Aces, Erks and Backroom Boys: Aircrew, ground staff and war plane builders remember the Second World War* (London: Cassell, 2002), p. 181.
6. IWM/DS 13265, Reel 6, Eric Marsden.
7. IWM/DS 13265, Reel 1, Eric Marsden.
8. SWWEC, Acc. No. 2000.676, Albert William Bennett, 'Memories of the RAF & S.E. Asia Command', p. 1.
9. Peter Jago quoted in Smithies, *Aces, Erks and Backroom Boys*, p. 198.
10. SWWEC, Acc. No. BAK001–02, Leslie F. Baker 'Untitled Memoir', p. 2.
11. Hughes, *An Erk Goes To War*, p. 7.
12. Author's interview: Wg Cdr Harry Blee, 12 August 2019.
13. IWM/DS 13265, Reel 2, Eric Marsden.
14. Hughes, *An Erk Goes To War*, pp. 9–10.
15. SWWEC, Acc. No. BOW001–1, Len Bower 'Untitled Handwritten Memoir', p. 29.
16. Ibid.
17. Mawdsley, *An Erk's Eye View of World War II*, p. 39.
18. Ibid, p. 177.
19. Anonymous, *Tattered Battlements: A Malta Diary by a Fighter Pilot* (London: Peter Davies, 1943), p. 8.
20. IWM/DS 13265, Reel 8, Eric Marsden.
21. Hughes, *An Erk Goes To War*, p. 101.
22. IWM/DS 13265, Reel 4, Eric Marsden.
23. Ibid.

24. Mawdsley, *An Erk's Eye View of World War II*, p. 40.
25. SWWEC Acc. No. BOW001–1, Len Bower 'Untitled Handwritten Memoir', p. 28.
26. Ibid, p. 19.
27. Mawdsley, *An Erk's Eye View of World War II*, pp. 44–5.
28. Hughes, *An Erk Goes To War*, pp. 9, 17.
29. Mawdsley, *An Erk's Eye View of World War II*, p. 21.
30. SWWEC, Acc. No. BOW001–1, Len Bower 'Untitled Handwritten Memoir', p. 24.
31. Mawdsley, *An Erk's Eye View of World War II*, p. 49.
32. See for example, 'App. F WAAF Branches and Trades 1939–45' & 'App. H Airwomen in Main Trade Groups 1939–45' in Beryl E. Escott, *Women in Air Force Blue* (Wellingborough, Nothamptonshire: PSL, 1989), pp. 298–9, 301.
33. Trixie Irving quoted in Escott, *Women in Air Force Blue*, p. 170.
34. Katherine Bentley Beauman, *Partners in Blue: The Story of Women's with the Royal Air Force* (London: Hutchinson, 1971), p. 165.
35. Ibid, pp. 164–6.
36. Trixie Irving quoted in Escott, *Women in Air Force Blue*, p. 170.
37. Hilda Bell quoted in Beryl E. Escott, *Our Wartime Days: The WAAF in World War II* (Stroud, Gloucestershire: Alan Sutton, 1995), pp. 89–90.
38. Hugh Verity, 'Some RAF Pick-ups for French Intelligence' in K.G. Robertson (Ed), *War, Resistance & Intelligence: Essays in Honour of M.R.D. Foot* (Barnsley: Leo Cooper, 1999), p. 183.
39. Correspondence between Mr A.E.R. Goulty and the author, 22 August 1995. (For a variety of reasons, my late grandfather didn't talk that much about his war, albeit he was proud to have served in the RAF. On the fiftieth anniversary of VJ-Day, he was moved to write to me about his experiences. I hope that he would not have minded me sharing some of that correspondence, and appreciated this book).
40. F.R. Chappell, *Wellington Wings: An RAF Intelligence Officer in the Western Desert* (London: William Kimber, 1980), p. 28.
41. Rita Symons quoted in Smithies, *Aces, Erks and Backroom Boys*, p. 253.
42. SWWEC, Acc. No. AMB001–2–1–1, J.M. Ambler Memoir entitled: 'Memories of my RAF Service during WW2', p. 2.
43. IWM/DS 11744, Reels 3 & 4, Stanley Wright.
44. SWWEC, Acc. No. BAK001–02, Leslie F. Baker 'Untitled Memoir', p. 4.
45. Harry Old quoted in Edward Smithies, *Aces, Erks and Backroom Boys*, p. 184.
46. Lawrence Wheatley, *An Erksome War* (Braunton, Devon: Merlin, 1991), pp. 39–40.
47. Henry Brown, *Per Astro Ad Asbestos* (New Waltham, nr. Grimsby, Lincs: Ashridge, 1999), p. 155.
48. A.E. Haarer, *A Cold-Blooded Business* (London: Staples, 1958), p. 16.
49. Ibid, p. 97.
50. Ibid, p. 37.
51. Brown, *Per Astro Ad Asbestos*, p. 33.
52. Ibid, p. 64.
53. Jackie Poulton, quoted in Beryl E. Escott, *Our Wartime Days*, p. 107.
54. Dorothea Barrie quoted in Escott, *Women in Air Force Blue*, p. 158.
55. Phyllis Cove quoted in Escott, *Our Wartime Days*, p. 141.
56. Morton Charlton, *Madalay and Beyond: Tales from a Medical Airman's diary* (Braunton, Devon: Merlin, 1996), p. 9.
57. Brown, *Per Astro Ad Asbestos*, p. 120.

58. See for example, Malcolm Fife, *RAF Acklington: Guardian of Northern Skies* (Fonthill Media, 2017).
59. SWWEC, Acc. No. BOW001–1, Len Bower 'Untitled Handwritten Memoir', p. 24.
60. Haarer, *A Cold-Blooded Business*, p. 92.
61. Wheatley, *An Erksome War*, pp. 28, 39.
62. Brown, *Per Astro Ad Asbestos*, p. 101.
63. Mawdsley, *An Erk's Eye View of World War II*, p. 11.
64. IWM/DS 13265, Reel 3, Eric Marsden.
65. SWWEC, Acc. No. BOW001–1, Len Bower 'Untitled Handwritten Memoir', p. 25.
66. IWM/DS 13265, Reel 17, Eric Marsden.
67. Ibid, Reel 3.
68. Charlton, *Madalay and Beyond*, p. 5.
69. SWWEC, Acc. No. AMB001-2-1-1, J. M. Ambler Memoir entitled: 'Memories of my RAF Service during WW2', p. 2.
70. SWWEC, Acc. No. BOW001–1, Len Bower 'Untitled Handwritten Memoir', p. 28.
71. IWM/DS 13265, Reel 4, Eric Marsden.
72. Haarer, *A Cold-Blooded Business*, pp. 52–3.
73. IWM/DS 11744, Reel 1, Stanley Wright.
74. Pip Beck, *A WAAF in Bomber Command* (London: Goodall, 1989), p. 65.
75. John Sharman quoted in Roger A. Freeman, *Chocks Away!*, p. 156.
76. Brown, *Per Astro Ad Asbestos*, p. 90.
77. Harry Blee, *Harry's Travels: History of William Harold Percival Blee* (Privately produced, 2004), p. 4.
78. IWM/DS 13265, Reel 18, Eric Marsden.
79. Ibid, Reel 24.
80. Brown, *Per Astro Ad Asbestos*, p. 65.
81. Jeanne Truman quoted in Edward Smithies, *Aces, Erks and Backroom Boys*, p. 248.
82. IWM/DS 11744, Reel 3, Stanley Wright.
83. Charlton, *Mandalay and Beyond*, p. 55.
84. H.C.B. Rogers, *Troopships and their history* (London: Seeley Service, 1963), p. 188.
85. Wheatley, *An Erksome War*, p. 42.
86. Peter Jago quoted in Smithies, *Aces, Erks and Backroom Boys*, p. 200.
87. Charlton, *Mandalay and Beyond*, p. 13.
88. Hughes, *An Erk Goes To War*, p. 26.
89. Charlton, *Mandalay and Beyond*, p. 15.
90. Wheatley, *An Erksome War*, p. 43.
91. See for example, Charlton, *Mandalay and Beyond*, p. 15; Hughes, *An Erk Goes To War*, p. 29; Wheatley, *An Erksome War*, pp. 43–4.
92. IWM/DS 13265, Reel 19, Eric Marsden.
93. Charlton, *Mandalay and Beyond*, p. 12.
94. Peter Jago quoted in Smithies, *Aces, Erks and Backroom Boys*, p. 206.
95. Dorothy Marsh quoted in Escott, *Women in Air Force Blue*, p. 200.
96. Hughes, *An Erk Goes To War*, p. 36.
97. Ibid, p. 45.
98. Ibid, p. 44.
99. Ibid, p. 78.
100. IWM/DS 11744, Reel 4, Stanley Wright.
101. SWWEC, Acc. No. 2000.676, Albert William Bennett, 'Memories of the RAF & S.E. Asia Command', p. 3.

102. Wheatley, *An Erksome War*, p. 94.
103. See for example, Ibid, p. 110.
104. Charlton, *Mandalay and Beyond*, p. 92.
105. IWM/DS 11744, Reel 4, Stanley Wright.
106. Author's correspondence: Wg Cdr Harry Blee, July 2019.
107. Hughes, *An Erk Goes To War*, p. 51.
108. Ibid, p. 56.
109. Wheatley, *An Erksome War*, p. 65.
110. SWWEC, Acc. No. 2000.676, Albert William Bennett, 'Memories of the RAF & S.E. Asia Command', p. 3.
111. Air Publication 1081 (reprinted February 1939), *RAF Pocket Book 1937*, Ch. XIV Medical, Section 74 Maintenance of Health: Venereal Disease, Paragraph 968, p. 244.

Chapter 7: Accidents, Crashes, Shot Down and Taken Prisoner

1. SWWEC, Acc. No. LEEWW 2006.597, Reminiscences of James Anthony Tooth (PO later Fl/Lt and Spitfire Pilot with 130, 152 & 287 Squadrons), p. 5.
2. Pip Beck, *A WAAF in Bomber Command* (London: Goodall, 1989), p. 152.
3. Flt/Lt Bill Bennée quoted in Mike Garbett and Brian Goulding, *Lancaster at War* (London: Guild, 1971), p. 97.
4. Air Commodore 'Taffy' Powell, *Ferryman: from Ferry Command to Silver City* (Shrewsbury: Airlife, 1982), pp. 114–15.
5. Author's interview: Wg Cdr Harry Blee, 12 August 2019.
6. See for example, Martin Middlebrook & Chris Everitt, *The Bomber Command War Diaries: An Operational Reference Book 1939–1945* (Barnsley: Pen & Sword, 2014), p. 24.
7. IWM/DS, 13265, Eric Marsden, Reel 2.
8. SWWEC, CAR005–1, E.F. Carlisle-Brown 8-page memoir entitled: 'World War II – 1939–46: Some Personal Memories of my Service', p. 3.
9. Roger A. Freeman, *Chocks Away!*, p. 132.
10. SWWEC, CAR005–1, E.F. Carlisle-Brown 8-page memoir entitled: 'World War II – 1939–46: Some Personal Memories of my Service', p. 3.
11. Author's interview: Wg Cdr Harry Blee, 12 August 2019.
12. See for example, Phillip J.R. Moyes, *Bomber Squadrons of the RAF and their Aircraft* (London: MacDonald, 1964), pp. 135–8.
13. Andrew Brookes, *Bomber Squadron at War* (London: Ian Allan, 1983), pp. 133–4.
14. SWWEC, FAU001–1 LEEWW:2006.510, C.A. Faulks, 83-page T/S Memoir Entitled: 'One Man's War: An Excerpt from the Memoirs of "Guy" Faulks: A Life Luckier than Most', July 2006, p. 44.
15. TNA, Kew, AIR 27/1758, Operations Record Book: 356 Heavy Bomber Squadron, May 1944, Entry for 7/5/44, p. 8.
16. Author's interview: Wg Cdr Harry Blee, 12 August 2019.
17. James Sanders, *Of Wind and Water: A Kiwi Pilot in Coastal Command* (Shrewsbury: Airlife, 1989), p. 59.
18. SWWEC, CUR002–3, Tape 1003, 687 continued: T/S of oral history interview: Des Curtis.
19. Beck, *A WAAF in Bomber Command*, p. 51.
20. SWWEC, AMB001–2–1–1, Jack M. Ambler, 6-page T/S Memoir entitled: 'Memories of my RAF Service during World War Two', p. 4.

21. Author's interview: Wg Cdr Harry Blee, 12 August 2019.
22. See for example, Middlebrook & Everitt, *The Bomber Command War Diaries*, p. 258; Jack Currie, *The Augsburg Raid: The Story of one of the most dramatic and dangerous raids ever mounted by RAF Bomber Command* (London: Goodall, 1987) passim.
23. Beck, *A WAAF in Bomber Command*, p. 53.
24. IWM/DS, 11744, Stanley Wright, Reel 2.
25. IWM/DS, 13265, Eric Marsden, Reel 5.
26. Plt Off J.R.A. Hodgson letter to his brother, Sgts Mess, RAF St Eval, 2 September 1942, quoted in David Hodgson, *Letters from a Bomber Pilot* (London: Thames Methuen, 1985), p. 50.
27. Paul Richey, *Fighter Pilot: A Personal Record of the Campaign in France 1939–1940* (Stroud, Gloucestershire, History Press, 2016), pp. 74–5.
28. SWWEC, Acc. No. LEEWW 2006.597, Reminiscences of James Anthony Tooth, p. 7.
29. Ibid, p. 8.
30. Ted Mawdsley, *An Erk's Eye View of World War II: A Former Airman's Experiences with 103 Squadron at RAF Elsham Wolds, Lincolnshire 1942–43* (Bognor Regis: Woodfield, 2003), p. 98.
31. Beck, *A WAAF in Bomber Command*, p. 141.
32. Lawrence Wheatley, *An Erksome War* (Braunton, Devon: Merlin, 1991), p. 82.
33. Ibid, pp. 62–3.
34. Ken Rees with Karen Arrandale, *Lie in the Dark and Listen: The Remarkable Exploits of a WWII Bomber Pilot and Great Escaper* (London: Grub Street, 2006), pp. 100, 105–106.
35. Carlton Younger, *No Flight from the Cage: The Compelling Memoir of a Bomber Command Prisoner of War during the Second World War* (Hitchin, Herts: Fighting High, 2013), p. 30; Middlebrook & Everitt, *The Bomber Command War Diaries*, p. 268.
36. Percy Wilson Carruthers DFM, *Ploughs, Planes & Palliasses: A WW2 Airman's Story of Survival* (Bognor Regis, W Sussex: Woodfield, 2009), p. 88.
37. See for example, Middlebrook & Everitt, *The Bomber Command War Diaries*, p. 329.
38. Henry Ord Robertson DFM, *Dangerous Landing: A first-hand story of evasion* (Wellingborough, Northamptonshire: PSL, 1989), pp. 33–5.
39. 'Blue' Rackley, 'Caterpillars Extraordinaire' in Mike Garbett & Brian Goulding, *Lancaster at War* (London: Book Club Associates, 1985), p. 99.
40. Tony Johnson, *Escape to Freedom: An Airman's Tale of Capture, Escape and Evasion* (Barnsley: Pen & Sword, 2009), p. 49.
41. Robertson, *Dangerous Landing*, pp. 36–7.
42. W.J. 'Jim' Hunter, *From Coastal Command to Captivity: The Memoir of A Second World War Airman* (Barnsley: Pen & Sword, 2003), pp. 56–8.
43. Ibid, p. 59.
44. SWWEC, Acc. No. LEEWW 2006.597, Reminiscences of James Anthony Tooth, p. 13.
45. William Ash, *Under the Wire: The Wartime Memoir of a Spitfire pilot, legendary escape artist and 'cooler king'* (London: Bantam, 2006), p. 109.
46. Ibid, pp. 110–11.
47. SWWEC, Acc. No. LEEWW 2006.597, Reminiscences of James Anthony Tooth, p. 13.
48. Denis Peto-Shepherd, *The Devil Take The Hindmost* (Durham: Pentland Press, 1996), p. 270.
49. See for example, Ian Dear, *Escape and Evasion: POW Breakouts in World War Two* (London: Cassell, 2002), pp. 14, 16.
50. Robertson, *Dangerous Landing*, p. 46.
51. Ibid, p. 114.

52. M.R.D. Foot & J.M. Langley, *MI9: Escape and Evasion 1939–1945* (London: Book Club Associates, 1979), p. 83.
53. See for example, Ibid, p. 83.
54. See for example, Ibid, pp. 73–6; Dear, *Escape and Evasion*, Ch. 3 'The PAT Line and its Traitors', pp. 35–49.
55. See for example, Ibid, pp. 79–82. Dear, *Escape and* Evasion, Ch. 11 'The Little Cyclone', pp. 135–47.
56. See for example, Oliver Clutton-Brock, *RAF Evaders: The Comprehensive Story of Thousands of Escapers and their Escape Lines, Western Europe 1940–1945* (London: Grub Street, 2009), pp. 167–72.
57. Rees with Arrandale, *Lie in the Dark and Listen*, p. 111.
58. Trevor Utton quoted in Stephen Darlow, *Lancaster Down! The extraordinary tale of seven young airmen at war* (London: Bounty, 2007), p. 123.
59. Denys Teare, *Evader* (Manchester: Goodall, 2008), p. 191.
60. Tom Cooke quoted in Norman Franks & Simon Muggleton, *Flying Among Heroes: The Story of Squadron Leader T.C.S. Cooke, DFC, AFC, DFM, AE* (Stroud, Gloucestershire: History Press, 2012), pp. 161–2.
61. Robertson, *Dangerous Landing*, p. 39.
62. Teare, *Evader*, p. 15.
63. See for example, J.M. Langley, *Fight Another Day* (London: Magnum, 1980), pp. 149–50.
64. Paul Brickhill, *Escape or Die: Authentic Stories of the RAF Escaping Society* (London: Evans Brothers, 1952), p. 162.
65. Teare, *Evader*, p. 21.
66. See for example, Dear, *Escape and Evasion*, Ch. 2 'Clutty and his Escape Devices', esp. pp. 29–30.
67. See for example, Foot & Langley, *MI9: Escape and Evasion 1939–1945*, p. 273.
68. Ibid, p. 261.
69. Ibid, p. 281.
70. J.V. Foster, *Sauerkraut & Boiled Potatoes* (Privately published, undated), p. 17.
71. Ibid, pp. 9–10.
72. Jim Burtt-Smith, *Memoirs of a 'Goldfish': The Life and times of a World War II Bomber Pilot* (Bognor Regis: Woodfield, 2000), p. 113.
73. Carruthers, *Ploughs, Planes & Palliasses*, p. 96.
74. See for example, Johnson, *Escape to Freedom*, p. 56; Darlow, *Lancaster Down!*, pp. 146–7.
75. Ash, *Under the Wire*, p. 134.
76. Brickhill, *Escape or Die*, p. 21.
77. Burtt-Smith, *Memoirs of a 'Goldfish'*, p. 115.
78. Johnson, *Escape to Freedom*, p. 80.
79. Adrian Gilbert, *POW: Allied Prisoners in Europe 1939–1945* (London: John Murray, 2007), p. 77.
80. Alan Carter, *Survival of the Fittest: A Young Englishman's Struggle as a Prisoner of War in Java and Japan* (Privately published, 2013), p. 71.
81. Ibid.
82. See for example, Brian MacArthur, *Surviving the Sword: Prisoners of the Japanese 1942–45* (London: Abacus, 2007), pp. 325–40.
83. Carter, *Survival of the Fittest*, p. 49.
84. Ibid, p. 55.
85. See for example, ibid, pp. 61–2.

86. Carruthers, *Ploughs, Planes & Palliasses*, pp. 97–8.
87. Trevor Utton quoted in Darlow, *Lancaster Down!*, p. 154.
88. Foster, *Sauerkraut & Boiled Potatoes*, pp. 15–16.
89. Cy Grant, *A Member of the RAF of Indeterminate Race: World War Two experiences of a West Indian Officer in the RAF* (Bognor Regis: Woodfield, 2006), pp. 60–1.
90. Younger, *No Flight from the Cage*, pp. 93–4.
91. Hunter, *From Coastal Command to Captivity*, p. 75.
92. Ibid, p. 88.
93. Foster, *Sauerkraut & Boiled Potatoes*, pp. 18–19.
94. For further discussion of these themes see: Ken Rees with Karen Arrandale, *Lie in the Dark and Listen: The Remarkable Exploits of a WWII Bomber Pilot and Great Escaper* (London: Grub Street, 2006).
95. Hunter, *From Coastal Command to Captivity*, p. 69.
96. Grant, *A Member of the RAF of Indeterminate Race*, p. 79.
97. Carter, *Survival of the Fittest*, p. 103.
98. Burtt-Smith, *Memoirs of a 'Goldfish,'* pp. 119–20.
99. Carter, *Survival of the Fittest*, p. 150.
100. Dear, *Escape and* Evasion, esp. p. 18.
101. See for example, Laddie Lucas, *Flying Colours: The Epic Story of Douglas Bader* (London: Granada, 1983), esp. p 252.
102. Richard Passmore quoted in Gilbert, *POW: Allied Prisoners in Europe 1939–1945*, pp. 266–7.
103. Gilbert, *POW: Allied Prisoners in Europe 1939–1945*, p. 255.
104. For details on Sgt Grimson see for example: ibid, pp. 274–8; Foot & Langley, *MI9: Escape and Evasion 1939–1945*, pp. 252–3; Ash, *Under the Wire*, pp. 267–70, 274–6.
105. See for example, Paul Brickhill, *The Great Escape* (London: Cassell, 2000); Rees with Arrandale, *Lie in the Dark and Listen*, pp. 145–96.
106. Ash, *Under the Wire*, p. 207.
107. Ibid, p. 215.
108. See for example, Appendix 3 'The Tunnel at Oflag XXIB, Schubin' in Hunter, *From Coastal Command to Captivity*, pp. 138–41.
109. Ash, *Under the Wire*, p. 228.

Chapter 8: Demobilisation and Coming Home

1. Pierre Clostermann, DSO, DFC, *The Big Show: Some Experiences of a French Fighter Pilot in the RAF* (London: Corgi, 1970), p. 250.
2. SWWEC, Acc. No. LEEWW 2006.597, Reminiscences of James Anthony Tooth (PO later Fl/Lt and Spitfire Pilot with 130, 152 & 287 Squadrons), p. 20.
3. Muriel Gane Pushman, *We All Wore Blue* (London: Futura, 1990), p. 177.
4. Miss Forbes quoted in Edward Smithies, *Aces, Erks and Backroom Boys: Aircrew, Ground Staff and Warplane Builders Remember the Second World War* (London: Cassell, 2002), p. 305.
5. Mr Waite quoted in Ibid, p. 301.
6. SWWEC, Acc. No. BAK001.02, Leslie F. Baker, 'Untitled Memoir', p. 8.
7. Mr Dale quoted in Smithies, *Aces, Erks and Backroom Boys*, p. 297.
8. See for example, 'The Royal Air Force Mutiny 1946' on Wikipedia (accessed 26 November 2019). This article contains advice on further reading about the subject.

9. SWWEC, Acc. No. LEEWW 2006.597, Reminiscences of James Anthony Tooth, p. 20.

10. Henry Brown, *Per Astro AD Asbestos* (New Waltham, nr Grimsby, Lincs: Ashridge, 1999), pp. 175–6.

11. Based on information in RAF Form 2520C: Officer, Royal Air Force Service and Release Book: 'under RAF Form 2520/122: Conditions of Release and Notes on Payment of Allowances and Release Benefits' and RAF Form 2520D: WAAF Officer, Royal Air Force Release Book: 'under RAF Form 2520/122 W: Conditions of Release and Notes on Payment of Allowances and Release Benefits.'

12. SWWEC, AMB001–2–1–1, J.M. Ambler, 'Memories of My RAF Service during WW2', p. 6.

13. SWWEC, CAR005–1–1 of 8, E.F. Carlisle-Brown, 8-page T/S Memoir Entitled: 'WWII 1939–46', p. 8.

14. Ted Mawdsley, *An Erk's Eye View of World War II: A Former airman's experiences with 103 Squadron at RAF Elsham Wolds, Lincolnshire 1942–43* (Bognor Regis: Woodfield, 2003), p. 183.

15. IWM/DS 11744, Reel 8, Stanley Wright.

16. Peter Wykeham, *Fighter Command* (London: Putnam, 1960), p. 273 (AVM Peter Wickham, DSO, OBE, DFC, AFC, Danish Order of Dannebrog, US Air Medal).

17. See for example, Michael Armitage, *The Royal Air Force: An Illustrated History* (London: Brockhampton, 1998), pp. 180–6 and Arthur Pearcy, *Dakota at War* (London: Ian Allan, 1982), pp. 104–107.

18. Mr A.E.R. Goulty, Letter to the author, 22 August 1995, p. 2.

19. Ibid, p. 3.

20. Author's interview: Wg Cdr Harry Blee, 12 August 2019.

21. SWWEC, AMB001–2–1–1, J.M. Ambler, 'Memories of My RAF Service during WW2', p. 6.

22. See Dick Ashley's comments in Smithies, *Aces, Erks and Backroom Boys*, pp. 193–7.

23. SWWEC, Acc. No. 2000.676, Albert William Bennett, 'Memories of the RAF & S.E. Asia Command', p. 5.

24. W.J. 'Jim' Hunter, *From Coastal Command to Captivity: The Memoir of A Second World War Airman* (Barnsley: Pen & Sword, 2003), pp. 117–18.

25. Carlton Younger, *No Flight from the Cage: The Compelling Memoir of a Bomber Command Prisoner of War during the Second World War* (Hitchin, Herts: Fighting High, 2013), pp. 227–8.

26. SWWEC, CUR002–3 Des Curtiss, DFC, Transcript of Tape 1003/687, Dr Peter Liddle Oral History Interview with Des Curtiss, July 2001.

27. See for example, Barry Turner & Tony Rennell, *When Daddy Came Home: How Family Life Changed Forever in 1945* (London: Hutchinson, 1995), esp. Ch. 1 'Call Me Mister', pp. 1–15; Juliet Gardiner, *Wartime Britain 1939–1945* (London: Review, 2005), esp. pp. 676–80.

28. IWM/DS 13265, Reels 33 & 34, Eric Marsden.

29. See J.V. Foster, *Sauerkraut & Boiled Potatoes* (Privately published).

30. Mr A.E.R. Goulty, Letter to the author, 22 August 1995, pp. 1–2.

Bibliography

The National Archives, Kew
Operations Record Books from AIR 27

The Imperial War Museum (Department of Sound), London
The following oral history interview recordings were consulted:

12524	Brown, (Air Commodore) Cyril Bob
12135	Budzik, Kazimierz
19585	Cooling, Rupert
12892	Drobinski, (Squadron Leader) Boleslaw Henryk
13265	Marsden, Eric
30386	Pate, Ronald Frederick
21291	Sanders, (Wing Commander) James Gilbert
9106	Saunders, Gwendoline
11744	Wright, Stanley

The Second World War Experience Centre, Otley
Material regarding the following individuals was consulted:

Allinson, K.
Ambler, J.M.
Baker, C.G.E.
Baker, L.F.
Barker, Ray
Bennett, Albert
Bower, Len
Brown, C.
Buchanan, J.K.
Cannings, A.V.
Carlisle-Brown, E.F.
Curtis, Des
Faulks, C.A.
Field, H.J.
Foster, Don
Grist, J.

Peto-Shepherd, (Squadron Leader) D.N.
Rivett, Rev. L.
Sibree, B.O.
Tooth, J.A.
Thomas, Richard
Quin, J.M.C.

Author's collection

Papers and photographs re: The wartime RAF/WAAF service and experiences of Mr and Mrs A.E.R. Goulty.
Interview: Wing Commander Harry Blee, 12 August 2019.
Air Publication 1081 (reprinted February 1939), *RAF Pocket Book 1937*.

Further reading

The wartime RAF is a vast subject, and researchers will soon find that they are confronted by a mass of published material. Below are listed titles that I've found particularly useful, plus others that provide further reading for anyone interested in the topic. Readers will also find full details of the various sources consulted in the accompanying chapter notes.

Official and semi-official works

Anon, *Air Sea Rescue*, HMSO, London, 1942.
Anon, *Atlantic Bridge: The Official Account of RAF Transport Command's Atlantic Ferry*, HMSO, London, 1945.
Anon, *Bomber Command: The Air Ministry Account of Bomber Command's Offensive Against the Axis, September, 1939–July, 1941*, HMSO, London, 1941.
Anon, *Coastal Command: The Air Ministry Account of the Part Played by Coastal Command in the Battle of the Seas 1939–1942*, HMSO, London, 1942.
Anon, *Fighter Pilot: A Personal Record of the Campaign in France, September 8th 1939, to June 13th 1940*, B.T. Batsford, London, 1942.
Anon, *RAF Middle East: The Official Story of Air Operations in the Middle East, from February 1942 to January 1943*, HMSO, London, 1945.
Anon, *Tattered Battlements: A Malta Diary by a Fighter Pilot*, Peter Davies, London, 1943.
Anon, *Winged Words: Our Airmen Speak For Themselves*, William Heinemann Ltd., London, 1941.
Dudley-Gordon, Tom, *Coastal Command at War*, Jarrolds, London, undated.
Macadam, John, *The Reluctant Erk: Stories of the RAF Airmen without Wings*, Jarrolds, London, undated.
Richards, Denis, *Royal Air Force 1939–1945 Volume I: The Fight at Odds*, HMSO, London, 1953.
Richards, Denis & St G. Saunders, Hilary, *Royal Air Force 1939–1945 Volume II: The Fight Avails*, HMSO, London, 1954.
St G. Saunders, Hilary, *Royal Air Force 1939–1945 Volume III: The Fight is Won*, HMSO, London, 1954.
Tilsley, Frank, *The Boys of Coastal Command*, Cassell, London, 1944.

Reference works

Bowyer, Chaz, *The Royal Air Force, 1939–1945*, Pen & Sword, Barnsley, 1996.

Delve, Kevin, *The Source Book of the RAF*, Airlife Publishing, Shrewsbury, 1994.

Falconer, Jonathan, *RAF Bomber Command 1939 to 1945 Operations Manual*, Haynes, Yeovil, 2018.

Middlebrook, Martin & Everitt, Chris, *The Bomber Command War Diaries: An Operational Reference Book 1939–1945*, Pen & Sword, Barnsley, 2014.

Mondey, David, *British Aircraft of World War II*, Chancellor Press, London, 1995.

Moyes, Philip, *Bomber Squadrons of the RAF and their Aircraft*, Macdonald & Co., London, 1964.

Histories/memoirs

Ash, William, *Under the Wire: The Wartime Memoir of a Spitfire pilot, legendary escape artist and 'cooler king'*, Bantam Books, London, 2006.

Baveystock, Leslie, DSO, DFC and Bar, DFM, *Wavetops At My Wingtips*, Airlife Publishing, Shrewsbury, 2001.

Beck, Pip, *A WAAF in Bomber Command*, Goodhall Publications, London, 1989.

Berryman, Nick, *In the Nick of Time: The Experiences of an RAF Air Sea Rescue Pilot with 276 Sqn*, Woodfield Publishing, Bognor Regis, 2000.

Bishop, Patrick, *Fighter Boys: Saving Britain 1940*, Harper Perennial, London, 2004.

Bishop, Patrick, *Bomber Boys: Fighting Back 1940–1945*, Harper Perennial, London, 2008.

Bishop, Patrick, *Air Force Blue: The RAF in World War Two – Spearhead of Victory*, William Collins, London, 2017.

Brickhill, Paul, *Escape or Die: Authentic Stories of the RAF Escaping Society*, Evans Brothers, London, 1952.

Brown, Henry, *Per Astro Ad Asbestos*, Ashridge Press, New Waltham, 1999.

Bungay, Stephen, *The Most Dangerous Enemy: A History of the Battle of Britain*, Arum Press, London, 2000.

Burtt-Smith, Jim, *Memoirs of a 'Goldfish': The Life and times of a World War II Bomber Pilot*, Woodfield Publishing, Bognor Regis, 2000.

Carter, Alan, *Survival of the Fittest: A Young Englishman's Struggle as a Prisoner of War in Java and Japan*, privately published, 2013.

Carruthers, Percy, Wilson, DFM, *Ploughs, Planes & Palliasses: A WW2 Airman's Story of Survival*, Woodfield Publishing, Bognor Regis, 2009.

Chappell, F.R., *Wellington Wings: An RAF Intelligence Officer in the Western Desert*, William Kimber & Co., London, 1980.

Charlton, Morton, *Mandalay and Beyond: Tales from a Medical Airman's Diary*, Merlin Books, Braunton, 1996.

Currie, Jack, *Wings Over Georgia*, Goodall Publications, London, 1989.

Currie, Jack, *Lancaster Target*, Goodall Publications, London, 2008.

Docherty, Tom, *Dinghy Drop: 279 Squadron RAF 1941–46*, Pen & Sword, Barnsley, 2007.

Duncan Smith, W.G.G., *Spitfire into Battle*, Isis Publishing, Oxford, 2003.

Gibbs, Patrick, DSO, DFC and Bar, *Not Peace But a Sword*, Grub Street Publishing, London, 1993.

Gibson, Guy, *Enemy Coast Ahead*, Goodhall Publications, Wilmslow, 1995.

Gilbert, Adrian, *POW: Allied Prisoners in Europe 1939–1945*, John Murray, London, 2007.

Grant, Cy, *A Member of the RAF of Indeterminate Race: World War Two experiences of a West Indian Officer in the RAF*, Woodfield Publishing, Bognor Regis, 2006.

Haarer, A.E., *A Cold-Blooded Business*, Staples Press, London, 1958.

Hastings, Max, *Bomber Command*, Pan Books, London, 1999.

Henry, Mike, DFC, *Air Gunner*, Goodhall Publications, Wilmslow, 1997.

Hough, Richard, *One Boy's War*, Pen & Sword, Barnsley, 2007.

Hudson, James, DFC, RAFVR, *There and Back Again: A Navigator's Story*, Tucann Books, Lincoln, 2001.

Hughes, Bertram, *An Erk Goes To War*, Navigator Books, Ringwood, 1996.

Hunter, W.J. 'Jim', *From Coastal Command to Captivity: The Memoir of A Second World War Airman*, Pen & Sword, Barnsley, 2003.

Johnson, J.E. 'Johnnie', *Wing Leader*, Chatto & Windus, London, 1956.

Johnson, Tony, *Escape to Freedom: An Airman's Tale of Capture, Escape and Evasion*, Pen & Sword, Barnsley, 2009.

Kent, J.A., *One of the Few*, William Kimber, London, 1971.

Lewis, Bruce, *Aircrew: The Story of the Men who Flew the Bombers*, Cassell, London, 2000.

Mawdsley, Ted, *An Erk's Eye View of World War II: A Former Airman's Experiences with 103 Squadron at RAF Elsham Wolds, Lincolnshire 1942–43*, Woodfield Publishing, Bognor Regis, 2003.

McVicar, Don, *Ferry Command*, Airlife Publishing, Shrewsbury, 1981.

Middlebrook, Martin, *The Battle of Hamburg: The Firestorm Raid*, Penguin, London, 1984.

Middlebrook, Martin, *The Nuremberg Raid 30–31 March 1944*, Penguin, London, 1986.

Middlebrook, Martin, *The Berlin Raids: RAF Bomber Command 1943–44*, Penguin, London, 1990.

Olive, Gordon, DFC, *Spitfire Ace: My Life as a Battle of Britain Fighter Pilot*, Amberley, Stroud, 2016.

Overy, Richard, *Why The Allies Won*, Pimlico, London, 1995.

Overy, Richard, *The Battle*, Penguin, London, 2000.

Peto-Shepherd, Denis, *The Devil Take the Hindmost*, The Pentland Press, Bishop Auckland, 1996.

Pitchfork, Graham, *Shot Down and on the Run: The RAF and Commonwealth aircrews who got home from behind enemy lines 1940–1945*, The National Archives, Kew, 2003.

Pitchfork, Graham, *Shot Down and in the Drink: RAF and Commonwealth aircrews saved from the sea 1939–1945*, The National Archives, Kew, 2005.

Powell, Griffith, 'Taffy', *Ferryman: From Ferry Command to Silver City*, Airlife Publishing, Shrewsbury, 1982.

Rayner, Ted, *Coastal Command Pilot 1939–1945: Wartime Experiences with 220 & 269 Squadrons*, Woodfield Publishing, Bognor Regis, 2001.

Rees, Ken with Arrandale, Karen, *Lie in the Dark and Listen: The Remarkable Exploits of a WWII Bomber Pilot and Great Escaper*, Grub Street, London, 2006.

Richards, Denis, *RAF Bomber Command in the Second World War: The Hardest Victory*, Penguin, London, 2001.

Sanders, James, *Of Wind and Water: A Kiwi Pilot in Coastal Command*, Airlife Publishing, Shrewsbury, 1989.

Smith, Ron, DFM, *Rear Gunner Pathfinders*, Goodhall Publications, London, 1989.

Smithies, Edward, *Aces, Erks and Backroom Boys: Aircrew, ground staff and war plane builders remember the Second World War*, Cassell, London, 2002.

Spooner, Tony, DSO, DFC, *In Full Flight*, Wingham Press, Canterbury, 1991.

Terrain, John, *The Right of the Line*, Wordsworth Editions, Ware, 1997.

Wellum, Geoffrey, *First Light*, Penguin, London, 2018.

Wheatley, Lawrence, *An Erksome War*, Merlin Books, Braunton, 1991.

Wilson, Kevin, *Men of Air: The Doomed Youth of Bomber Command*, Cassell, London, 2011.

Index